Solemn Words and
Foundational Documents

Solemn Words and Foundational Documents

An Annotated Discussion of Indigenous-Crown Treaties in Canada, 1752–1923

JEAN-PIERRE MORIN

UNIVERSITY OF TORONTO PRESS

Toronto Buffalo London

© University of Toronto Press 2018
utorontopress.com

All rights reserved. The use of any part of this publication reproduced, transmitted in any form or by any means, electronic, mechanical, photocopying, recording, or otherwise, or stored in a retrieval system, without prior written consent of the publisher – or in the case of photocopying, a licence from Access Copyright (Canadian Copyright Licensing Agency), 320 – 56 Wellesley Street West, Toronto, Ontario, M5S 2S3 – is an infringement of the copyright law.

Library and Archives Canada Cataloguing in Publication

Morin, Jean-Pierre, 1974–, author
    Solemn words and foundational documents : an annotated discussion of Indigenous-Crown treaties in Canada, 1752–1923 / Jean-Pierre Morin.

Includes bibliographical references and index.
Issued in print and electronic formats.

ISBN 978-1-4875-9445-9 (softcover). ISBN 978-1-4875-9446-6 (hardcover).
ISBN 978-1-4875-9447-3 (HTML). ISBN 978-1-4875-9448-0 (uPDF).

    1. Indians of North America—Canada—Treaties. 2. Indians of North America—Legal status, laws, etc. 3. Indians of North America—Canada—Government relations. I. Title.

KE7709.M67 2018   342.7108'72   C2018-904069-6
KF8205.M67 2018

We welcome comments and suggestions regarding any aspect of our publications – please feel free to contact us at news@utorontopress.com or visit our Internet site at utorontopress.com.

North America
5201 Dufferin Street
North York, Ontario, Canada, M3H 5T8

2250 Military Road
Tonawanda, New York, USA, 14150

ORDERS PHONE: 1-800-565-9523
ORDERS FAX: 1-800-221-9985
ORDERS E-MAIL: utpbooks@utpress.utoronto.ca

UK, Ireland, and continental Europe
NBN International
Estover Road, Plymouth, PL6 7PY, UK

ORDERS PHONE: 44 (0) 1752 202301
ORDERS FAX: 44 (0) 1752 202333
ORDERS E-MAIL: enquiries@nbninternational.com

Every effort has been made to contact copyright holders; in the event of an error or omission, please notify the publisher.

The views and opinions expressed in this publication are those of the author and not necessarily those of the Government of Canada.

University of Toronto Press acknowledges the financial assistance to its publishing program of the Canada Council for the Arts and the Ontario Arts Council, an agency of the Government of Ontario.

Canada Council for the Arts
Conseil des Arts du Canada

ONTARIO ARTS COUNCIL
CONSEIL DES ARTS DE L'ONTARIO
an Ontario government agency
un organisme du gouvernement de l'Ontario

Funded by the Government of Canada
Financé par le gouvernement du Canada

For my parents, Judy and Jean-Marie.

Contents

List of Primary Documents   ix
List of Illustrations   xiii
Acknowledgments   xv

Introduction: Reading a Treaty   1
Further Readings   12
Legal Principles of Treaty Interpretation Used by the Supreme Court of Canada   12
Timeline   13

1 The Making of the Peace and Friendship Treaties, 1725–1779   21
   Oral and Written Accounts of the 1752 "Cope" Treaty   24
   The 1752 Treaty and the Courts   31
   Further Readings   35
   Questions for Discussion   35
   Documents   36
   Cast of Characters: 1752 Cope Treaty   43

2 The Making of the Huron-British Treaty of 1760   49
   Oral and Written Accounts of the Huron-British Treaty, 1760   52
   The Huron-British Treaty and the Courts   58
   Further Readings   63
   Questions for Discussion   63
   Documents   64
   Cast of Characters: Huron-British Treaty of 1760   69

3 Upper Canada Land Surrenders: Rice Lake Treaty of 1818   75
   Oral and Written Accounts of Rice Lake Treaty no. 20   79
   Rice Lake Treaty no. 20 and the Courts   85
   Further Readings   88
   Questions for Discussion   88
   Documents   89
   Cast of Characters: Rice Lake Treaty no. 20, 1818   96

4 The Making of the Robinson-Huron Treaty, 1850   99
   Oral and Written Accounts of the Robinson-Huron Treaty, 1850   105
   The Robinson-Huron Treaty and the Courts   112
   Further Readings   117
   Questions for Discussion   117
   Documents   119
   Cast of Characters: Robinson-Huron Treaty, 1850   130
5 The Making of the Vancouver Island Treaties: Saanich Treaties, 1852   135
   Oral and Written Accounts of the 1852 Saanich Treaties   138
   The Saanich Treaties and the Courts   144
   Further Readings   146
   Questions for Discussion   146
   Documents   147
   Cast of Characters: 1852 Saanich Treaties   153
6 The Early Numbered Treaties: Treaty no. 6, 1876   157
   Oral and Written Accounts of Treaty 6, 1876   163
   Treaty 6 and the Courts   173
   Further Readings   175
   Questions for Discussion   176
   Documents   177
   Cast of Characters: Treaty 6   188
7 The Northern Numbered Treaties: Treaty no. 8, 1899   193
   Oral and Written Accounts of Treaty 8, 1899   196
   Treaty 8 and the Courts   203
   Further Readings   208
   Questions for Discussion   208
   Documents   209
   Cast of Characters: Treaty 8   222
8 The Making of the Williams Treaties, 1923   227
   Oral and Written Accounts of the Williams Treaties, 1923   231
   The Williams Treaties and the Courts   238
   Further Readings   241
   Questions for Discussion   241
   Documents   243
   Cast of Characters: Williams Treaties   251

Index   253

List of Primary Documents

CHAPTER 1
1. Treaty Text: "Cope Treaty," 1752, Peace and Friendship Treaties, Nova Scotia Archives, RG 1, vol. 430, no. 2   36
2. Excerpts from "Minutes of Council Held at Halifax," 1752, in *Selections of Documents from the Province of Nova Scotia*, ed. Thomas B. Akins (Halifax: Charles Annand, 1869)   39
3. Excerpts from "Testimony of Joe Christmas, Gabriel Sylliboy, and Ed Christmas, Proceedings of the Sylliboy Case of 1928, Port Hood, July 4, 1928," in Ruth Holmes Whitehead, *The Old Man Told Us: Excerpts from Mi'kmaw History, 1500–1950* (Halifax: Nimbus, 1991)   40
4. Excerpts from *Simon v. The Queen*, [1985] 2 S.C.R. 387   41

CHAPTER 2
1. Treaty Text: Huron-British Treaty of 1760. As transcribed in the May 24, 1990, *R. v. Sioui* decision of the Supreme Court of Canada, and originating in Archives nationales du Québec, Records of notary Barthélémy Faribault fils, deposited on August 4, 1810, CN301, S99   64
2. "Indian of Lorette," *The Star and Commercial Advertiser*, February 27, 1828, AMICUS: 8396067   64
3. Excerpts from the Journal of James Murray (vol. III, p. 331) and the Journal of Captain John Knox, September 6, 1760 (vol. I, p. 516), in *An Historical Journal of the Campaigns in North America for the Years 1757, 1758, 1759 and 1760 by Captain John Knox*, ed. A.G. Doughty (Toronto: Champlain Society, 1916)   66
4. Excerpt from *R. v. Sioui*, [1990] 1 S.C.R. 1025   67

CHAPTER 3
1. Treaty Text: Rice Lake Treaty, no. 20, November 5, 1818, LAC, RG10, vol. 1842, IT160, IA 20, T-9938   89
2. William Claus, Deputy Superintendent General of Indian Affairs, to Major Bowles, Military Secretary, November 10, 1818, LAC, RG10, vol. 489, pp. 29439–41, C-13339   91

3. Minutes of Council Meeting, November 5, 1818, LAC, RG10, vol. 790, pp. 7029–32   92
4. Account by Chief George Paudash, date unknown, A.E. Williams/United Indian Bands of the Chippewas and the Mississaugas Collection, Provincial Archives of Ontario, F 4337-11-0-8   94
5. Excerpt from *R. v. Taylor and Williams*, 1981, CARSWELLONT 641, 62 C.C.C. (2d) 227 (Ont. C.A.)   95

CHAPTER 4

1. Treaty Text: Robinson Treaty Made in the Year 1850 with the Ojibewa Indians of Lake Huron Conveying Certain Lands to the Crown, September 9, 1850, LAC, RG10, vol. 1844, IT 148, IA 61, T-9938   119
2. William Benjamin Robinson, Treaty Commissioner's Report, September 24, 1850, LAC, RG10, vol. 191, no. 54001–5500, pp. 111709–17, reel C-11513   121
3. Wa-ge-ma-ke and Pa-pa-seance to Governor General, August 17, 1851, LAC, RG10, vol. 572, reel C-13373   125
4. Michel Le Aigle Dokis to Governor General, Marquis of Lorne, 1878, LAC, RG10, vol. 2067, file 10,307, pt. 1, pp. 21762–3, reel C-11149   126
5. Chiefs of Parry Island to Department of Indian Affairs, 1887, LAC, RG10, vol. 2369, file 74,634, p. 75579, reel C-11209   127
6. Information of John Mashekyash – Batchewana Bay, Archives of Ontario, Irving Papers 20/36/3(3), June 1, 1893   128
7. Excerpt from *Ontario (Attorney General) v. Bear Island Foundation*, [1991] 2 S.C.R., 570   129

CHAPTER 5

1. Treaty Text: Treaties with Saanich Tribe, 1852, "Conveyance of Land to Hudson's Bay Company by Indian Tribes," in *Papers Connected with the Indian Land Question, 1850–1875* (Victoria: R. Wolfenden, 1875)   147
2. Excerpt from an interview with Chief David Latasse, conducted by Frank Pagett, "105 Years in Victoria and Saanich!," *Victoria Daily Times*, July 4, 1934, AMICUS: 7727707   148
3. Excerpt from letter from James Douglas to Archibald Barclay, March 18, 1852, HBC Archives reel 1M11.G1/140 / BC Archives A/C/20/Vi2   150
4. Excerpt from *Saanichton Marina Ltd. v. Claxton*, British Columbia Court of Appeal, March 30, 1989 (*Saanichton Marina Ltd. v. Claxton*, 1989 CanLII 2721 (BC CA))   151

CHAPTER 6

1. Treaty Text Excerpts: Treaty No. 6, LAC, RG10, vol. 1847, IT 296, IA 157A, T-9940   177
2. Excerpts from an interview with Elder Fred Horse, Frog Lake First Nation, February 18, 1974, "Indian History Film Project," Canadian Plains Research Centre, University of Regina   181
3. Excerpts from Treaty Commissioner's Report, December 4, 1876, Alexander Morris, *The Treaties of Canada with the Indians of Manitoba and the North-West Territories* (Toronto: Belfords, Clarke and Co., 1880), 180–96   184
4. Excerpt from *R. v. Sundown*, [1999] 1 S.C.R. 393   186

CHAPTER 7

1. Treaty Text Excerpts: Treaty No. 8, LAC, RG10, vol. 1848, IT 415, IA 428, T-9941   209
2. Report of Commissioners for Treaty No. 8   214
3. Excerpts from an interview with Elder William Okeymaw, Sucker Creek First Nation, March 27, 1975, "Indian History Film Project," Canadian Plains Research Centre, University of Regina   217
4. Excerpts from an interview with Elder Felix Gibot, Fort Chipewyan First Nation, February 5, 1974, "Indian History Film Project," Canadian Plains Research Centre, University of Regina   218
5. Excerpt from *R. v. Badger*, [1996] 1 S.C.R. 771   220

CHAPTER 8

1. Treaty Text Excerpts: Treaty Made November 15, 1923, between His Majesty the King and the Mississauga of Rice Lake, Mud Lake, Scugog Lake, and Alderville, LAC, RG10, vol. 1853, IT 483, IA 1080, T-9941   243
2. Excerpt from Williams Commission Report, December 1, 1923, LAC, RG10, vol. 2330, file 67,071–3, pt. 1, reel C-11202   247
3. Statement by Chief John Bigwin, "Indians Claim Right to Fish and Hunt Not Given Up," *Orillia Packet and Times*, June 13, 1938, LAC, RG10, vol. 6960, file 475/20–2, pt. 1   248
4. Excerpts from *R. v. Howard*, [1994] 2 S.C.R. 299, pp. 299–309   250

List of Illustrations

MAPS
Map 1   Historic Treaties of Canada   2

FIGURES
Figure 1.1   A proclamation from Governor Peregrine Hopson, 1752   46
Figure 1.2   A Mi'kmaq family with their chief in Nova Scotia, c. 1801   47
Figure 2.1   James Murray, c. 1770   72
Figure 2.2   Nicolas Vincent (Tsaouenhohoui), c. 1825   73
Figure 3.1   Treaty no. 20, "Lake Rice Purchase," 1818   98
Figure 4.1   William B. Robinson, Chief Shingwauk, and Chief Nenaigooching, 1850   133
Figure 4.2   Robinson-Huron Treaty, September 9, 1850   134
Figure 5.1   Chief David Latasse, 1932   155
Figure 5.2   James Douglas   156
Figure 6.1   Peter Hourie with Chief O'Soup (Chippewa), Chief Flying in a Circle (Ka-ka-wista-ha), Chief Big Child (Mistawasis), and Chief Starblanket (Ahtahkakoop), November 1886   190
Figure 6.2   Alexander Morris   191
Figure 6.3   Western Treaty no. 6, August 23, 1876   192
Figure 7.1   David Laird explaining the terms of Treaty 8, Fort Vermilion, Alberta, 1899   224
Figure 7.2   Treaty 8, June 21, 1899   225
Figure 8.1   Williams Treaty, October 31, 1923   252

Acknowledgments

As a historian working in the public service, I never really thought that I'd ever get around to writing this book. One specific opportunity presented itself that permitted me to have the time and resources to put onto the page what had been running around my head for years. I also had just the right combination of people around me to ensure that I finished what I started.

I would like to express my sincere gratitude to Colleen Swords, former deputy minister of Indigenous Affairs and Northern Development Canada, and Hélène Laurendeau, deputy minister of Crown-Indigenous Relations and Northern Affairs, who allowed me to participate in the Public Servant in Residence program of the Canada School of the Public Service and encouraged me to write this book. I must also express my gratitude to the History Department of Carleton University, which not only hosted me during my residency but also welcomed me as a member of the Ravens family. Special thanks to David Dean, Dominique Marshall, and John Walsh for taking a chance on a government flunky.

As this book was being conceived, I received wise counsel and excellent advice from people with much deeper experience than me. Of special note, I thank Matthew Hayday both for guiding me through my transition into academic life and for helping me understand how to write a book, as well as my colleagues at Crown-Indigenous Relations and Northern Affairs, Keriana McGregor, Kim Robinson, and Tara Jane Hayward, who help me craft my understanding of treaties over a 15-year career.

This work went through several different drafts and revisions along the way, constantly being improved by those who volunteered their precious time. Thanks to Michel Hogue, Jill St. Germain, and Michelle Hamilton for reviewing early drafts of my chapters and providing invaluable comments and suggestions. A special thank you goes to Susan Ward Bond and Kirsten Campbell, who reviewed every sentence, searching out overly complicated sentences, pointing out comma splices, and correcting my tendency for overly complicated words.

Finally, I would like to thank my family, who put up with my constant chatter about this treaty or that one, random quotations from chiefs and commissioners, or arcane archival documents. Thank you to Jeanette Steffler, who has listened to me talk about this topic for far too long, told me to write this book, acted as my sounding board, worked with me to make sense of my ideas, and supported me throughout the entire project. Without her, this book would not exist.

Introduction: Reading a Treaty

In 2011, the Nishnawbe-Aski Nation, an organization representing Treaty 5 and Treaty 9 First Nations of Northern Ontario, held a treaty symposium with the theme "Sharing the History – What Is the Future?" Academic historians, community leaders, government representatives, Treaty Elders, and Lakehead University students gathered to discuss the historical significance of Treaties 5 and 9, the opportunities to strengthen communities through treaty teachings, and the challenges created by the differing interpretations of the spirit and intent of treaties by First Nation signatories and the Crown. As the staff historian of the now defunct Treaty Policy Directorate of Indian and Northern Affairs Canada (now Crown-Indigenous Relations and Northern Affairs Canada), I had been asked to participate in a panel to discuss how the treaty terms have been historically understood by Canada.

As a non-Indigenous person working for the "Department" and discussing the history of treaties with Indigenous partners for over a decade, I was well aware that my statements would be challenged by competing perspectives of other panelists. In short order, the topic of discussion shifted away from how the treaty terms have been understood to who had the "right history" of the treaties, with some panelists stating that the Crown's perspective was based on a false history and me replying that the Crown's perspective on the terms was informed by the limited historical record. As the tension between us increased, an Anishinaabe Elder sitting in the audience had had quite enough of our bickering and strode up onto the stage to quiet us. He bluntly told us that our discussion was not being held in the spirit of the treaty relationship, as no one truly had an open mind to listen to the other. He reasoned that the point of our argument was irrelevant, as we both had the "right" history – my Indigenous co-panelists had the "right" First Nation history of the treaty, and I had the "right" Crown history. He ended his intervention with the blunt assessment that so long as both "histories" are kept separate, we will never have the complete history of the treaties.

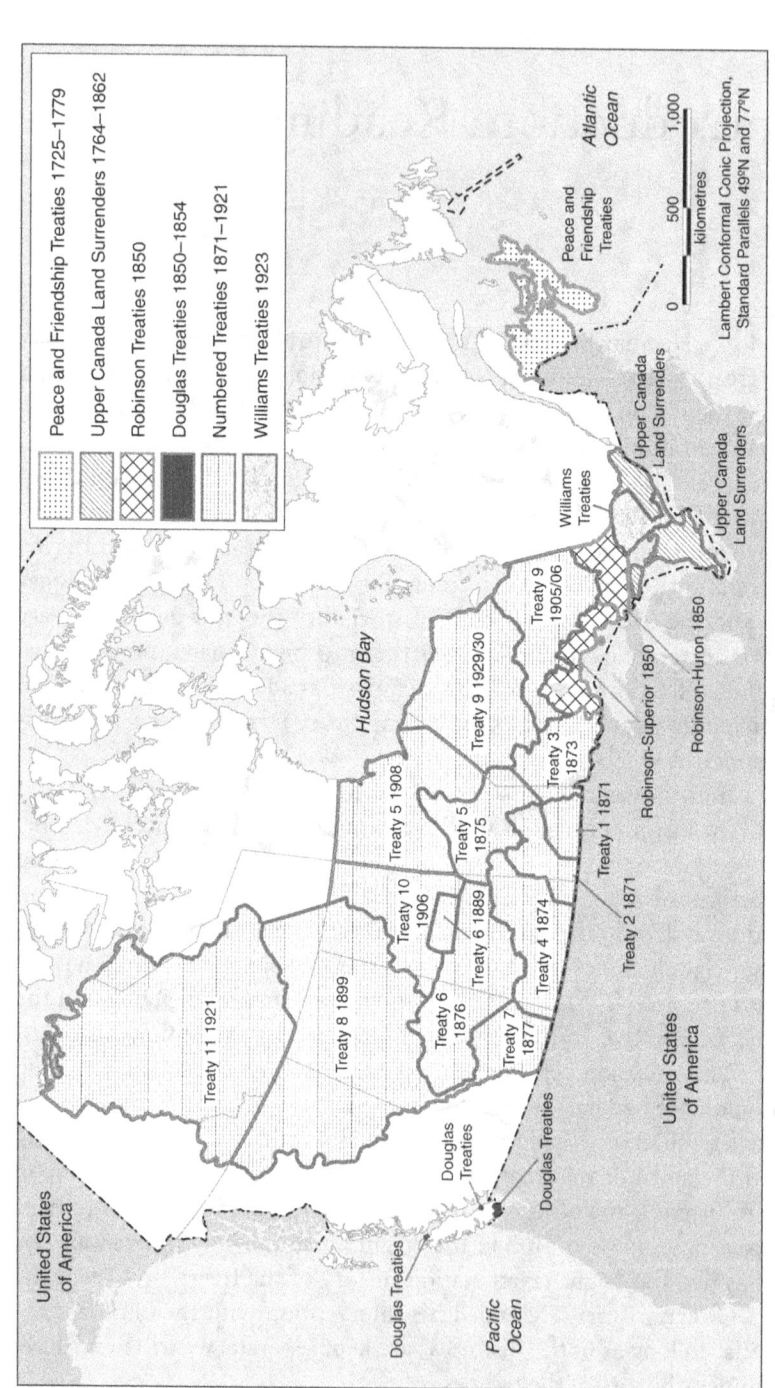

Map 1 Historic Treaties of Canada

Source: Adapted from *Historic Treaties of Canada*, map produced by Indian and Northern Affairs Canada, Lands Directorate.

As has happened many times during my career as a historian and public servant, the wisdom of an Elder forced me to re-examine how I do my work. I realized very quickly that while I thought I was incorporating Indigenous perspectives on treaties in my work, I continued to place an "our history vs. their history" qualification on the different perspectives, limiting my understanding of the meaning, significance, and lasting impact of treaties on Canadian society. In the years since that tense panel discussion in Thunder Bay, I have tried to challenge and change my own narrow perspective on the history of treaties, and consequently to influence the perspectives of my colleagues to see treaty history as a history built on a mutual understanding of treaties. Our understanding of long-standing treaties concluded between the Crown and Indigenous nations is incomplete, and we must strive to work with treaty partners to create a shared understanding of the spirit and the intent of treaties. In my mind, this is part of reconciliation, as creating a complete understanding of the relationships that exist between Indigenous and non-Indigenous peoples will help all peoples in Canada to determine our future together.

In 2015, the Truth and Reconciliation Commission (TRC) issued its final report on the experiences of Indigenous peoples in Canada's residential schools system. The Commission said that reconciliation is an ongoing process "about establishing and maintaining a mutually respectful relationship between Aboriginal and non-Aboriginal peoples in this Country."[1] The commissioners went on to say that to establish such a relationship, there must be an "awareness of the past, acknowledgement of the harm inflicted, atonement for the causes and action to change behaviour." Through the work of the Commission and countless others, we have come to understand that reconciliation is a continuous process that aims to transform our current relationships into ones built on respect and mutual understanding.

Throughout the report's six volumes, the TRC commissioners told Canadians that they needed to be better educated on the impact of residential schools and assimilationist policies if there is ever to be reconciliation within Canadian society. In its calls to action, specifically calls 62 to 65, the Commission invites Canadian educational institutions to develop curriculum on residential schools, treaties, and the history of Indigenous peoples in Canada.[2] Although a number of universities have increased

---

[1] Truth and Reconciliation Commission, *Canada's Residential Schools: Reconciliation*, vol. 6 (Montreal and Kingston: McGill-Queen's University Press, 2015), 3.
[2] Ibid., 235.

the number of Indigenous studies courses, there is still a need for reference materials specifically designed to support the Commission's calls to action. This is especially the case with respect to treaties, despite the fact that they are part of the foundational relationship with Indigenous peoples in Canada.

In its sixth volume, the Commission stated that it was "important for all Canadians to understand that without treaties, Canada would have no legitimacy as a nation."[3] Awareness and knowledge of treaties among Canadians, however, are very low. If we are to properly respond to the Commission's calls to action and build reconciliation between Canadians and Indigenous peoples, a better understanding of the significance and relevance of treaties is essential.

If one of the central tenets of reconciliation is to bring disparate and conflicting perspectives together to create new shared ideas, values, and goals, then that lens must be applied to the differing understandings of treaty history as it defines the relationship between the Crown and over two-thirds of all First Nations in Canada. The Office of the Treaty Commissioner of Saskatchewan describes this as a solemn and political relationship between the Treaty First Nations and the Crown, created by the obligation to mutually respect the treaty, where both parties have benefits and responsibilities in regards to the other.[4] This treaty relationship is bound and defined by the agreements but hampered by the rift between the treaty parties. The history of treaty making is contentious, with differing interpretations and understanding of the "spirit and intent" of treaties depending on one's world view. While both government and Indigenous representatives were seeking to conclude agreements, the reasons behind that intent differed greatly, and these differences continue to influence how they are understood. Healing this rift can be done only through a better understanding of the differences and similarities of historical interpretation and the enduring impact on current understanding of treaties. To create a shared history of treaties, we must look to how the understanding of the treaties by the parties has changed and how this difficult history affects the current treaty relationship. As the Truth and Reconciliation Commission stated, "History plays an important role in reconciliation; to build for the future, Canadians must look to, and learn from, the past."[5]

---

[3] Ibid., 33.
[4] Office of the Treaty Commissioner, *Statement of Treaty Issues: Treaties as a Bridge to the Future* (Saskatoon: OTC, 1998), 67.
[5] Truth and Reconciliation Commission, *Canada's Residential Schools: Reconciliation*, vol. 6, p. 4.

If you were to pick up and read one of the over 70 treaties concluded between Indigenous nations and British authorities, and later the government of Canada between 1701 and 1923, it may appear to be fairly straightforward. Everything is right there, written on paper. The terms are spelled out, the signatories are listed, the monarch's name invoked as the ultimate authority. Some treaties indicate that there will be "peace and friendship" between the parties, such as in the treaty concluded at Halifax in 1752.[6] Other treaties state that the First Nation signatories will have "the full and free privilege to hunt over the Territory now ceded by them, and to fish in the waters thereof, as they have heretofore been in the habit of doing," as in the 1850 Robinson Treaties signed at Sault Ste. Marie.[7] Still others indicate that the government will "lay aside reserves for such bands as desire reserves, the same not to exceed in all one square mile for each family of five," as it does in Treaty 8, concluded in 1899.[8]

The text alone does not provide the definitive understanding of the treaty, as there is very little consensus about the meaning, the scope, and the intent behind these words. These agreements bear witness to the interactions of different cultures and world views, and the differing understandings of the treaty terms are also influenced by these views. Over the course of nearly three centuries, agreements were concluded from the Atlantic coast, across the Great Lakes Basin and into the Prairies, and down to the Pacific coast and up through the Mackenzie Valley. The practice of concluding treaties was not new, as there was a long-standing diplomatic practice of treaty making among Indigenous nations prior to the arrival of Europeans. Hundreds of different Indigenous communities met, discussed, and negotiated agreements with, depending on the time period, representatives of colonial administrations, and finally the agents of the Dominion of Canada. Just as the different Indigenous parties represented vastly different cultural beliefs and understandings from one region to the next, the representatives of the "Crown," either the British or the Canadian authority, also had views of the world that changed over the course of time. As a result, each treaty has terms that must be understood in relation to its specific circumstances: why the treaty was needed; the nature of the relationship between the parties; who participated in the negotiation; and what was happening outside of the treaty discussions.

---

[6] "Cope Treaty," November 22, 1752, Nova Scotia Archives, Peace and Friendship Treaties, RG 1, vol. 430, no. 2.

[7] "Robinson-Huron Treaty," September 9, 1850, Library and Archives Canada, Treaties and Surrenders, RG10, vol. 1844, IT 148, R216-79-6-E, MIKAN: 3963991.

[8] "Treaty 8," June 21, 1899, Library and Archives Canada, Treaties and Surrenders, RG10, vol. 1851, IT 415, R216-245-8-E, MIKAN: 2061036.

Asking these questions challenges long-held historical and legal positions that the terms of treaties and their interpretation are limited by the scope and extent of the actual text. As J.R. Miller notes in *Compact, Contract and Covenant: Aboriginal Treaty-Making in Canada*, governments have long limited their interpretation of treaties by focusing "on the language of their own treaty texts, with their descriptions of alienating Indian lands and subordinating First Nations to the authority of the queen's [sic] government."[9] Government largely viewed treaties as contracts dealing primarily with land cession. In contrast to this primarily legal view of treaty interpretation, Treaty Elders from the different regions of Canada have criticized this legalistic and narrow position, arguing that "treaty rights, obligations, duties and relationships cannot be determined solely by references to the written articles of treaty."[10] As Harold Cardinal and Walter Hildebrandt note in their commentary on Elders' teachings in Saskatchewan, the written text is not reflective of the "spirit and intent" of the agreements made, and the written treaty "distorts or misrepresents the understandings" of the parties.[11] This reliance on the written text also attacks Indigenous agency, as it overlooks the long-standing diplomatic and political activities of Indigenous parties, such as treaty making.[12]

In several cases, the Supreme Court of Canada has ruled that a limited interpretation based solely on the text is incorrect. In its 1983 *Nowegijick* and 1985 *Simon* decisions, the Supreme Court stated that treaties needed to be "liberally construed,"[13] and in the subsequent *Badger* decision it recognized that the text itself did not "always record the full extent of the oral agreements" and that the treaties must "be interpreted in the sense that they would naturally have been understood by the Indians at the time of the signing."[14] In 1999, Supreme Court Justice Beverly McLachlin summarized the various legal arguments into nine principles of interpretation, such as that treaties constitute a unique type of agreement and attract special principles of interpretation, that courts must be sensitive

---

[9] J.R. Miller, *Compact, Contract, Covenant: Aboriginal Treaty-Making in Canada* (Toronto: University of Toronto Press, 2009), 191.
[10] Harold Cardinal and Walter Hildebrandt, *Treaty Elders of Saskatchewan: Our Dream Is That Our Peoples Will One Day Be Clearly Recognized as Nations* (Calgary: University of Calgary Press, 2000), 50.
[11] Ibid.
[12] Adam Gaudry, "Fantasies of Sovereignty: Deconstructing British and Canadian Claims to Ownership of the Historic North-West," *Native American and Indigenous Studies* 3, no. 1 (2016): 47.
[13] *Nowegijick v. The Queen*, [1983] 1 S.C.R. 29, [1983] 2 C.N.L.R. 89 (S.C.C.).
[14] *R. v. Badger*, [1996] 1 S.C.R. 771, para. 52.

to the unique cultural and linguistic differences between the parties, and that treaty rights must not be interpreted in a static or rigid way.[15] While, as Aimée Craft noted, these principles summarize and refine the interpretive canons of treaty in a way that brings greater weight to Indigenous understandings, they have not remediated the tendency of privileging the Crown's interpretation of treaties.[16] These interpretive principles are also limited by the very nature of the judicial system as an extension of the settler state; as John Borrows has noted, "the source of judicial power often cascades from the dominant group's ideological headwaters," often reinforcing colonial bias in legal decisions.[17] This power imbalance is also demonstrated by the constant need for nations, groups, communities, and individuals to assert recognition of their rights, but also their Indigenous identity. Taiaiake Alfred and Jeff Corntassel have argued that this formal recognition of the Indigenous identity as part of settler judicial systems distorts the true identity of communities by forcing this identity to meet the criteria imposed by the settler state.[18]

Indigenous legal scholar James (Sakej) Youngblood Henderson and colleagues have indicated that rulings from the Canadian courts mean that the context in which a treaty was discussed, agreed upon, and written must be taken into consideration to properly understand the significance of treaty terms.[19] Furthermore, as Janna Promislow notes in her commentary "Treaties in History and Law," treaties are "dynamic, ongoing relationships anchored by shared commitment to that relationship and the attendant mutual recognition and respect" that "present both legal and political problems that demand solutions that take the past, present and future into account."[20] For good or ill, the courts have provided us with a framework to help us reconcile the Eurocentric and Indigenous perspectives of treaties.

For Elders, historians, and the courts, reading a treaty concluded between Indigenous nations and the Crown also necessitates going beyond

---

[15] *R. v. Marshall*, [1999] 3 S.C.R. 456, para. 78. The full list of the interpretative principles can be found at the end of this chapter.

[16] Aimée Craft, "Breathing Life into the Stone Fort Treaty" (MLaw thesis, University of Victoria, 2011), 8.

[17] John Borrows, "Constitutional Law from a First Nation Perspective: Self-Government and the Royal Proclamation," *UBC Law Review* 28, no. 1 (1994): 2.

[18] Taiaiake Alfred and Jeff Corntassel, "Being Indigenous: Resurgences against Contemporary Colonialism," *Government and Opposition* 40, no. 4 (2005): 601.

[19] James (Sakej) Youngblood Henderson, Marjorie L. Benson, and Isobel M. Findlay, *Aboriginal Tenure in the Constitution of Canada* (Scarborough, ON: Carswell Thomson, 2000), 244.

[20] Janna Promislow, "Treaties in History and Law," *UBC Law Review* 47, no. 3 (2014): 1086.

the limits of the written text. Based on their work with Saskatchewan Treaty Elders, Cardinal and Hildebrandt tell us that to know the true understanding of treaties, one needs the oral evidence and oral histories of Treaty First Nations, the treaty commissioners' reports and other documents, the records of other non-Indigenous witnesses such as missionaries and North-West Mounted Police officers, and the official written versions.[21] In other words, to understand the treaty terms, we need to consider what was said, by whom, and for what reasons. Couple this with the directions of the Supreme Court to "liberally construe" treaty terms, to seek the understanding of the parties at the time of treaty making, and to be sensitive to the cultural and linguistic differences between the parties,[22] and we can start to form a much broader approach to help us read these treaties. This approach creates the framework for the chapters of this book.

While there are several different starting points to read a treaty, such as from an oral history or a court ruling, the most common approach is to start with the treaty text based on the original archival document. One reason to do so stems from the fact that government relies on the text as the basis for its understanding, while Indigenous understandings are often expressed as an opposition to the Crown's interpretation based on that text. Furthermore, the fact that the written texts have formed an important part of the court process has made them the "official" record of the agreements between the parties.

Each chapter covers one specific treaty, starting with the 1752 Cope Treaty and concluding with the 1923 Williams Treaties, and a brief analysis of the documents, discussion questions, and the full text of the sources. The analysis discusses the differing perspectives on the meaning of the terms of the treaty and allows for the juxtaposition of sources from "both sides of the treaty table" in order to uncover the understanding both of the parties at the time of signing and of how the courts have used these interpretations in their rulings. Individual chapters also include four different sources in their examination of a treaty: the treaty text, a published or archived oral history of the treaty, the formal settler account or report of the treaty negotiation, and a court ruling dealing with the treaty in question. It should be noted that the text of the treaties discussed in a specific chapter is a transcription of the original signed document, when possible, or the oldest existing archival version. Every effort has been made to ensure the accuracy and integrity of the text, including spelling and punctuation

---

[21] Cardinal and Hildebrandt, *Treaty Elders of Saskatchewan*, 50.
[22] *R. v. Marshall*, para. 75.

style. Of the over 70 agreements that could have been examined here, eight treaties have been selected as case studies. The treaties cover nearly the complete time period (1701–1923) of treaty making prior to the current comprehensive land-claims process, the so-called "modern treaties." In addition, the selected treaties all have strong archival records, along with archived and published oral histories, and are central elements in legal decisions and jurisprudence.

The first two chapters examine treaties concluded during the height of colonial competition between France and Britain, where each sought to solidify its relationships and alliances with Indigenous nations. Chapter 1 looks at the 1752 treaty signed at Halifax, one of the so-called Peace and Friendship Treaties concluded between 1725 and 1779, between Major Jean Baptiste Cope of the Mi'kmaq community of Shubenacadie and British governor Peregrine Hopson. The 1752 "Cope Treaty" not only is typical of the treaty-making process in the Atlantic region at that time but also shows how new clauses were added and later understood by the parties as the Indigenous-settler relationship changed. In Chapter 2, the unique nature of the Huron-British Treaty of 1760 is examined. It is representative of the changing nature of military alliances and the motivation of both parties – the Huron of Lorette and the British commanders trying to secure the last territories of New France during the Seven Years' War. It is a controversial agreement long denied by the Crown, and the struggle for treaty recognition by the Huron-Wendat highlights how the courts have influenced treaty interpretation by the very act of recognizing an agreement as a treaty.

The third chapter focuses on one of the treaties covering southern Ontario and negotiated under the protocols established by the Royal Proclamation of 1763. Concluded in 1818, the Rice Lake Treaty was one of the first agreements concluded after the War of 1812 – a period when the British were reconsidering the nature of the military alliance with the region's Indigenous nations. The differing words of the Crown's representative and the treaty text had a profound impact on the Indigenous signatories' understanding of the treaty, an understanding that continues to affect the current relationship between signatory First Nations and settler governments.

Building on the process of treaty making for land in what is today Ontario, Chapter 4 focuses on the understanding of the Robinson-Huron Treaty of 1850. As a somewhat different model of treaty making with a broader range of rights and promises that would influence later agreements, the examination of the Robinson-Huron Treaty will shed light on the changing nature of the Indigenous-Crown relationship and how differing perspectives continue to have an impact upon modern-day treaty interpretation.

By turning to the treaties concluded by the Hudson's Bay Company on Vancouver Island, specifically the 1852 Saanich Treaties, Chapter 5 offers a view into a period of early contact and how settlers and Indigenous peoples saw one another. An examination of some of the "Douglas" or "Vancouver Island" treaties also allows for a discussion of how treaties can be understood when there is a paucity of written records but a rich oral history. The unique nature of these treaties, as compared to those east of the Rockies, also provides some insight into the ongoing land question in British Columbia.

In Chapters 6 and 7, some of the best-known treaties – Treaty 6 of 1876 and Treaty 8 of 1899 – will be considered. Treaty 6, covering the central parts of Saskatchewan and Alberta, is an excellent case study of the first phase of treaty making in the years after Confederation, which was based largely on the Robinson Treaties of 1850. With its unique clauses and long legal history, the debates around the meaning and intent of Treaty 6 are rich and diverse. Treaty 8 is the first agreement of the second phase of post-Confederation treaty making, covering the mineral- and resource-rich lands of the Athabasca and Peace rivers. In this case, the treaty negotiations marked a new approach by Canada that profoundly shaped both Indigenous and settler perspectives of the treaty.

In the final chapter, the last treaties concluded prior to the modern treaty-making policies of the 1970s have our attention. Concluded after the last western treaty in 1921, the Williams Treaties saw a reversion in the Crown's treaty making, as they have fewer specified rights and promises. Overlapping with a number of earlier agreements, including the Rice Lake Treaty of 1818 and the Robinson-Huron Treaty of 1850, the Williams Treaties present a unique case of competing treaties, radically different interpretations, and a unique legal history.

Each chapter flows from the treaty text and moves through other supporting documents toward the court ruling, thus enabling an understanding and comparison of the differing perspectives and their legacy. In order to make comparisons between the various understandings of a treaty, we can be guided by these specific questions in three key areas:

- **What is the context of the treaty?** What were the events that led to the conclusion of the agreement? What were the "geopolitical" considerations of the parties? Who was present at the treaty negotiations? As the agreements concluded are the result of specific circumstances that brought certain peoples together, the reasons that led to the very creation of the treaty are part of the perspectives held by the parties.

- **How were the agreements recorded?** In what medium are the treaty terms preserved: oral or textual? Who was the intended audience? Why were the treaties being recorded in the first place? Any attempt at reconciling the differing perspectives must be based on what the parties themselves believe they concluded in the agreements. It is therefore necessary to understand what was included or omitted from the record, and how they compare and contrast to one another.
- **How have these documents been used?** What has been said about the documents? How have they been used by the courts? How have they been challenged, rejected, or supported? Treaties are agreements that establish both rights and obligations. As a result, the courts play a significant role in helping define and interpret their scope and meaning. How court rulings use the treaty texts and the record shapes, for good or ill, the way in which treaties are understood, their terms applied, and their relationships respected.

Similar to the approach of assessing historical records by "reading against the grain," the treaty text, oral and textual records, and court rulings around a treaty all require a critical approach to bring a clearer understanding of the differing perspectives. As Keith D. Smith notes in his introduction to *Strange Visitors: Documents in Indigenous-Settler Relations in Canada from 1876*, students of Indigenous history must strive to "read against the grain" and try to "understand the author's overt message and endeavour to unmask or uncover contradictions, inconsistencies, absences, preconceptions, and biases even if these may not have been intentional."[23] In the specific case of "reading a treaty," we are seeking to look beyond what is in the limited words of the treaty text and place the agreement within the competing world views of the treaty parties, identify where understandings converge, and examine how these differing perspectives have influenced the Indigenous-settler relationship.

This means using official reports and settler documents created around the time of the events, oral histories and teachings of the treaties shared among Indigenous communities, Indian Affairs records and reports, newspaper articles about the treaty meetings and interviews with

---

[23] Keith D. Smith, *Strange Visitors: Documents in Indigenous-Settler Relations in Canada from 1876* (Toronto: University of Toronto Press, 2014), xxi.

Indigenous Elders, court proceedings and testimonies of treaty-related litigation, and the work of historians, legal scholars, and community leaders. The four specific documents in each chapter (treaty text, settler written account, unrestricted recorded Indigenous oral history, and court decision) are but a small sample of all the sources that could be used to help students better understand the place of treaties in Canadian history and ongoing Indigenous-settler relations. Choices were made to focus on the most accessible sources that built on one another and culminated in a court process. The goal here is to show one way to "read a treaty" and help students understand that we are all Treaty Peoples, as all Canadians continue to benefit from treaties. Such an understanding is part of the process of moving toward reconciliation in Canada.

It should be noted that in this reader, the term "Indigenous" has been chosen when broadly referring to the First Peoples of Turtle Island/North America; however, the terms preferred by specific groups, communities, and nations will be used. For example, "Anishinaabeg" will be used for the Indigenous communities inhabiting the Kawartha Lakes region of Ontario, while the specific community will be referred to by the names they use, such as Hiawatha First Nation or Curve Lake First Nation.

FURTHER READINGS

Harold Cardinal and Walter Hildebrandt. *Treaty Elders of Saskatchewan: Our Dream Is That Our Peoples Will One Day Be Clearly Recognized as Nations.* Calgary: University of Calgary Press, 2000.

J.R. Miller, *Compact, Contract, Covenant: Aboriginal Treaty-Making in Canada.* Toronto: University of Toronto Press, 2009.

Janna Promislow. "Treaties in History and Law." *UBC Law Review* 47, no. 3 (2014): 1085–1111.

Truth and Reconciliation Commission. *Canada's Residential Schools: Reconciliation.* Vol. 6. Montreal and Kingston: McGill-Queen's University Press, 2015.

LEGAL PRINCIPLES OF TREATY INTERPRETATION USED BY THE SUPREME COURT OF CANADA[24]

1. Aboriginal treaties constitute a unique type of agreement and attract special principles of interpretation.
2. Treaties should be liberally construed and ambiguities or doubtful expressions should be resolved in favour of the aboriginal signatories.

---

[24] *R. v. Marshall*, [1999] 3 S.C.R. 456.

3. The goal of treaty interpretation is to choose from among the various possible interpretations of common intention the one which best reconciles the interests of both parties at the time the treaty was signed.
4. In searching for the common intention of the parties, the integrity and honour of the Crown is presumed.
5. In determining the signatories' respective understanding and intentions, the court must be sensitive to the unique cultural and linguistic differences between the parties.
6. The words of the treaty must be given the sense which they would naturally have held for the parties at the time.
7. A technical or contractual interpretation of treaty wording should be avoided.
8. While construing the language generously, courts cannot alter the terms of the treaty by exceeding what "is possible on the language" or realistic.
9. Treaty rights of aboriginal peoples must not be interpreted in a static or rigid way. They are not frozen at the date of signature. The interpreting court must update treaty rights to provide for their modern exercise. This involves determining what modern practices are reasonably incidental to the core treaty right in its modern context.

TIMELINE

1500–1600s	Indigenous peoples of the Atlantic coast undertake trade with French and Basque fishers and whalers, exchanging furs and food from the mainland for European finished goods.
1534	St. Laurent Iroquois encounter Jacques Cartier's expedition near Stadacona, the current site of Quebec City.
1605	Founding of Port-Royal on the shore of the Bay of Fundy.
1650s	Dispersal of the Huron-Wendat from Huronia by the Iroquois. A group of Huron resettle near Quebec City.
1670	The Company of Adventurers of England Trading into Hudson's Bay, commonly known as the Hudson's Bay Company, receives a Royal Charter granting it exclusive British trading rights to the Hudson Bay watershed.
1701	With the goal of ending the Franco-Iroquois wars as well as conflicts between the Haudenosaunee and the nations

of the Great Lakes allied with New France, the Great Peace of Montreal is concluded between New France and over 40 Indigenous nations.

1713   Great Britain and France conclude the Treaty of Utrecht to end the War of Spanish Succession, which cedes French-claimed territories of Acadia on the peninsula of Nova Scotia to Britain. France retains its claim on Île Royale (Cape Breton Island) and Île St-Jean (Prince Edward Island), as well as lands on the north shore of the Bay of Fundy. The region's Mi'kmaq and Maliseet peoples are not consulted or party to the negotiations.

1725–79   The Maritime Peace and Friendship Treaties are negotiated between the Mi'kmaq and Maliseet peoples of the Maritimes and the British, to re-establish peaceful relations between them during a period marred by colonial military conflict.

1752   The chief of Shubenacadie, Jean Baptiste Cope, concludes a Peace and Friendship treaty at Halifax with Governor Hopson that recognizes continued hunting and fishing rights and peaceful relations between the Mi'kmaq and the British in Nova Scotia.

1754–63   The struggle for European colonial domination erupts again into warfare. Considered the first "global war," the Seven Years' War sees Indigenous warriors participating on both sides of the conflict.

1755   As a response to the growing colonial conflict with the French, British officials create an Indian Department to manage the military relationship between colonial officials and their Indigenous allies. William Johnson is appointed superintendent for the Northern District.

1760   The Indigenous allies of New France abandon the French and call upon the British to recognize their neutrality in the Seven Years' War. Two treaties are concluded in 1760: the Treaty of Swegatchie and the Huron-British Treaty between the British and the Confederacy of Seven Fires and the Huron-Wendat.

1763–6   In an effort to ensure control over their lands from British claims after the fall of New France, a coalition of nations in the Great Lakes and Ohio Valley rally around the leadership of Odawa chief Obwandiyag, known as Pontiac by the British, and attempt to dislodge British

	troops now occupying former French trading posts and forts.
1763	After the transfer of New France to the United Kingdom, a Royal Proclamation is issued to establish the new administrative structure of the British North American colonies. The Proclamation also establishes an Indigenous territory outside of the colonial boundaries to be protected from encroachment. Rules and protocols for the acquisition of Indigenous lands by Crown officials are also set out, and they become the basis for all future lands treaties.
1764	Representatives of some 24 different nations meet with Sir William Johnson at Niagara to discuss trade and diplomatic relations throughout the Great Lakes region. In light of the ongoing conflict in the Great Lakes region, Johnson uses the Royal Proclamation to forge a new alliance between the British and Indigenous nations.
1764–1862	In an effort to open new lands for a growing colony, the Indian Department negotiates a series of land-surrender treaties throughout the St. Lawrence Valley and the Great Lakes Basin. These treaties cover relatively small parcels of land and exchange Indigenous rights and title to the British in exchange for a one-time payment or annuity.
1805	The Anishinaabeg inhabiting the north shore of Lake Ontario and Deputy Superintendent William Claus conclude a renewal of previous agreements to transfer parts of the north shore of Lake Ontario to the British, including the site of the Toronto Carrying Place.
1812–14	War of 1812 between the British and the United States. Nearly 10,000 Indigenous warriors fight alongside the British regulars and local militias to defend their homes and lands against the Americans, notably Shawnee leader Tecumseh, who sought to confirm an independent Indigenous territory around the Ohio and Mississippi river valleys.
1817	The Earl of Selkirk, in his attempt to establish a colony on the Red River, concludes a treaty with five Chiefs for the purchase of land along the shores of the Red and Assiniboine rivers.
1816–30s	With the end of military threats from the United States, British administrators believe that there is no longer

	a military role for Indigenous nations in the colonies. Now viewed as a burden upon the development of the colonies, the Indian Department begins initiatives to help settle and "civilize" Indigenous peoples.
1818	The Anishinaabeg of the Kawartha Lakes region and William Claus conclude the "Rice Lake Treaty" to open up the lands north of Rice Lake to European settlement in exchange for payments, reserve lands, and hunting and fishing rights.
1821	A revision to the Hudson's Bay Company Charter grants the company an exclusive monopoly of trade in lands west of the continental divide to the Pacific coast.
1849	The Hudson's Bay Company makes Fort Victoria on Vancouver Island its primary post on the Pacific coast as part of its obligation to establish a colony on the Pacific coast.
1850	The Robinson Treaties are concluded in 1850 at Sault Ste. Marie for the lands around lakes Superior and Huron, creating a new model for future negotiations.
1850–4	On Vancouver Island, a series of 14 treaties are concluded between the Salish and Kwakiutl peoples and the governor and chief factor of the HBC, James Douglas, for the lands around the new settlement at Victoria, as well as near Fort Rupert and Nanaimo further to the north of the Island.
1857	House of Assembly of the Province of Canada adopts the *Gradual Civilisation Act* to incentivize the assimilation of Indigenous peoples in the province of Canada by granting land to those deemed sufficiently integrated into colonial society.
1860	After more than 100 years of British administration, management of Indian affairs is transferred from the Home Office in Britain to each individual colony.
1867	The colonies of Canada, New Brunswick, and Nova Scotia merge to form the Dominion of Canada. Under Section 91, paragraph 24 of the *British North America Act*, responsibility for "Indians" and their lands resides with the federal government – only Canada has the authority to negotiate treaties with Indigenous nations.
1869	The Dominion of Canada and the Hudson's Bay Company conclude the purchase of the Company's

	Charter to Rupert's Land in exchange for £300,000. No consultation was undertaken with the region's Indigenous peoples.
1871–1921	Concerned by American expansionism and the need to assert its sovereignty across the Northwest Territories, Ottawa undertakes the negotiation of seven treaties across the southern Prairies. The transfer of Indigenous title to the Crown allows for agricultural settlement and the construction of the Canadian Pacific Railway. After 1899, four more treaties are concluded to cover the resource-rich northern lands.
1876	Alexander Morris, lieutenant-governor of Manitoba and the Northwest Territories, concludes a treaty at Fort Carlton and Fort Pitt with the Cree, Assiniboine, and Saulteaux of the Saskatchewan River region.
1876	The House of Commons passes legislation, the *Indian Act*, consolidating existing acts and regulations relating to Indigenous peoples and reserve lands. The Act also defines who is an Indian and what constitutes a band.
1880	Because of the growth and complexity of Indian affairs, the Department of Indian Affairs is created as a separate department from the Department of the Interior.
1898	After the gold strike at Bonanza Creek leads to the Klondike Gold Rush and the arrival of thousands of miners and prospectors, Canada establishes the Yukon as a separate territory from the Northwest Territories.
1899	In response to growing demands from Indigenous communities and fearing a disruption of access to the Klondike, David Laird leads negotiations to conclude a new treaty with the peoples of the Peace and Athabasca river regions.
1905	The provinces of Alberta and Saskatchewan are created out of the Northwest Territories, but the provincial governments have no control over most of the provinces' natural resources.
1914–19	Over 4,000 Indigenous men serve during the First World War.
1916	Justice R.V. Sinclair leads a commission of inquiry in central Ontario and determines that earlier colonial treaties in the region had not fully addressed Indigenous rights and interests. He proposes that a new treaty

	be negotiated with the Anishinaabeg (Chippewa and Mississauga) peoples.
1923	Following the recommendation of his commission to establish new treaties to address the shortcomings of treaties concluded in the nineteenth century, A.S. Williams concludes treaties with the Anishinaabeg peoples of the Lake Simcoe and Kawartha Lakes regions, for their rights and title in exchange for a one-time payment.
1923–75	The Government of Canada ends large-scale treaty making with Indigenous nations, believing that costs were too high and the process was no longer necessary.
1927	Under the direction of Duncan Campbell Scott, deputy superintendent general of Indian Affairs, the *Indian Act* is amended, making it illegal for litigators to solicit funds from a First Nation without the expressed approval of the superintendent of Indian Affairs. The amendment effectively prevents First Nations from using the courts to advance any claims or defend treaty rights. The amendment is repealed in 1951.
1930	The federal government and the provinces of Manitoba, Saskatchewan, and Alberta finalize the *Natural Resources Transfer Agreement* to transfer control of natural resources to provincial jurisdiction. The agreement also unilaterally limits Indigenous hunting and fishing rights under the Numbered Treaties to non-commercial purposes.
1938	The first attempts at commercial extraction of oil from the Athabasca oil sands are undertaken by Abasand Oils Ltd., in the Treaty 8 territory of Alberta.
1939–45	Over 4,000 Indigenous men serve during the Second World War.
1946–8	Following a shift in public perception toward Indigenous peoples, a Joint Committee of the Senate and the House of Commons on Indian Affairs is convened to examine the needs and requirements of Canada's Indigenous peoples. Its eventual committee report opens the way to major changes in Indian Policy.
1951	As a response to the Special Committee's recommendations, amendments are made to the *Indian Act* to remove some overtly paternalistic and coercive

	elements and to create the Indian Registry. Federal control of local affairs and residential schools are unaffected.
1966	After being reduced to the level of a branch, Indian Affairs regains its status as a department when it is merged with Northern Affairs.
1969	The Pierre Trudeau government introduces its "Statement of the Government of Canada on Indian Policy," commonly known as the "White Paper," that proposes abolishing Indian Status, repealing the *Indian Act*, dismantling the Department of Indian Affairs, and terminating treaties. Faced with overwhelming Indigenous resistance, the proposals are withdrawn in 1971.
1970	Harold Cardinal publishes *The Unjust Society* as a rebuttal to the White Paper and spearheads the Indian Association of Alberta's response, *Citizens Plus*, which becomes the driving message of resistance against the government's proposal.
1973	In the *Calder* decision, the Supreme Court recognizes that Indigenous land title may still exist in British Columbia and that it is not incompatible with common law. The federal government establishes the Comprehensive Land Claims process to address outstanding Indigenous rights to lands and natural resources in areas not covered by existing treaties. The claims are called "comprehensive" because of their wide scope and the fact that they address such things as land title, fishing and trapping rights, and financial compensation.
1973	A separate policy, the Specific Claims Policy, is developed to address grievances that First Nations have regarding the fulfilment of treaties and claims relating to the administration of First Nations lands and assets under the *Indian Act*.
1980–1	In the lead-up to the repatriation of the Canadian Constitution, Indigenous leaders charter two trains, known as the "Constitution Express," carrying nearly 1,000 people from Vancouver to Ottawa to publicize concerns that Aboriginal and treaty rights could be abolished by the proposed draft of the Constitution. As the demonstrations continue to the United Nations and

	London, the Trudeau Government agrees to recognize Aboriginal and treaty rights in the Constitution.
1982	The repatriation of the Constitution and the inclusion of Section 35 enshrines the protections of existing Aboriginal and treaty rights.
1985	Bill C-31 receives Royal Assent to modify the *Indian Act* to remove discrimination against women whose Indian Status was lost through marriage to non-status men. The amendment also establishes a process to grant status to the children of these women.
1995	The adoption of the Inherent Right Policy marks a major shift in Indigenous policy in Canada by making a clear break in a long line of paternalistic and controlling policies by recognizing Indigenous nations' right to be self-governing.
1996	The Royal Commission on Aboriginal Peoples issues its final report and tackles nearly every issue affecting Indigenous peoples in Canada. At its core, the RCAP report calls on Canada and Indigenous peoples to create a new and stronger relationship.
1998	Canada issues *Gathering Strength* as a response to the RCAP report, where it states that Canada will work toward strengthening its relationship with Indigenous peoples and bridging the gap between them and non-Indigenous Canadians.
1999	The Supreme Court of Canada rules in the *Marshall* decision that the "truck house" clause of the Peace and Friendship Treaty of 1760–61 guarantees a "right to a moderate livelihood" for Indigenous signatories.
2008	Prime Minister Stephen Harper formally apologizes to all residential school survivors for their experiences, and establishes a Truth and Reconciliation Commission.
2015	The Truth and Reconciliation Commission releases its final report and presents its 94 calls to action. Several of its calls to action emphasize the need for greater understanding of treaties concluded between Indigenous nations and the Crown.

Chapter 1
The Making of the Peace and Friendship Treaties, 1725–1779

Throughout the seventeenth and eighteenth centuries, the empires of France and Britain continued their struggle for colonial domination of North America. The coast of the Gulf of St. Lawrence, the isthmus of Chignecto, the peninsula of Nova Scotia, and the Bay of Fundy were of particular strategic importance to the European colonizers because these territories were the entrance to the interior of the continent and valued for the economic wealth of its forests, furs, and fishing. Since 1605, the burgeoning French colony of "Acadie" had outgrown its first settlement, the Habitation de Port Royal on the shores of the Bay of Fundy, and the French wanted to expand the settlement. The English Crown had granted a colonial charter for New Scotland (*Nova Scotia*) in 1621 to William Alexander (who had previously led two failed settlements on the peninsula). As European nations eyed their maps, and claimed and affixed new names to territories, the Mi'kmaq continued to live on their ancestral land, the Mi'kma'ki – the peninsula and the coastal lands of the Gulf of St. Lawrence and the Atlantic. Divided into different communal territories, the Mi'kmaq saw relatively little disruption from the newcomers in those early years of European presence.[1] Through their long period of coastal contact with European fishers and explorers, a long-standing trade relationship brought new goods into communities, decades prior to the first permanent European settlements. While a European presence along the coast brought trade, it also brought others seeking to enslave the region's Indigenous population. The presence of British slavers raiding along the coast of the Mi'kma'ki

---

[1] L.F.S. Upton, "Contact and Conflict on the Atlantic and Pacific Coasts of Canada," *Acadiensis* 9, no. 2 (1980): 5.

and kidnapping Mi'kmaq since the 1600s created considerable and lasting distrust of later British settlers.[2]

European conflicts continuously spilled over into North America, including Mi'kma'ki lands. The French, having established stronger relations with the Mi'kmaq, the Malecite, and Passamaquoddy than the British, often called upon their Indigenous allies for support in these ongoing conflicts. They ensured the security of French activity in the area.[3] Due to strong kinship and growing religious ties with the newcomers, Mi'kmaq warriors took up arms in support of their allies. The French routinely encouraged guerrilla warfare, pushing the Mi'kmaq to harass the British, and sporadically attacked New England fishing boats and trade vessels. The attacks continued until 1713, when hostilities in Europe and the Americas ended with the signing of the Treaty of Utrecht.

With no consultation or consideration for its Indigenous allies, France relinquished its claims to the part of Acadia constituting present-day Nova Scotia to Britain in 1713, when its military campaigns suffered defeat in the latter part of the war. France retained Île Royale (Cape Breton Island), Île St-Jean (Prince Edward Island), and present-day New Brunswick.[4] The Treaty of Utrecht did not settle all tension in the peninsula. The allegiance of the Mi'kmaq to the French and the presence of a fair-sized Acadian population in the isthmus of Chignecto and into the Annapolis Valley made British administrators uncertain and uneasy. In the years following the transfer, and despite the promises made in the 1713 treaty, France continued to support both its former settlers and its Indigenous allies in Nova Scotia against British authority. By providing arms, supplies, and missionaries, the French administrators at Louisbourg hoped to use the Mi'kmaq in future campaigns. The long-standing relations between the Mi'kmaq and the Acadians, as well as French administrators, kept the Mi'kmaq firmly in the French camp, a bond reinforced by the more profitable trade being done with French traders over the few British merchants in the region.[5]

In an effort to regularize trade and ensure a stable peace, the British governor in Boston sought out the region's Indigenous nations, and on

---

[2] Bonita Lawrence, "Rewriting Histories of the Land: Colonization and Indigenous Resistance in Eastern Canada," in *Race, Space, and the Law: Unmapping a White Settler Society*, ed. Sherene Razack (Toronto: Between the Lines, 2002), 34.

[3] Stephen Patterson, "Indian-White Relations in Nova Scotia, 1749–61: A Study in Political Interaction," *Acadiensis* 23, no. 1 (1993): 25.

[4] Bill Wicken and John G. Reid, *An Overview of the 18th Century Treaties Signed Between the Mi'kmaq and Wuastukwiuk Peoples and the English Crown, 1725–1928*, submission to the Royal Commission on Aboriginal Peoples, 1993, p. 4.

[5] Patterson, "Indian-White Relations," 27.

December 15, 1725, negotiated a "Peace and Friendship" treaty with them. The 1725 Treaty of Boston, or Dummer Treaty, included the Indigenous nations of Maine, New Hampshire, Acadia, and Nova Scotia.[6] Under the terms of the treaty, the Indigenous signatories agreed to "forbear All Acts of Hostility, Injuries and discords towards all the Subjects of the Crown of Great Britain and not offer the least hurt, violence, or molestation of them or any of them in their persons or Estates."[7] With the treaty, Governor Dummer intended to prevent conflict between British settlers and the region's Indigenous peoples by establishing trade relations with them and by acquiring their consent for British colonization in the region.

Although the region was generally peaceful in the following two decades, the 1725 treaty did not prevent Mi'kmaq and Maliseet from being drawn back into colonial conflicts. By the 1740s, tensions rose again as French forces moved against British positions such as during the sieges of Annapolis Royal in 1744 and 1746. French administrators at Louisbourg, through agents such as Father Le Loutre, sought out Mi'kmaq support in Nova Scotia against the British.[8] The British were viewed with high levels of suspicion and distrust by the region's original peoples as they openly harassed Mi'kmaq communities and hunting parties. These conflicts intensified after the founding of Halifax in 1749 due to the open aggression of the colony's governor, Edward Cornwallis, against the Mi'kmaq, and the complete lack of consultation with the area's Mi'kmaq communities. The British were intruders in Mi'kmaq territories, and the settlement was seen as an attempt to usurp their lands.[9] In attempts to end the violence, the British and representatives from various Mi'kmaq, Maliseet, and Passamaquoddy nations renewed the 1725 agreement on several occasions, such as in 1726, 1749, 1752, 1760, and 1761. Hostilities in the region continued until Britain and France ended their conflict in North America at the end of the Seven Years' War in 1760.

The Peace and Friendship Treaties, as they have come to be known, all followed a similar pattern.[10] Based on the agreement made in 1725, the subsequent treaties called on the parties to re-establish peaceful and

---

[6] Wicken and Reid, *An Overview*, 5.
[7] Treaty of 1725 for Ratification at Annapolis Royal, National Archives, Colonial Office Papers, CO 217, vol. 4, no. 349.
[8] Patterson, "Indian-White Relations," 32.
[9] Daniel N. Paul, *We Were Not the Savages: A Micmac Perspective on the Collision of European and Aboriginal Civilization* (Halifax: Nimbus, 1993), 112.
[10] Wayne Daugherty, *Maritime Indian Treaties in Historical Perspective* (Ottawa: Indian and Northern Affairs Canada, 1983), 30.

commercial relations. In all cases, the terms were relatively clear: the parties would not "molest" the other, the Mi'kmaq and Maliseet affirmed a continued relationship with the British Crown just as there had been with the French Crown, assistance would be brought to shipwrecks, and trade would resume.[11] Contrary to future treaties in the Great Lakes region, the Peace and Friendship Treaties contained no clauses relating to the sale or surrender of lands or resources by Indigenous nations. While the majority of the agreements were largely reaffirming the 1725 treaty, two treaties had additional clauses relating to hunting and fishing, and trade: the so-called "truck house" clauses. In the 1752 treaty, the British promised to ensure "free liberty of Hunting & Fishing as usual" and to establish a truck house, or trading post, for the use of the Indigenous signatories.[12] The "truck house" clause was again repeated in 1760. As one of the primary goals of the treaties was to re-establish trade within the colony, these "truck houses" would serve to encourage a commercial relationship between the Mi'kmaq, the Maliseet, and British settlers. While the actual operation of trading posts was short lived, these clauses would become the central focus of court cases in the 1980s and 1990s.

ORAL AND WRITTEN ACCOUNTS OF THE 1752 "COPE" TREATY

In the fall of 1752, Major Jean Baptiste Cope, leader of the Mi'kmaq community on the Shubenacadie River, met with the new governor of Nova Scotia, Peregrine Hopson, and his assembled council in an effort to end the sporadic violence occurring throughout the central region of the colony. Since the end of the last French-British conflict in the region and the establishment of Halifax by Edward Cornwallis in 1749, tensions between the British settlers and administrators and the various Mi'kmaq communities had remained high. As Mi'kmaq historian Daniel Paul recounts, the conflicts and violent encounters increased as a result of the new settlement, and by September 1749 the Mi'kmaq were in a state of war against the British, a cycle of violence that would end only in 1760 with the fall of the French in North America.[13] Just a few months after the arrival of 2,000 settlers at Halifax, a group of Mi'kmaq warriors were reported to have killed four men at a saw mill in Halifax Harbour, an attack for which there is little

---

[11] Treaty of 1725 for Ratification at Annapolis Royal, National Archives, Colonial Office Papers, CO 217, vol. 4, no. 349.
[12] "Cope Treaty," 1752, Nova Scotia Archives, Peace and Friendship Treaties, RG 1, vol. 430, no. 2.
[13] Paul, *We Were Not the Savages*, 107.

existing context but that was used as an excuse for Cornwallis and his council to issue a bounty on Mi'kmaq scalps and encourage settlers to "annoy, destroy, take or destroy the savage commonly called Micmacks wherever they are found."[14] Over the course of two years, British colonial administrators increasingly asserted their claims over the Mi'kma'ki through renaming and encouraging attacks on Mi'kmaq communities, and the number of conflicts grew as Mi'kmaq defended their traditional lands from invaders.[15]

By the summer of 1752, the situation had reached a tipping point for the British. Cornwallis, having resigned over criticism of his administration of the colony, was replaced by a veteran of the colonies, Peregrine Hopson, who held a somewhat more conciliatory view of the colony's Indigenous inhabitants. Convinced that the current situation was unsustainable, he quietly began to spread word that he wanted to renew the peace established in 1725.[16] By September, after an encounter with Halifax ship-owner William Piggott, who convinced him to speak to the British, Cope arrived in Halifax to negotiate terms. Between his arrival on September 14 and the ratification of the treaty on November 22, discussions were held between Cope and Peregrine to re-establish peaceful relations, reopen trade, and protect Mi'kmaq interests throughout the colony.

The only existing written accounts of those meetings of the fall of 1752 are the minutes of the Nova Scotia executive council. In three separate entries dated September 14 and 16, and November 22, 1752, the council minutes reported on Cope's initial reception and Governor Hopson's response to calls for peace, and then in November recorded the final version of the treaty and the governor's enacting proclamation. In the first entry, the minutes recounted how "one of the Mickmack Indians, who calld himself one of their Chiefs, was come in, with proposals of renewing a peace" and appeared before the Governor and council. When questioned by Hopson as to the nature of the proposals, Cope, who is not identified as the individual in question until the next entry, responded "[t]hat the Indians should be paid for the land the English had settled upon in this Country."[17] Cope was clear that he was only representing his own community as they had "empowerd him to treat in behalf of them" but that he was also willing to try to bring the other Mi'kmaq communities to come and meet with the British at Halifax.

---

[14] Council Minutes, Province of Nova Scotia, October 1–2, 1749, CO. 217/9, pp. 117–18.
[15] Paul, *We Were Not the Savages*, 109.
[16] Patterson, "Indian-White Relations," 36.
[17] "Minutes of Council held at Halifax," 1752, in *Selections of Documents from the Province of Nova Scotia*, ed. Thomas B. Akins (Halifax: Charles Annand, 1869), 671.

While it is difficult to ascertain the true intent of Cope's statement regarding compensation for British land occupation, William Wicken, in his work *Mi'kmaq Treaties on Trial*, argues that Cope's primary interest was to "define the territories where the Mi'kmaq and the British would live in the future."[18] As the Mi'kmaq on the Shubenacadie River were the closest to the new settlement at Halifax, they had the most interest in getting recognition for their lands and establishing division of lands in the peninsula. The governor and council's response to Cope's initial proposal did not quite match up with his request for compensation. Rather, the counterproposal sought to re-establish peaceful relations, stating that "what is passed shall be buried in Oblivion, and for the time to come we shall be pleasd & charmed to live together as Friends." While not directly making a statement about the division of the territories between the Mi'kmaq and the British, Hopson does appear to recognize Mi'kmaq lands by encouraging further settlement around the growing Shubenacadie community, indicating that "no person shall hinder it, nor shall meddle with the lands where you are."[19] In a change from previous negotiations between the British and the region's Indigenous communities, Hopson offered to protect some harvesting rights, as the Mi'kmaq would not "be hinderd from Hunting, or Fishing in this Country, as you have been used to do." In addition, the British offered to establish a "Truck house of Merchandise," or trading post, at Shubenacadie to facilitate trade. Hopson ended his proposal with the request that any agreement would be renewed yearly by the parties and confirmed by the giving of "annual presents," an uncommon British practice in Nova Scotia, despite its wide use in the interior of North America. The final entry in the council minutes closed off with a purported statement by Cope that he would go out and "engage to do my utmost Endeavours to bring here the other Tribes of Micmacks to make a peace."[20] If Cope made any comments on the absence of a reply to his request for compensation, it was not recorded in the council minutes.[21]

As Stephen Patterson notes in his study *Indian-White Relations in Nova Scotia, 1749–1761*, Hopson's response appears to have been influenced by the proposal of British officer Major George Scott.[22] In a letter to Hopson a month prior to Cope's arrival in Halifax, Scott argued that the most effective way to achieve peaceful relations with the Mi'kmaq was by "removing

---

[18] William Wicken, *Mi'kmaq Treaties on Trial: History, Land, and Donald Marshall Junior* (Toronto: University of Toronto Press, 2002), 184.
[19] "Minutes of Council held at Halifax," 1752, pp. 672–3.
[20] Ibid., 674.
[21] Wicken, *Mi'kmaq Treaties on Trial*, 185.
[22] Patterson, "Indian-White Relations," 38.

them from the French Interest, Attaching them to ours, and making them usefull in Point of Trade."[23] Scott, who was a member of Nova Scotia's 40th Regiment of Foot and likely had some experience with the French-Mi'kmaq relationship, believed that the British needed to adopt French methods of gift giving, to make agreements with constant renewals, and to create a trade relationship that would be more advantageous to the Mi'kmaq. To that end, Scott's proposal rested on two main points: establishing trading posts close to communities and the offering of annual presents. In his mind, "supplying the Indians with European Commodities much cheaper than the French can, and being strictly honest in all our dealings with them is the surest method, and that which I propose for bringing them over to our interest."[24]

Two months later, the council minutes returned to the topic of peace between the Shubenacadie Mi'kmaq and the British as Jean Baptiste Cope was again in Halifax. Although he had promised to try to convince other leaders to join him, Cope was accompanied by only three other individuals: Andrew Hodley, François Jeremie, and Gabriel Martin, noted in the minutes as members of his community. Despite the fact that Cope had arrived in Halifax some two weeks prior,[25] the November 22 council meeting does not recount any of the discussions or negotiations that led to the final treaty text included in the council minutes. It simply stated that "the following Treaty of Peace was Signed, Ratified and Exchanged with the Mick Mack Tribe of Indians, Inhabiting the Eastern Parts of this Province."[26] This wording recognizes the internal divisions between communities within the Mi'kma'ki. As Wicken and Reid describe in *An Overview of 18th Century Treaties Signed Between the Mi'kmaq and Wastukwiuk Peoples and the English Crown*, the Mi'kmaq did not have one representative who spoke for all communities. Rather, each community selected its own representatives, and they could not conclude final terms until consultation had been undertaken with their specific communities.[27] Consequently, Cope and his colleagues could speak only for their own community members, and no others, regardless of the council's statement referring to the Mi'kmaq of the eastern peninsula.

The treaty text, included in the November council minutes, and preserved in Hopson's personal papers, further develops the counterproposal

---

[23] Major George Scott to Peregrine Hopson, August 17, 1752, LAC, C.O. Nova Scotia "A" Hopson 1752, MG11, NS, "A" vol. 49, p. 8.
[24] Ibid., 9.
[25] *Halifax Gazette*, November 11, 1752, p. 2.
[26] "Minutes of Council held at Halifax," 1752, p. 682.
[27] Wicken and Reid, *An Overview*, 122–3.

made by the governor on September 16. The agreement renews peaceful relations between the parties as first established by the 1725 agreement made at Boston, and it calls on Cope to encourage other communities to do the same. A second clause affirms the "free liberty of Hunting and Fish as usual" and pledges to build a truck house at Shubenacadie and to encourage trade with British settlements. As suggested by Major Scott, the treaty also includes a yearly renewal of the peace and the distribution of presents on October 1. In addition to the early proposal, two additional clauses call on the Mi'kmaq to come to the aid of shipwrecks and to use the colony's courts to resolve disputes.[28] Two days later, a governor's proclamation was issued announcing the signing of the treaty and warning British subjects of prosecution for violating the peace. As Wicken notes, the agreement provides a process for building a relationship with the Shubenacadie Mi'kmaq but is entirely silent on the issues of compensation for settlement and control of the land.[29]

The immediate impact of the treaty's signing is debatable. In his report to the Lords of Trade, Hopson acknowledged that only a small group had signed the treaty. He hoped that "it may have the good effect to bring over the Rest but this is more to be hoped for than trusted to."[30] Broadsheets of the governor's treaty proclamation were widely distributed throughout the region, but there appears to have been little interest, as only two other communities asked to sign on to the 1752 agreement.[31] Whether the agreement firmly established peaceful relations is also debatable, as Jean Baptiste Cope himself was accused of being involved in the disappearance of a group of British officials, and as was the case with the early tensions of the Seven Years' War, he appears to have again sided with the French.[32]

As the agreement signed by Jean Baptiste Cope and Peregrine Hopson was replaced by later treaties, the 1752 treaty, the council minutes remained the only written source for the agreement. Like other treaties, it would be replaced and buried by subsequent agreements. The outbreak of the Seven Years' War and the eventual British victory across the region brought about a new round of treaties in 1760, again building on the 1725 treaty and including the additional clauses from the 1752 agreement.

---

[28] "Minutes of Council held at Halifax," 1752, pp. 683–5.
[29] Wicken, *Mi'kmaq Treaties on Trial*, 187.
[30] Peregrine Hopson to Lords of Trade, December 6, 1752, LAC, C.O. Nova Scotia "A" Hopson 1753, MG11, NS, "A" vol. 50, p. 26.
[31] Peregrine Hopson to Lords of Trade, April 14, 1753, LAC, C.O. Nova Scotia "A" Hopson 1753, MG11, NS, "A" vol. 52, pp. 134–5.
[32] Geoffrey Plank, "The Two Majors Cope: The Boundaries of Nationality in Mid-18th Century Nova Scotia," *Acadiensis* 25, no. 2 (1996): 36.

For the Mi'kmaq, these agreements were more than simple cessations of violence between warring parties. They were official recognitions of their rights to the lands of the Mi'kma'ki and assurances that they would be unmolested by British settlers in their traditional pursuits and land usage. As the treaties stipulated, they were to be long lasting, with yearly efforts to reinvigorate the relationship between the British and the Mi'kmaq through annual presents. To the British of Nova Scotia, however, the significance and the relevance of the treaties faded quickly when colonial officials changed and attitudes toward Mi'kmaq hardened as the number of new settlers increased. As settler interests shifted more toward assimilation instead of relationship building, the region's Indigenous peoples became increasingly marginalized.

The first written record of the oral history shared by the Mi'kmaq occurred over 150 years later during proceedings of a 1928 court case centred on the prosecution of Gabriel Sylliboy, grand chief of the Mi'kmaq, for hunting muskrat out of season. Six Mi'kmaq men testified to the longstanding significance of the treaty concluded between Cope and Hopson. During the trial, summaries of the testimony of the Mi'kmaq witnesses were made, possibly by the judge hearing the case, George G. Patterson.[33] Five of the six gave their testimony in Mi'kmaq, which was translated and summarized by Mi'kmaq interpreter John Gould. Despite being a summarized version of their testimony, this account represents one of the earliest records of Mi'kmaq oral history of the 1752 treaty for non-Mi'kmaq. The six witnesses, four of whom were in their 70s (Joe Christmas, Andrew Alek, Andrew Bernard, and Francis Gould), were all prominent leaders in their communities across the island.[34] Joe Christmas had been the Grand Captain of the Mi'kmaq Grand Council, while Gabriel Sylliboy was the sitting grand chief of the Mi'kmaq at the time, and Ben Christmas was the chief of the community at Sydney, Nova Scotia.

The testimony of the Indigenous leaders presented at trial not only revealed their understanding of the treaty and its terms but also spoke to how that knowledge was transferred across the generations. From their perspective, a treaty had definitely been concluded between the Mi'kmaq and the British in the mid-1700s, and their communities relied on it. As Joe Christmas stated, "the King of England made treaty with Micmacs, with the whole tribe" and because of the treaty, they "had right to hunt

---

[33] William Wicken, "Heard It from Our Grandfathers: Mi'kmaq Treaty Tradition and the Sylliboy Case of 1928," *UNB Law Review* 44 (1995): 156.
[34] Ibid., 148.

& fish at anytime."[35] The testimony also challenged the British account of who participated in the discussions in November 1752. While the council minutes associate those accompanying Jean Baptiste Cope as members of his community, Chief Ben Christmas noted that two of the three individuals who signed the treaty were from Cape Breton: "Two of chiefs whose signature appears on Treaty [of 1752] was Andrew Hadley Martin [Andre Martin; André is 'Antle' in Micmac, often corrupted further into 'Hadley' by English speakers, who then compound it as 'Andrew Hadley']. He came from Nyanza Victoria Co. And Gabriel Martin. He came from Escasoni."[36] For all of them, the primary right protected by the Treaty of 1752 was that the "Indians got from King free hunting and fishing at all times" and that prior to Gabriel Sylliboy's arrest, the exercise of this right had never been infringed upon. They also stressed that they saw the treaty as still being in effect as the promised yearly presents were still being received, as noted by Gabriel Sylliboy: "Still believe Treaty good … Under Treaty get from Gov't blankets and flour and some shoes & long coats. Still get them."[37] The recorded testimony, despite its summarized nature, clearly shows that the treaty remained central to the Mi'kmaq understanding of their relationship with the rest of the settler state. As Francis Gould testified, the treaty was still in effect because they "promised to keep Treaty & got these things in return" such as yearly supplies of food, clothing and gear.[38] Both Christmas and Sylliboy also understood the treaty to be in force. Christmas testified, "Treaty never revoked so far as they are concerned. Still believe they have rights of hunting and fishing at all times,"[39] while Sylliboy referred to the written treaty text to back up his claim to a right to hunt: "I sd. let me go and I'll show you copy of treaty."[40]

As William Wicken notes in his examination of the trial, the testimony demonstrated how information about and understandings of the treaty had been transmitted through the generations. Joe Christmas stated that he "Heard it from our grandfathers," while Gabriel Sylliboy recounted hearing about the treaty from a young age: "Since I was boy heard that Indians got from King free hunting and fishing at all times."[41] All the witnesses were raised at a time when the majority of the Mi'kmaq

---

[35] Ruth Holmes Whitehead, *The Old Man Told Us: Excerpts from Mi'kmaw History, 1500–1950* (Halifax: Nimbus, 1991), 327.
[36] Ibid., 330.
[37] Ibid., 329
[38] Ibid., 330.
[39] Ibid.
[40] Ibid., 328.
[41] Wicken, "Heard It from Our Grandfathers," 149.

communities in Unamaki (Cape Breton Island) still spoke almost exclusively Mi'kmaq, and information was transmitted and recorded "orally by parents, grandparents and community elders."[42] Knowledge of the treaty went well beyond families and isolated communities. Readings and discussions of not only the 1752 treaty but all the treaties concluded between Mi'kmaq and the British were a regular occurrence during community meetings and annual gatherings of the Mi'kmaq.[43] In her examination of the annual feast of Ste. Anne gatherings, Janet Chute notes that the feast "provided a forum in which Micmac leadership could discuss and promote exclusively Micmac goals and aspirations."[44] While the feast day was observed locally, the Chapel Island community in Cape Breton also hosted a gathering of the Mi'kmaq leadership on July 26 for over two centuries. The gathering served as an important part in the sharing of information and knowledge, as it was a time where the community leaders could "review and act upon their shared understandings [of] treaties entered into with the British colonial government during the 18th century."[45] The practice of "reading" the treaties continued to be a central element of the events well into the 1930s.

The sharing of oral history continues today throughout Mi'kmaq communities, especially as traditional practices are increasingly linked to easing intergenerational trauma created by assimilationist policies such as residential schools.

THE 1752 TREATY AND THE COURTS

While the Peace and Friendship Treaties formed part of the identity of the Mi'kmaq through the continuous sharing of teaching and other oral traditions, they were viewed by the rest of Canadian society largely as relics of the past with little significance. As with other treaties, the treaty concluded at Halifax on November 22, 1752, was forced back into the consciousness of non-Mi'kmaq parties by way of the courts. In particular, two cases dealt with the 1752 agreement: the aforementioned *R. v. Sylliboy* of 1928, and the 1985 ruling of the Supreme Court of Canada in *R. v. Simon*. The contradictory decisions in the two cases also show how legal interpretations of treaties have changed in the last century.

---

[42] Ibid., 150.
[43] Paul, *We Were Not the Savages*, 117.
[44] Janet Chute, "Ceremony, Social Revitalization and Change: Micmac Leadership and the Annual Festival of St. Anne," in *Papers of the 23rd Algonquian Conference*, ed. W. Cowan (Ottawa: Carleton University Press, 1992), 45.
[45] Ibid., 57.

In the *Sylliboy* case, Judge George Patterson's ruling represented a narrow interpretation of the treaty, based on the text itself and with little regard for the oral testimony of the six Mi'kmaq witnesses.[46] In Patterson's opinion, the agreement made in 1752 could not apply to the Mi'kmaq in Unamaki/Cape Breton as it was outside the colony of Nova Scotia at the time. He further argued that the language of the treaty limited its application to Shubenacadie, the community said to be represented by Jean Baptiste Cope in the text, and that the treaty "was not made with the Micmac Tribe as a whole but with only small body of that Tribe living in the Eastern Part of Nova Scotia proper" in 1752.[47] As Sylliboy was not a member of that specific community, but rather from Eskasoni in Cape Breton Island, he could not be entitled to the specified right to hunt and fish. Not satisfied with excluding Unamaki inhabitants from the treaty, Patterson further declared that due to the violent actions by Mi'kmaq from Shubenacadie in the years after the signing, the treaty "was almost at once put to an end by the breaking out of war." Patterson also held that the treaty itself had long since lost its enforceability, as it was never referenced in any of the various game laws that were enacted after 1794. By doing so, he implied that a right could be recognized only by the state. As a final attack on the treaty, Patterson's ruling stripped the Mi'kmaq of any authority to even enter into a treaty, since "the Indians were never regarded as an independent power ... The savage's rights or sovereignty, even ownership were never recognized." From where he sat on the bench, Patterson determined that the Mi'kmaq actually had no authority to negotiate a treaty, and that the "Treaty of 1752 is not a treaty at all and is not to be treated as such." In his opinion, Gabriel Sylliboy had been misguided in thinking that the agreement in question was a treaty at all.[48]

The *Sylliboy* ruling formed the basis of policy in the Maritimes for nearly six decades before the decision in the *Simon* case in 1985. *Sylliboy* reinforced the Crown's tendency to value Eurocentric and written interpretations of treaties above oral histories and tradition. As Wicken stresses, governments used court rulings such as *Sylliboy* to "emphasize European-produced documentation for understanding both the British and the Mi'kmaq perspectives of treaty-making."[49] Through this ruling, provincial governments vigorously applied wildlife management

---

[46] Wicken, "Heard It from Our Grandfathers," 145.
[47] *R. v. Sylliboy*, [1928] 50 C.C.C. 889, p. 308.
[48] Ibid., 313.
[49] Wicken, "Heard It from Our Grandfathers," 146.

legislation to the point where Mi'kmaq hunters and fishers were feeling harassed and targeted.[50]

The Supreme Court of Canada's ruling in *Simon v. The Queen* in 1985 challenged Eurocentric perspectives that often invalidated the Indigenous experience and pushed legal interpretation toward greater alignment with Mi'kmaq oral testimony. James Simon, a registered member of the Shubenacadie band, had been convicted under the Nova Scotia *Lands and Forests Act* of being in possession of a rifle and cartridges. Through the preceding trials, Simon admitted to having the rifle and shells but argued that under the terms of the 1752 Treaty, he had "free liberty of Hunting and Fishing as usual."[51] In essence, this case was based on the same arguments as the 1928 *Sylliboy* case. However, contrary to the latter ruling, the Supreme Court sided with the Mi'kmaq and their understanding of the treaty.

In a decision written by Chief Justice Brian Dickson, the Supreme Court revisited the core elements of the *Sylliboy* decision, effectively refuting the near entirety of the earlier ruling. With respect to the parties' capacity and authority to conclude a treaty, Justice Dickson concluded that "both the Governor and the Micmac entered into the Treaty with the intention of creating mutually binding obligations which would be solemnly respected." Chief Jean Baptiste Cope had been chosen as a representative of his community, and Governor Hopson had full authority as colonial governor to negotiate an agreement.[52] The ruling also rejected Judge Patterson's position on hunting rights by stating that the

> Treaty, by providing that the Micmac should not be hindered from but should have free liberty of hunting and fishing as usual, constitutes a positive source of protection against infringements on hunting rights. The fact that the right to hunt already existed at the time the Treaty was entered into by virtue of the Micmac's general aboriginal right to hunt does not negate or minimize the significance of the protection of hunting rights expressly included in the Treaty.[53]

---

[50] Grand Chief Donald Marshall, Sr. Grand Captain Alexander Denny, and Putus Simon Marshall of the Executive of the Grand Council of the Mi'kmaw Nation, "The Covenant Chain," in *Drum Beat: Anger and Renewal in Indian Country*, ed. Boyce Richardson (Toronto: Summerhill Press, 1989), 91.
[51] *Simon v. The Queen*, [1985] 2 S.C.R. 387.
[52] Ibid., para. 24.
[53] Ibid., para. 26.

The ruling in *Simon* also allowed the Supreme Court to clarify the growing legal principles surrounding treaty interpretation. Building on the previous year's *Nowegijick* decision, Chief Justice Dickson wrote that attempts to limit the extent of a treaty or a right "run contrary to the principle that Indian treaties and statutes relating to Indians should be liberally construed and uncertainties resolved in favour of the Indians."[54] In other words, instead of applying a limited Eurocentric interpretation to treaty terms based on a narrow use of language, more weight must be placed upon the Indigenous perspective.

The ruling also rejected the Crown's argument that the existence of the treaty right was moot as the treaty had actually been terminated by the outbreak of war.[55] Again, Chief Justice Dickson indicated that "an Indian treaty is unique; it is an agreement *sui generis* which is neither created nor terminated according to the rules of international law."[56] As a result, treaties between Indigenous nations and the Crown are "subject to special rules of interpretation."[57] It would take another case dealing with the Peace and Friendship Treaties, *R. v. Marshall* of 1999, to bring even greater clarity to these broader, interpretive principles. In *Marshall*, Justice McLachlin developed nine core principles flowing from court decisions. These continue to guide legal interpretation of treaties and treaty rights.

The Supreme Court's ruling in *R. v. Simon* was an interesting legal test because it was one of the first significant rulings following the passage of the *Constitution Act, 1982*, and Section 35 protecting and enshrining Aboriginal and treaty rights. Here, the ruling not only stepped in to clarify that a treaty with no land provisions could still be considered valid, but it also reaffirmed that treaty rights could not be infringed upon by provincial regulations.[58] The ruling strengthened both the legal argument and the historical reality that Indigenous nations had the capacity to enter into "binding treaties with the Crown."[59] It also reinforced earlier rulings, such as the 1969 *White and Bob* decision, that Indigenous

---

[54] Ibid., para. 50.
[55] Philip M. Saunders, "Getting Their Feet Wet: The Supreme Court and Practical Implementation of Treaty Rights in the *Marshall* Case," *Dalhousie Law Journal* 23 (2000): 54.
[56] *Simon v. The Queen*, para. 33.
[57] Saunders, "Getting Their Feet Wet," 54.
[58] Bruce W. Hodgins, "Aboriginal Peoples and Their Historic Right to Hunt: A Reasonable Symbiotic Relationship," in *The Culture of Hunting in Canada*, ed. Jean L. Manore and Dale G. Miner (Vancouver: University of British Columbia Press, 2006), 199.
[59] Diana Ginn, "Indian Hunting Rights: *Dick v. R., Jack and Charlie v. R.*, and *Simon v. R.*," *McGill Law Journal* 31 (1986): 540.

understandings of the treaty-making process must be considered when determining the validity of a treaty. This was again reinforced in the *Sioui* decision of 1990.[60] The decision also created a legal test to help determine future cases relating to methods of hunting and activities considered to be "incidental" to hunting activities, relied upon in the *R. v. Sundown* decision in 1999.[61]

FURTHER READINGS

Wayne Daugherty. *Maritime Indian Treaties in Historical Perspective*. Indian and Northern Affairs Canada, 1983.

Ruth Holmes Whitehead. *The Old Man Told Us: Excerpts from Mi'kmaw History, 1500–1950*. Halifax: Nimbus, 1991.

Stephen Patterson. "Indian-White Relations in Nova Scotia 1749–1761: A Study in Political Interaction." *Acadiensis* 23, no. 1 (1993): 23–59.

Daniel Paul. *We Were Not the Savages: A Micmac Perspective on the Collision of European and Aboriginal Civilization*. Halifax: Nimbus, 1993.

William Wicken. *Mi'kmaq Treaties on Trial: History, Law and Donald Marshall Jr*. Toronto: University of Toronto Press, 2002.

QUESTIONS FOR DISCUSSION

1. What do the accounts tell us about how the treaty of 1752 was negotiated?
2. Based on the following passages, identify points of similarities and points of divergence between the account of the council minutes of 1752 and the oral testimony given by Gabriel Sylliboy.

> **"Minutes of Council Held at Halifax," 1752, in *Selections of Documents from the Province of Nova Scotia*, ed. Thomas B. Akins (Halifax: Charles Annand, 1869)**
>
> We will not suffer that you be hinderd form Hunting, or Fishing in this Country, as you have been used to do, and if you shall think fit to settle your Wives & Children upon the river Shibenaccadie, no person shall hinder it, nor shall meddle with the lands where you are, and the Governour will put up a Truck house of Merchandise there, where you may have everything you stand in need of at a reasonable price, and where shall be given unto you the full value of the peltrie, Feathers, or other Things

---

[60] See Chapter 2.
[61] See Chapter 6.

which you shall have to sell ... And we hope to brighten the Chain in our Hearts and to confirm our Friendship every year; and for this purpose we shall expect to see here some of your Chiefs to receive annual presents whilst you behave yourselves as good, and faithful children of our great King.

Testimony of Gabriel Sylliboy, Proceedings of the Sylliboy Case of 1928, Port Hood, July 4, 1928

Since I was boy heard that Indians got from King free hunting and fishing at all times. Still believe Treaty good. When officer took pelts I told him I had treaty. He sd he knew nothing about that. I sd. let me go and I'll show you copy of treaty. I sd. if I wanted to I cd. prevent him taking furs but as he didn't know about Treaty I wd let him take furs. Under Treaty get from Gov't blankets and flour and some shoes & long coats. Still get them. Haven't got any for a year. From Mr. Boyd Indian Superintendent River Bourgoise. Where there is no game in hard months {?} get order for $10.00 for goods in store. In Spring, get seeds. Gov't put up & maintain schools on every reservation. Putting up Home at Shubenacadie. All by virtue of Treaty.

3. Can you identify other similarities and differences in the accounts of the treaties?
4. How do the courts reconcile the competing perspectives of these treaties?

DOCUMENTS

Treaty Text: "Cope Treaty," 1752, Peace and Friendship Treaties, Nova Scotia Archives, RG 1, vol. 430, no. 2

Treaty or Articles of Peace and Friendship Renewed between His Excellency Peregrine Thomas Hopson Esquire Captain General and Governor in Chief in and over His Majesty's Province of Nova Scotia or Acadie. Vice Admiral of the same & Colonel of one of His Majesty's Regiments of Foot, and His Majesty's Council on behalf of His Majesty.
　　and
Major Jean Baptiste Cope, chief Sachem of the Tribe of Mick Mack Indians Inhabiting the Eastern Coast of the said Province, and Andrew Hadley Martin, Gabriel Martin & Francis Jeremiah, Members and Delegates of the

said Tribe, for themselves and their said Tribe their Heirs, and the Heirs of their Heirs forever, Begun made and concluded in the manner, form and Tenor following, vizt:

1. It is agreed that the Articles of Submission and Agreement, made at Boston in New England by the Delegates of the Penobscot Norridgwolk & St. John's Indians, in the year 1725 Ratified & Confirmed by all the Nova Scotia Tribes, at Annapolis Royal, in the month of June 1726, & lately renewed with Governor Cornwallis at Halifax, & Ratified at St. John's River, now read over, Explained and Interpreted, shall be and are hereby from this time forward Renewed, Reiterated, and forever Confirmed by them and their Tribe; and the said Indians for themselves and their Tribe and their Heirs aforesaid Do make & Renew the same Solemn Submissions and promises for the Strickt observance of all the Articles therein contained as at any time heretofore hath been done.
2. That all Transactions during the late War shall on both sides be buried in Oblivion with the Hatchet, and that the said Indians shall have all favour, Friendship & Protection shewn them from this His Majesty's Government.
3. That the said Tribe shall use their utmost endeavours to bring in the other Indians to Renew and Ratify this Peace, and shall discover and make known any attempts or designs of any other Indians or any Enemy whatever against His Majestys Subjects within this Province so soon as they shall know thereof and shall also hinder and Obstruct the same to the utmost of their Power, and on the other hand if any of the Indians refusing to ratify this Peace, shall make War upon the Tribe who have now confirmed the same; they shall upon Application have such aid and Assistance from the Government for their Defence, as the case may require.
4. It is agreed that the said Tribe of Indians shall not be hindered from, but have free liberty of Hunting & Fishing as usual: and that if they shall think a Truckhouse needful at the River Chibenaccadie or any other place of their resort, they shall have the same built and proper Merchandize lodged therein, to be Exchanged for what the Indians shall have to dispose of, and that in the mean time the said Indians shall have free liberty to bring for Sale to Halifax or any other Settlement within this Province, Skins, feathers, fowl, fish or any other thing they shall have to sell, where they shall have liberty to dispose thereof to the best Advantage.

5. That a Quantity of Bread, Flour, & such other Provisions as can be procured, necessary for the Familys, and proportionable to the number of the said Indians, shall be given them half yearly for the time to come; and the same regard shall be had to the other Tribes that shall hereafter agree to Renew and Ratify the Peace upon the Terms and Conditions now Stipulated.
6. That to Cherish a good Harmony & mutual Correspondance between the said Indians & this Government, His Excellency Peregrine Thomas Hopson Esqr. Captain General & Governor in Chief in & over His Majesty's Province of Nova Scotia or Accadie, Vice Admiral of the same & Colonel of one of His Majesty's Regiments of Foot, hereby Promises on the Part of His Majesty, that the said Indians shall upon the first day of October Yearly, so long as they shall Continue in Friendship, Receive Presents of Blankets, Tobacco, and some Powder & Shot; and the said Indians promise once every Year, upon the first of October to come by themselves or their Delegates and Receive the said Presents and Renew their Friendship and Submissions.
7. That the Indians shall use their best Endeavours to save the lives and goods of any People Shipwrecked on this Coast, where they resort, and shall Conduct the People saved to Halifax with their Goods, & a Reward adequate to the Salvadge shall be given them.
8. That all Disputes whatsoever that may happen to arise between the Indians now at Peace, and others His Majesty's Subjects in this Province shall be tryed in His Majesty's Courts of Civil Judicature, where the Indians shall have the same benefit, Advantages and Priviledges, as any others of His Majesty's Subjects.

In Faith and Testimony whereof, the Great Seal of the Province is hereunto Appended, and the party's to these presents have hereunto interchangeably Set their Hands in the Council Chamber at Halifax this 22nd day of Nov. 1752, in the twenty-sixth year of His Majesty's reign.

P. T. Hopson	Jean Baptiste Cope, his Mark
Chas. Lawrence	Andrew Hodley, his Mark
Benj. Green	Francois Jeremie, his Mark
Jno. Salusbury	Gabriel Martin, his Mark
Willm. Steele	
Jno. Collier	

Excerpts from "Minutes of Council Held at Halifax," 1752, in *Selections of Documents from the Province of Nova Scotia*, ed. Thomas B. Akins (Halifax: Charles Annand, 1869)

September 14, 1752

... one of the Mickmack Indians, who calld himself one of their Chiefs, was come in, with proposals of renewing a peace &c., who was sent for before the Council ... Then the Governour desired he would acquaint the Council what proposals he had to make, who replyed that he was come in upon the Encouragement given him in a letter from Govr. Cornwallis, and that his proposals were – That the Indians should be paid for the land the English had settled upon in this Country. He was asked if he was one of the Chiefs, who replyd, That he was chief of that part of the Nation that lived in these parts of the province and had about forty men under him. He was then askd why no more of them came in with him? who replyd That they had empowerd him to treat in behalf of them all ... That he would return to his own people and inform them what he had done here, and then would go to the other Chiefs, and propose to thein [sic] to renew the peace, and that he thought he should be able to perform it in a month, and would bring some of them with him if he could, and if not would bring their answer.

September 16, 1752

The following answer to the proposal of the Indian Chief Was interchangeably signed & seald ...

    Friend,

    It is with pleasure that We see thee here to commune with us touching the burying of the Hatchet between the British Children of his puissant Majesty King George and the Children of the Mickmacks of this Country. We do assure you that he had declared unto us, that you are his Children, and that you have acknowledg'd his for your great chief and Father. He ordered us to treat you as dear Brethren, and we did not commence any new Dispute wit you upon our arrival here – but what is passed shall be buried in Oblivion, and for the time to come we shall be pleasd & charmed to live together as Friends.

    We will not suffer that you be hinderd form Hunting, or Fishing in this Country, as you have been used to do, and if you shall think fit to settle your Wives & Children upon the river Shibenaccadie, no person shall hinder it, nor shall meddle with the lands where you are, and the Governour will put up a Truck house of Merchandise there, where you may have everything you stand in need of at a reasonable price, and where shall be given unto you the full value of the peltrie, Feathers, or other Things which you shall have to sell.

We approve of your Engagement to go and inform your people of this our answer and then the other Tribes, with the promise of your endeavours to bring them to a Renewal of ye peace ... and each one of us will put our Names to the Agreement that shall be made between us. And we hope to brighten the Chain in our Hearts and to confirm our Friendship every year; and for this purpose we shall expect to see here some of your Chiefs to receive annual presents whilst you behave yourselves as good, and faithful children of our great King.

Excerpts from "Testimony of Joe Christmas, Gabriel Sylliboy, and Ed Christmas, Proceedings of the Sylliboy Case of 1928, Port Hood, July 4, 1928," in Ruth Holmes Whitehead, *The Old Man Told Us: Excerpts from Mi'kmaw History, 1500–1950* (Halifax: Nimbus, 1991). Reprinted by permission of the publisher.

Testimony of Joe Christmas, p. 327

I am a Micmac and was chief for six years. Became chief in 1909. Heard that according to treaty we had right to hunt & fish at anytime. I cannot read. Heard it from our grandfathers. Heard that King of England made treaty with Micmacs, with the whole tribe. (Objected to.) Remember hearing that goods were given – blankets – under treaty. (Objected to.) About 65 years ago. In the fall before Christmas. Big coats and old fashioned guns & powder horns also. And some hide to make moccasins. And some food. In the spring potatoes & [?] some for seed. Tobacco too. And some spears for spearing eels. Where people had little farms they got oats. These goods distributed every six months. Where people hunting they were supplied with powder shot & guns.

Testimony of Gabriel Sylliboy, p. 328

Am a Micmac Indian of Nova Scotia tribe. Never interfered with in my hunting before. Heard of some Indians on other side of Truro being interfered with a year ago. Since I was boy heard that Indians got from King free hunting and fishing at all times. Still believe Treaty good. When officer took pelts I told him I had treaty. He sd he knew nothing about that. I sd. let me go and I'll show you copy of treaty. I sd. if I wanted to I cd. prevent him taking furs but as he didn't know about Treaty I wd let him take furs. Under Treaty get from Gov't blankets and flour and some shoes & long coats. Still get them. Haven't got any for a year. From Mr. Boyd Indian Superintendent River Bourgoise. Where there is no game in hard months [?]

get order for $10.00 for goods in store. In Spring, get seeds. Gov't put up & maintain schools on every reservation. Putting up Home at Shubenacadie. All by virtue of Treaty. In Treaty promised to teach us. Did not know nor believe I was breaking any law in taking muskrats when I did.

Testimony of Francis Gould, p. 330.

Remember my grandfather going to Sydney & getting blankets long coat corn (3 bushels) gun powder flour sometimes seed corn beads for moccasins. He told me he got these from the King. Under the Treaty. We promised to keep Treaty & got these things in return. That is what my grandfather told me.

Testimony of Ben Christmas, p. 330

Chief of that band nearly six years. Two of chiefs whose signature appears on Treaty [of 1752] was Andrew Hadley Martin [Andre Martin; Andre is "Antle" in Micmac, often corrupted further into "Hadley" by English speakers, who then compound it as "Andrew Hadley"]. He came from Nyanza Victoria Co. And Gabriel Martin. He came from Escasoni. Indians believe Treaty still in force. Nothing ever pd. Indians for cancellation or revoking of treaty. Treaty never revoked so far as they are concerned. Still believe they have rights of hunting and fishing at all times.

Excerpts from *Simon v. The Queen*, [1985] 2 S.C.R. 387

24. The Treaty was entered into for the benefit of both the British Crown and the Micmac people, to maintain peace and order as well as to recognize and confirm the existing hunting and fishing rights of the Micmac. In my opinion, both the Governor and the Micmac entered into the Treaty with the intention of creating mutually binding obligations which would be solemnly respected. It also provided a mechanism for dispute resolution. The Micmac Chief and the three other Micmac signatories, as delegates of the Micmac people, would have possessed full capacity to enter into a binding treaty on behalf of the Micmac. Governor Hopson was the delegate and legal representative of His Majesty The King. It is fair to assume that the Micmac would have believed that Governor Hopson, acting on behalf of His Majesty The King, had the necessary authority to enter into a valid treaty with them. I would hold that the Treaty of 1752 was validly created by competent parties.

25. Article 4 of the Treaty of 1752 states, "It is agreed that the said Tribe of Indians shall not be hindered from, but have free liberty of Hunting &

Fishing as usual" What is the nature and scope of the "liberty of Hunting & Fishing" contained in the Treaty?

26. The majority of the Nova Scotia Court of Appeal seemed to imply that the Treaty contained merely a general acknowledgement of pre-existing non treaty aboriginal rights and not an independent source of protection of hunting rights upon which the appellant could rely. In my opinion, the Treaty, by providing that the Micmac should not be hindered from but should have free liberty of hunting and fishing as usual, constitutes a positive source of protection against infringements on hunting rights. The fact that the right to hunt already existed at the time the Treaty was entered into by virtue of the Micmac's general aboriginal right to hunt does not negate or minimize the significance of the protection of hunting rights expressly included in the Treaty.

27. Such an interpretation accords with the generally accepted view that Indian treaties should be given a fair, large and liberal construction in favour of the Indians. This principle of interpretation was most recently affirmed by this Court in Nowegijick v. The Queen, [1983] 1 S.C.R. 29 ...

31. It should be clarified at this point that the right to hunt to be effective must embody those activities reasonably incidental to the act of hunting itself, an example of which is travelling with the requisite hunting equipment to the hunting grounds. In this case, the appellant was not charged with hunting in a manner contrary to public safety in violation of the Lands and Forests Act but with illegal possession of a rifle and ammunition upon a road passing through or by a forest, wood or resort of moose or deer contrary to s. 150(1) of the same Act. The appellant was simply travelling in his truck along a road with a gun and some ammunition. He maintained that he was going to hunt in the vicinity. In my opinion, it is implicit in the right granted under article 4 of the Treaty of 1752 that the appellant has the right to possess a gun and ammunition in a safe manner in order to be able to exercise the right to hunt. Accordingly, I conclude that the appellant was exercising his right to hunt under the Treaty ...

50. In my view, Parliament intended to include within the operation of s. 88 all agreements concluded by the Crown with the Indians that would otherwise be enforceable treaties, whether land was ceded or not. None of the Maritime treaties of the eighteenth century cedes land. To find that s. 88 applies only to land cession treaties would be to limit severely its scope and run contrary to the principle that Indian treaties and statutes relating to Indians should be liberally construed and uncertainties resolved in favour of the Indians.

51. Finally, it should be noted that several cases have considered the Treaty of 1752 to be a valid "treaty" within the meaning of s. 88 of the

Indian Act (for example, R. v. Paul, supra; and R. v. Atwin and Sacobie, supra). The Treaty was an exchange to solemn promises between the Micmacs and the King's representative entered into to achieve and guarantee peace. It is an enforceable obligation between the Indians and the white man and, as such, falls within the meaning of the word "treaty" in s. 88 of the Indian Act.

CAST OF CHARACTERS: 1752 COPE TREATY

Jean Baptiste Cope: b. unknown; d. c. 1759–60

Jean Baptiste Cope (Cop, Copt, Coptk, Kopit) was a member of the Mi'kmaq community of Shubenacadie (Sipekne'katik) who likely first appeared in the documentary record in 1726 as one of the signatories to the 1726 Peace and Friendship treaty at Annapolis Royal in Nova Scotia. Throughout the British-French conflicts in the Maritime region, Cope, sometimes referred to as "Major Cope," was closely associated with the French-Mi'kmaq alliance, especially as Father Jean-Louis Le Loutre operated his mission out of Cope's home community. By 1752, Cope was recognized as the Chief of the Segepenegatig region of Mi'kma'ki, the land of the Mi'kmaq, covering what is today central Nova Scotia. In September 1752, Cope came to Halifax to negotiate a renewal of the Peace and Friendship treaties with Nova Scotia's governor, Peregrine Thomas Hopson. As well as renewing the earlier treaty, the 1752 agreement recognized continued rights to hunt and fish as well as the establishment of a British trading post in Shubenacadie. Despite this agreement, the relationship with the central Mi'kmaq and the British remained uneasy and tense. By the end of active warfare in the Maritimes during the Seven Years' War in 1758, Cope and many Mi'kmaq from Sipekne'katik are recorded as seeking refuge among the French on the Miramichi River. As his name does not appear on any of the treaties concluded after the conflict, it is likely that Cope died prior to 1760.

Edward Cornwallis: b. February 22, 1713; d. January 14, 1776

Edward Cornwallis was born in an influential military and political family in London in 1713. After a time at the Royal Court as a page, Cornwallis entered a military career at a young age and was promoted to captain by 1734 and a major by 1742. After serving in diplomatic roles early on, Cornwallis participated in several armed conflicts, including battle in Flanders, as well as the "pacification" of Scotland and the battle of Culloden in 1745. After a further promotion to colonel in 1749, he was appointed governor of Nova Scotia, with instructions to establish a military stronghold to protect trade routes to New England. In May of that year, he and 2,576 settlers landed in Chebucto Bay to establish a new settlement, named "Halifax" in honour of the then-president of the Board of Trade, Lord Halifax. Cornwallis was soon embroiled in the seemingly unending conflicts between France and Britain in the region. Blaming the French and its agents, specifically Father Jean-Louis Le Loutre, for encouraging Mi'kmaq to attack British settlers and posts, Cornwallis aimed to "root out" the Indigenous population, including a bounty on Mi'kmaq scalps, which encouraged a series of raids throughout the colony. By 1751, his fiscal management of the colony came under criticism, and he eventually left the colony in 1752.

Peregrine Thomas Hopson: b. unknown; d. February 27, 1759

While little is known of his early life, Peregrine Thomas Hopson was a career military officer who first appears in the records through his appointment as a lieutenant in 1703, and again in 1738 as a major in the 14th Regiment of Foot, having served much of his career at Gibraltar. After the fall of Louisbourg to the British in 1745, Hopson's regiment was transferred from Gibraltar to reinforce the occupying forces. Through the intervention of the Duke of Newcastle, Hopson was appointed first as lieutenant-governor of Louisbourg, and later succeeded Charles Knowles as governor in 1747. After the 1748 Treaty of Aix-la-Chapelle returned Louisbourg to France, Hopson negotiated the transfer, relocated the garrison to the new settlement at Halifax, and briefly returned to England. Hopson was named as a replacement for Edward Cornwallis and returned to Halifax in 1752, with the goal of bringing in both the Acadians and the Mi'kmaq into the British fold. In 1752, he met with Jean Baptiste Cope of the Shubenacadie (Sipekne'katik) Mi'kmaq to renew and extend the terms of early Peace and Friendship treaties. Although he officially held the position of governor of Nova Scotia, poor health forced him to return to Britain, while Lieutenant-Colonel Charles Lawrence became acting governor. He returned briefly to Halifax in 1757 during the Seven Years' War and died of illness during the British attack on Guadeloupe in 1758.

Jean-Louis Le Loutre: b. September 26, 1709; d. September 30, 1772

After the death of both of his parents, Jean-Louis Le Loutre entered the Séminaire du St-Esprit in Paris in 1730, later transferring to the Séminaire des Missions Étrangères in 1737 in the hope of becoming a missionary in North America. Soon after his ordination in 1737, he sailed to Acadia, where he was originally to be the parish priest to the Catholic Acadians at Annapolis Royal. As priorities had changed in that parish, Le Loutre was sent instead to the new Catholic mission on the Shubenacadie River in the heart of Nova Scotia after having learnt Mi'kmaq. His close links with the French administration in Louisbourg and his interactions with the colonies' Acadian population worried British administrators. With the War of Austrian Succession spilling over into the colonies by the mid-1740s, French missionaries, such as Le Loutre, were called upon to encourage their Indigenous congregations to harass British positions and ships throughout the region. Le Loutre quickly became one of the primary intermediaries between the French and the Mi'kmaq, especially after the fall of Louisbourg in 1745, going so far as to coordinate French naval forces during the 1746 attack on Annapolis Royal. After a brief trip back to France, Le Loutre returned to Acadia where he continued to foment Mi'kmaq opposition to British rule in Nova Scotia, actions that led British authorities, such as Edward Cornwallis, to seek his capture.

Gabriel Sylliboy: b. August 18, 1874; d. March 4, 1964

Gabriel Sylliboy (Kaplie'l Silipay) was born in 1874 at the Whycocomagh Reserve in Cape Breton Island (Onamag). By the time he was in his early 40s, Sylliboy was a respected religious leader of his community. After the death of Mi'kmaq grand chief John Denny Jr., who had advised his sons not to accept the hereditary chieftainship of the Mi'kmaq, Gabriel Sylliboy was the person to be elected grand chief in 1919 at the age of 44. Throughout his tenure as grand chief, Sylliboy strove to protect Mi'kmaq language and culture. In 1927, he was arrested for hunting out of season and argued that he had a right to hunt based on the 1752 Cope Treaty. While his conviction was upheld by courts, this decision was to be the first of a series that would lead to the recognition of the Peace and Friendship treaties by the Supreme Court of Canada. In February 2017, the government of Nova Scotia granted a free pardon that recognized Sylliboy's innocence and issued a formal apology for the arrest and conviction.

46 SOLEMN WORDS AND FOUNDATIONAL DOCUMENTS

Figure 1.1 A proclamation from Governor Peregrine Hopson, 1752. After the agreement was made in November 1752, the colonial administration of Nova Scotia printed and distributed, in both English and French, a proclamation announcing the new treaty.

Source: Nova Scotia Archives (NSA), RG1, vol. 430, no.2 – Commissioner of Public Records, Proclamation for Treaty of 1752.

THE MAKING OF THE PEACE AND FRIENDSHIP TREATIES 47

Figure 1.2 A Mi'kmaq family with their chief in Nova Scotia, c. 1801. Despite the growing British settlements such as Halifax and Annapolis Royal, Mi'kmaq continued to use and occupy their traditional territories of the Mi'kma'ki. As the number of settlers increased throughout the nineteenth century, access to these lands was greatly diminished.

Source: Library and Archives Canada, Acc. No. 1990-497-7, C-003135.

Chapter 2
The Making of the Huron-British Treaty of 1760

For 150 years, France and Britain, not to forget Spain and the Netherlands, continuously laid claim to more and more lands in the New World, pushing deeper into the interior along its waterways. Each fought to push out other European parties and secure control of the lands and their resources. By the mid-1750s, the French and the British had already seen three major conflicts between the colonies (King William's War, 1689–97; the War of the Spanish Succession, 1702–11; and, the War of Austrian Succession, 1744–8), as well as numerous skirmishes, raids, and attacks by one colonial force against the other. As L.C. Green notes in *Law of Nations and The New World*, European powers saw North America as something to claim and control for their own benefit, with little regard to the continent's Indigenous inhabitants.[1] The Seven Years' War, sometimes known as the "first" world war due to its global players and the numerous theatres of battle in Europe, North America, the Indian subcontinent, and at sea, was changing the geopolitical landscape of the so-called New World. Late in the summer of 1760, after six years of warfare for European dominance of eastern North America, the final stage between Britain and France was set in the area around Montreal.

By the mid-eighteenth century, complex systems of alliances between different and competing Indigenous communities and European colonizers were established. Throughout the lands claimed by France, from Acadia to New France down to Louisiana, French authorities developed mutually dependent relationships, such as with what came to be known by the 1760s as the Confederacy of Seven Nations and composed of Huron, Algonquin, Abenaki, Nipissing, and the Christianized Haudenosaunee who settled

---

[1] L.C. Green and Olive P. Dickason, *The Law of Nations and the New World* (Edmonton: University of Alberta Press, 1993), 50.

in French Catholic missions.² With the constant threat of conflict with the British colonies, France's Indigenous allies proved to be indispensable, as their highly effective tactics against the British bolstered the small number of French soldiers in New France. For their part, and prior to the Seven Years' War, there was no centralized approach to Indigenous-settler relations, and individual British colonies established relationships and alliances with the communities closest to them, such as the one between the colony of New York and the Six Nations Confederacy. With the outbreak of war in 1754, British colonial leaders discovered that the growing tensions between their colonies and the Indigenous communities due to land encroachment had eroded their relationships to the point where the Indigenous allies now preferred to remain neutral rather than support the British in the growing conflict with the French.³ Concerned that their military success would be threatened without Indigenous support, General Edward Braddock, Britain's military commander in the Americas, consolidated the British-Indigenous relationship under the Indian Department and appointed William Johnson as superintendent of the northern district of the colonies.

In the first years of the war, France dominated the conflict in large part because of the superior fighting skills of its Indigenous allies, the lack of Indigenous support to the British, and Britain's poorly organized defences, a situation that was due to the diffused nature of colonial defence resting with individual colonies. The establishment of the Indian Department in 1755 and William Johnson's skillful use of kinship relations through his marriage to Molly (Mary) Brant of the Mohawk nation, as well as diplomacy and Indigenous protocols, played a significant role in shoring up the colonies' defences, leading to British victories as Indigenous allies returned to the British camp, led by the Haudenosaunee Confederacy. As Denys Delâge, historian of Indigenous-settler relations at the time of the war, notes, part of the British strategy aimed to break France's Indigenous alliance by attacking it directly.⁴ By 1758, Britain, coupled with an increasingly effective naval blockade, better military strategy, and ranks strengthened by Indigenous warriors, was pushing the French and their allies out of long-held positions. One after another, French strongholds, such as Louisbourg (1758), Fort Frontenac (1758), and Fort Niagara and Québec (1759), fell to

---

² Jean-Pierre Sawaya, *Les Sept Nations du Canada: Tradition d'alliance dans le nord-est*, report for the Royal Commission on Aboriginal Peoples, 1993, p. 9.
³ Denys Delâge, "Les Premières Nations et la Guerre de la Conquête (1754–1765)," *Les Cahiers des dix* 63 (2009): 16.
⁴ Ibid., 10.

advancing British forces.⁵ By the summer of 1760, Montreal was the sole surviving French position of any importance.

That summer, three separate British armies, nearly 18,000 men, converged on Montreal for the final assault. General James Murray, commander at Quebec since the fall of Wolfe on the Plains of Abraham, came up the St. Lawrence. Jeffrey Amherst, commander of the British forces in North America, and William Johnson, who had been commissioned a colonel at the start of the conflict, moved their forces across Lake Ontario and down the St. Lawrence, while the army of William Haviland descended the Richelieu River.⁶ As a testament to the renewed alliances with Indigenous communities, William Johnson noted that nearly 800 warriors accompanied the British to Montreal. Although the French troops were cut off from supply or reinforcement, British commanders were still concerned that France's Indigenous allies would harass their troops and camps, especially as forces attempted to navigate the dangerous rapids of the St. Lawrence River. In August 1760, William Johnson sought to remove this threat by offering to recognize the neutrality of all those who abandoned the French.⁷ Johnson's tactic proved to be an effective one; by the end of August, a delegation of some 30 representatives from France's Indigenous allies, later known as the Confederacy of Seven Nations, met with him at Swegatchy on the southeastern shore of Lake Ontario to negotiate their neutrality prior to the final battle at Montreal.

By the first days of September, the three British armies were nearly upon Montreal. The Huron-Wendat, who had moved with the French retreating to Montreal from their village of Lorette near Quebec, realized quickly that the defeat of the French was inevitable, as news spread of the Confederacy's move to neutrality. On September 5, just three days prior to the surrender of the besieged city, Huron-Wendat leaders met with James Murray to conclude their own agreement of neutrality.⁸ Through the agreement, the Huron-Wendat were assured that they would be able to return to their village at Lorette and that they would have the right to exercise their religion and customs, as well as trade with the British. With the agreement in hand, the Huron-Wendat, the longest-standing and last Indigenous allies

---

⁵ Jean-François Lozier, "History, Historiography, and the Courts: The St. Lawrence Mission Villages and the Fall of New France," in *Remembering 1759: The Conquest of Canada in Historical Memory*, ed. P. Buckner and J.G. Reid (Toronto: University of Toronto Press, 2012), 111.
⁶ Alain Beaulieu, "Les garanties d'un traité disparu: le traité d'Oswegatchie, le 30 août, 1760," *Revue Juridique Thémis* 34 (2000): 376.
⁷ Ibid., 379.
⁸ Cornelius J. Jaenan, "Rapport historique sur la nation huronne-wendate," report prepared for the Huron-Wendat First Nation and the Government of Canada, 1994, p. 92.

of France, stood aside from the conflict. One week later, William Johnson convened the former French allies for a final meeting in mid-September at Kahnawake to reconfirm the original agreements and start a new relationship between the Indigenous nations of the St. Lawrence Valley and the British Crown.[9] These treaties brought an end to more than 150 years of relations and alliances between France and the Indigenous nations in the St. Lawrence Valley.

While the Huron-Wendat and the other communities in the newly named Province of Quebec constantly reminded the British of their agreements, especially the protection of their lands and respect for their way of life, their words fell on mostly deaf ears.[10] The realities of the administration of the occupied territory of New France, the political need to manage the expectations of some 80,000 French and Catholic colonists, the demands for access to the rich fur-bearing grounds of the interior by British and American merchants, and the political expediency of ignoring the treaties pushed these agreements out of the minds of most British administrators. Furthermore, the "calm" nature of the relationship with the communities of New France was in marked contrast to the violence between the British and the former French Indigenous allies in the Great Lakes region. It would take another two centuries for these agreements even to be recognized, and then only after being taken up by the Supreme Court of Canada.

ORAL AND WRITTEN ACCOUNTS OF THE HURON-BRITISH TREATY, 1760

The British accounts of the agreement concluded on September 5, 1760, are virtually non-existent except for two notes found in the papers of General James Murray and Captain John Knox. In his diary, Murray notes that on September 5, while positioning his troops on the south shore of the St. Lawrence River near Longueuil, he encountered Indigenous leaders who were apparently seeking him out:

> Sepr 5th March'd with them myself and on the road, met the Inhabitants who were coming to deliver their arms, and take the oaths, there two nations of Indians, of Hurons and Iroquois, came in & made their Pace,

---

[9] Alain Beaulieu, "Les suites du traité de Swegatchie (30 août 1760): Recherche sur la nature des pourparlers entre les Indiens du Québec et les autorités britanniques (1760–1774)," report prepared for Indian and Northern Affairs Canada, 1996, p. 5.

[10] Lozier, "History, Historiography, and the Courts," 110.

at the same time Three of Sir William Johnstons Indians came in wth a letter from General Amherst ...[11]

The General's brief words provide little information as to the nature of the meeting, simply indicating that they made their "pace" (peace).

In the journal of Captain John Knox, who was accompanying Murray, there is a little more detail. While Murray specifically notes that the representatives were Huron and Iroquois, Knox makes no mention of origins but indicates that "eight Sachems, of different nations, lately in alliance with the enemy" had come to surrender to Murray.[12] Knox's entry implies that the meeting was more than a simple acceptance of the Indigenous party's surrender to the British, as he states that "after conferring with his Excellency [Murray], ... all matters had been adjusted to their satisfaction."[13] Interestingly, the captain's account offers no details of the exchanges between the leaders and Murray or of the nature of the agreement made, simply stating that the "Chieftains were negotiating a peace." On September 5, a document was issued by Murray stating that the Huron had made "peace" with the British Crown, that they were under Murray's protection and should not be "molested" as they returned to their village at Lorette, and that they would be allowed the "free exercise of their Religion; their Customs, and Liberty of trading with the English."[14] No other written record by any known witnesses provides details of the meeting, the discussions, or the nature of the agreement.

In the days after the surrender of Montreal, William Johnson and his agents in the Indian Department focused on ensuring the continued loyalty of the so-called "domiciliés Indians" – the resettled Indigenous communities around Montreal, Trois-Rivières, and Quebec. On September 15 and 16, Johnson convened a conference with the "Eight nations of Canada," referred to as the "treaty held at Caghnawagey" in Johnson's papers, where the terms concluded with the Confederacy of Seven Nations at Swegatchy on August 30 were reaffirmed and renewed. The former French allies once again vowed to keep a "firm peace wth the Engl^sh ... [and] shall endeavour all in our Pow^r to keep it inviolably."[15] For the British occupiers of New

---

[11] Journal of James Murray, September 5, 1760, in *An Historical Journal of the Campaigns in North America for the Years 1757, 1758, 1759 and 1760 by Captain John Knox*, vol. III, ed. A.G. Doughty (Toronto: Champlain Society, 1916), 331.

[12] Journal of Captain John Knox, September 6, 1760, *An Historical Journal of the Campaigns in North America for the Years 1757, 1758, 1759 and 1760 by Captain John Knox*, vol. I, p. 516.

[13] Ibid.

[14] "Murray Treaty," Records of notary Barthélémy Faribault fils, Archives nationales du Québec, deposited on August 4, 1810, CN301, S99.

[15] "Indian Conference, Montreal, September 16, 1760," in *The Papers of Sir William Johnson*, vol. 13, ed. M.W. Hamilton and A.B. Corey (Albany: University of the State of New York, 1962), 164.

France, with the constant fear of renewed French attempts to recapture the colony and internal uprisings by the French colonists, securing this peace was of fundamental priority.

While the surrender of Montreal effectively brought an end to the conflict between Britain and France in the St. Lawrence Valley and strengthened relations between Britain and the Indigenous communities in this region, the same cannot be said for the ongoing conflict between the British and the Indigenous nations of the Great Lakes and Upper Mississippi. As Denys Delâge notes in his examination of the role of First Nations in the war, even prior to the surrender of Montreal there was a dramatic change in the balance of power in the interior of the continent as Indigenous warriors and communities lost French support and supplies. Furthermore, as British troops rooted out French positions and occupied French forts, a "wave of pan-amerindian resistance" began to form against the British invaders.[16]

In the aftermath of the surrender of Montreal and prior to the signing of the Treaty of Paris in 1763, British forces were in a state of occupation in New France. While William Johnson's attention was turned to rebuilding alliances and to counter the resistance attributed to Pontiac in the Great Lakes, the management of the new relationship with the "domiciliés" communities was left in the hands of Daniel Claus, Johnson's first lieutenant, in Montreal. Focused on the much larger communities around Montreal and the agreement made at Kahnawake, Claus and officials from the Indian Department showed little interest in the Huron-Wendat at Lorette and apparently had no memory of an agreement made by James Murray. In the years that followed, the Huron-Wendat, and consequently their agreement of 1760, increasingly fell by the wayside as matters around Montreal occupied Claus's attention.[17] Seven years after receiving Murray's assurances, the Huron-Wendat complained to Claus that he had never set foot in their community.[18] Five years later, he returned admitting that he had not been to Lorette since his first visit in 1767.[19] There is no written account of discussions that likely took place during either of those meetings with Claus.

While the British may have forgotten the treaty, the same cannot be said for the Huron-Wendat. As with other Indigenous communities, oral traditions long persisted among the Huron-Wendat at Lorette. On

---

[16] Delâge, "Les Premières Nations," 63.
[17] Beaulieu, "Les suites du Traité de Swegatchie," 7.
[18] Daniel Claus to William Johnson, August 22, 1767, *The Papers of Sir William Johnson*, vol. 5, ed. A.C. Flick (Albany: University of the State of New York, 1927), 635.
[19] Daniel Claus to William Johnson, July 3, 1772, *The Papers of Sir William Johnson*, vol. 8, ed. A.C. Flick (Albany: University of the State of New York, 1933), 525.

February 27, 1828, a journalist, whose name is not recorded, from the fledgling *The Star and Commercial Advisor/L'Étoile et Journal du Commerce*, a short-lived bilingual newspaper out of Quebec City, met and published an interview with Petit-Étienne, one of the oldest "chiefs" in the Huron settlement of Lorette.[20] As UQAM historian Alain Beaulieu indicates in his article "Les Hurons et la Conquête: un nouvel éclairage sur le 'traité Murray,'" the journalist, described as a "gentleman" in the article, was initially seeking information from a community Elder on the great Huron chief Atsistari. The interview quickly became about Chief Petit-Étienne's personal experiences during the last year of the Seven Years' War in New France.[21] Chief Petit-Étienne recounted how, as a young man, he had witnessed the fall of Quebec, the Huron-Wendat trek to Montreal, just as the British armies were converging on the city, culminating with an account of the peace agreement made with James Murray on September 5, 1760, and the subsequent abandonment of their community by the British.

At the time of the publication of the interview, Petit-Étienne, also known as Étienne Ondiaraété, was 91 years old. As well as participating in some of the most important moments in the colonial history of the St. Lawrence, Petit-Étienne was a member of the Council of Chiefs at Lorette. By 1791, his name appears as a Chief in a petition to the British Crown seeking protection of Huron-Wendat lands.[22] Over the course of the next 40 years, Petit-Étienne's name appeared on nearly all documents, petitions, and correspondence between the community and British officials. By 1810 and at the age of 71, he was briefly grand chief of the Huron of Lorette before Nicolas Vincent assumed the title.[23] In 1819 and again in 1823, he was part of the delegation led by Grand Chief Nicolas Vincent that appeared before a committee of the Legislative Assembly of Lower Canada.[24]

The published account by Petit-Étienne in the interview offers a rare glimpse into the impact of the Seven Years' War on the Indigenous peoples of the St. Lawrence Valley. He described his participation in the two sieges of Quebec, and the events following the fall of Quebec. Petit-Étienne recalled that a French agent called a meeting of the Huron "Council and

---

[20] "Indian of Lorette," *The Star and Commercial Advertiser*, February 27, 1828.
[21] Alain Beaulieu, "Les Hurons et la Conquête: un nouvel éclairage sur le 'traité Murray,'" *Recherches Amérindiennes au Québec* 30, no. 3 (2000): 54.
[22] Serge Goudreau, "Etienne Ondiaraété (1742–1830): un chef huron du village de Lorette," *Mémoire de la Société généalogique canadienne-francaise* 54, no. 4, cahier 238 (2003): 279.
[23] Ibid., 287.
[24] Ibid., 285.

told us the orders of the General were that we should follow him; – By 12 o'clock that night we and our women and children had commenced our march; but before doing so, we concealed all that we had in the woods, in the neighbourhood of the Village, taking nothing with us but the ornaments and sacred vessels of our Church."[25] After a hard winter to the west of Cap Rouge on the St. Lawrence, the Huron followed the retreating French army toward Montreal, "but the English Army had started before us in batteaux, and we travelled with our wives and children in our canoes, and on land; following as close to them as we could, 'till we reached Pointe-du-Lac" near Trois-Rivières. As their chiefs had "ordered us to follow the English army without firing upon them," Petit-Étienne indicated a reluctance by the Huron to engage the British. Petit-Étienne's account points to Huron uncertainty in their support for the French in the conflict, stating: "We were unwilling latterly to take any active part in the War by opposing the English, – our council of Chiefs thought our force too small to effect much for our own safety, they determined upon being neutral. – We knew our weakness and observed that neutrality which did not endanger us with the conquerors." As Beaulieu comments in his examination of this source, the Huron had already questioned the wisdom of following the French into battle since the fall of Quebec in 1759.[26]

Despite a few skirmishes along the way, Petit-Étienne indicated that they eventually arrived at Montreal and set up their camp at the village of the Iroquois at the Sault St. Louis (Kahnawake). They found the "Village deserted like our own, there was nobody in it."[27] The account makes no mention of why the village may have been abandoned, although the empty village could indicate that the Iroquois of Kahnawake had abandoned the French to the British siege, having already agreed to their neutrality on August 30, 1760.[28] After waiting several days in the village of Kahnawake located on the south shore of the St. Lawrence River, Petit-Étienne reported that they "heard that the War was at an end," although without telling the provenance of this information to his interviewer. It is possible that news of the treaty concluded at Swegatchy had finally reached the Huron, as the French also heard the news on September 2.[29] He then recounted how the Huron-Wendat chiefs sought to make peace with the British:

---

[25] "Indian of Lorette."
[26] Beaulieu, "Les Hurons et la Conquête," 58.
[27] "Indian of Lorette."
[28] Beaulieu, "Les Hurons et la Conquête," 59.
[29] Ibid., 59–60.

Our Chiefs immediately on hearing the news mounted their horses and went to Laprairie where the English General was. Upon their arrival at the quarters of the General, their horses were taken care of by the soldiers; the Officers took our Chiefs by the arm and led them to their General. As soon as he [Murray] saw them he cried out "These are the Huron! Why did you leave your village? You have nothing to fear from us, go back to your Village, you are safe" and he turned around to some one near him and gave an order.

We received the next morning a paper from him, which we understood to mean that Peace was made.[30]

In an interesting side question, the interviewer asked if Petit-Étienne still had the treaty paper given by General Murray. Replying that he did not have the document, he stated that "it belongs to the Nation" held in trust by the leaders of the community, and that only the Council itself can grant access to it. In 1810, as the property of the Jesuits were being confiscated, the Huron-Wendat Council had a copy of this document verified and deposited with the notary firm Barthélémy Faribault Fils for safekeeping.[31]

Petit-Étienne's oral history provides some of the contextual information not captured by the written record of Murray and Knox, such as the growing shift toward neutrality by the Huron-Wendat, the reasons for their presence on the south shore of the river, and the confirmation that the Huron-Wendat chiefs openly sought out Murray to conclude peace with him. Just as in other Indigenous communities, the oral transmission of information was a vital component of the Huron-Wendat way of life. During his 1819 appearance before the Lower Canada Legislative Assembly, Grand Chief Nicolas Vincent stated that his "Ancestors could not write: we have no books, we have it by tradition. In times of old our Chiefs assembled the nation to hear from its Chiefs the history of our nation: we follow the same customs and relate to our children the affairs of our nation within our own times."[32] The transmission of this specific aspect of the community's history, along with the marked importance of the treaty, continues to resonate in the community. For example, Huron-Wendat historian Marguerite Vincent Tehariolina indicates that the September 1760 document was frequently used by her community as it pressed government

---

[30] "Indian of Lorette."
[31] Goudreau, "Etienne Ondiaraété," 285.
[32] Testimony of Grand Chief Nicolas Vincent Tsawanhouhi, February 2, 1819, *Appendix to the XXVIII[h] Volume of the Journals of the House of Assembly of the Province of Lower Canada*, Third Session, Ninth Provincial Parliament, 1819, Appendix R.

officials to protect their lands and interests.[33] As George Sioui notes in *Pour une auto-histoire amérindienne*, the agreement made on September 5, 1760, "both then and now, [it] constitutes recognition of a sovereignty they have never ceded or sold" and is held as a foundational document supported by a strong oral tradition.[34]

THE HURON-BRITISH TREATY AND THE COURTS

Until the arrest of Régent, Conrad, Georges, and Hugues Sioui in 1982, few people outside the Huron-Wendat community of Lorette were aware of the discussions between James Murray and the leaders of the Huron-Wendat prior to the surrender of Montreal in 1760. While the various rulings, appeals, and the final decision by the Supreme Court of Canada in 1990 brought some legal clarity to the document issued by Murray in 1760, it also created considerable debate within the historical community.

Four brothers from the prominent Sioui family at Lorette, along with their families, had gone into the Parc Jacques-Cartier, a provincial park some 35 kilometres north of Quebec City, to engage in fasting, meditation, and traditional teachings. As the trip was to be an overnight excursion, a camp was struck inside the boundaries of the park, where small trees were cut to make tent poles and cooking fires were lit.[35] The Sioui brothers were subsequently charged under the Quebec *Parks Act* for cutting trees in the park and lighting fires outside of designated areas. Where the defendants had initially built their argument on the infringement by the *Parks Act* on Aboriginal rights to hunt and fish, as well as Charter rights to freedom of religion, during the appeal to the Superior Court of Quebec, legal arguments changed as new documents were filed, including a copy of the September 5, 1760, certificate issued by Murray. The Siouis' argument from this point forward was that the document was a "valid treaty the effect of which, by virtue of section 88 of the *Indian Act* and section 35 of the *Constitution Act, 1982*" was that the Quebec *Parks Act* therefore violated treaty rights to the religious practices of the Sioui brothers.[36]

After the Quebec Court of Appeal recognized that the submitted certificate, being referred to as the "Murray Treaty" at the time, was a valid

---

[33] Marguerite Vincent Teharionlina, *La nation huronne: son histoire, sa culture, son esprit* (Quebec: Éditions du Pélican, 1984), 145.

[34] George E. Sioui, *Pour une auto-histoire amérindienne* (Quebec: Presses de l'Université Laval, 1991), 126.

[35] Franklin S. Gertler and Peter W. Hutchins, "The Marriage of History and Law in R. v. Sioui," *Native Studies Review* 6, no. 2 (1990): 115.

[36] Ibid., 116.

treaty with the Huron,[37] the province of Quebec appealed to the Supreme Court. At the core of the province's appeal was questioning whether the document in question was truly a valid treaty or a simple "laissez-passer," a document ensuring safe passage from Longueuil to Lorette for the Huron-Wendat.[38] Agreeing to hear the case, the Supreme Court then focused on three specific questions: (1) was the certificate issued by James Murray a valid treaty?; (2) if yes, was it still in effect?; and (3) if yes, did it have the effect of making the Quebec *Parks Act* unenforceable upon the Sioui brothers?[39] Subsequent to a lengthy set of hearings, the Supreme Court of Canada tabled a unanimous ruling, written by Chief Justice Antonio Lamer, supporting the validity of the certificate as a treaty between the British and the Huron-Wendat.

In explaining the ruling, Chief Justice Lamer stated that in order to determine the validity of the document as a treaty, it was necessary to ensure that the parties in question had the capacity to conclude a treaty. Where the province argued that James Murray did not have authority to conclude any treaties, Lamer stated that "Murray was the highest ranking British officer with whom the Hurons could have conferred. The circumstances prevailing at the time, in my view, thus support the respondents' proposition that Murray in fact had the necessary capacity to enter into a treaty."[40] He further concluded that the Huron-Wendat themselves likely believed him to have been the right officer with whom to deal, because "Murray, as Governor of the Quebec district, might reasonably have been regarded by the Hurons living in that district as the person most competent to sign a treaty with them." Responding to the Crown's position that the Huron had no capacity to enter into a treaty because they did not have "historical occupation or possession" in the St. Lawrence Valley, the Supreme Court rebuffed the province again by stating that treaties between the Crown and Indigenous communities are not always about land. As the purported treaty was not about addressing land issues but establishing a peaceful relationship between the parties, and as this legal question had already been addressed in the *Simon* decision of 1985, the Huron-Wendat had full authority to do so.[41]

---

[37] *Sioui v. Le procureur général de la province de Québec*, [1987] RJQ, 1722, [1987] 4 CNLR 118 (Que. CA).
[38] Rachel Chagnon, "Clio et Thémis, la place de l'histoire dans le processus judiciaire," *Bulletin d'histoire politique* 9, no. 2 (2001): 112.
[39] *R. v. Sioui*, [1990] 1 S.C.R., p. 1026.
[40] Ibid., 1041.
[41] Ibid., 1043.

As Lamer turned to consider whether the certificate issued by Murray constituted a valid treaty, he took the opportunity to place this case within the existing jurisprudence of "treaty law." When dealing with historical records relating to Indigenous rights, and especially treaties, he said that

> a more flexible approach is necessary as the question of the existence of a treaty within the meaning of s. 88 of the *Indian Act* is generally closely bound up with the circumstances existing when the document was prepared (*White and Bob, supra*, at pp. 648–49, and *Simon, supra*, at pp. 409–10). In any case, the wording alone will not suffice to determine the legal nature of the document before the Court. On the one hand, we have before us a document the form of which and some of whose subject matter suggest that it is not a treaty, and on the other, we find it to contain protection of fundamental rights which supports the opposite conclusion.[42]

Arguing that as the text alone is insufficient to allow for a proper decision, the court must consider other extrinsic evidence to help bring clarity to the meaning of the text. Looking specifically at the few contemporary British documents addressing the September 5, 1760, encounter, namely the journal entries of James Murray and John Knox, Lamer ruled that these two records, especially Knox's reference to "all matters had been adjusted to their satisfaction," supported the fact that

> the document of September 5 was not simply an expression of General Murray's wishes, but the result of negotiations between the parties. This document was thus not simply a unilateral act, a simple acknowledgment or safe conduct, but the embodiment of an agreement reached between the representative of the British Crown and the representatives of the Indian nations present, including the representative of the Lorette Hurons.[43]

Ultimately, the Supreme Court upheld the Quebec Court of Appeal ruling that the certificate issued by James Murray on September 5, 1760, constituted a valid treaty under section 88 of the *Indian Act*. After reminding the parties that a treaty between Indigenous nations and the Crown could not be unilaterally extinguished without the consent of the Indigenous

---

[42] Ibid., 1049
[43] Ibid., 1057.

party, Lamer ruled the provincial legislation unenforceable upon the Sioui, as their rights to exercise "traditional customs" was protected by the treaty.

The Supreme Court's *Sioui* decision reinforced the growing jurisprudence relating to the interpretation and validation of treaties. Like the 1985 *Simon* decision on the 1752 Cope treaty in Nova Scotia,[44] it confirmed that a treaty did not need to involve land to be valid. The ruling also provided a new precedent for determining what could be a treaty, through "a broad and generous interpretation of what constitutes a treaty."[45] More important, the ruling broadened the use of other forms of evidence that could be used in cases dealing with treaties. In their analysis of Chief Justice Lamer's ruling, lawyers Franklin Gertler and Peter Hutchins, who had represented the National Indian Brotherhood/Assembly of First Nations as intervenors during the *Sioui* case, noted,

> It is clear from the judgement of Mr. Justice Lamer that mere analysis of the words of the document of 5 September 1760 might not have been sufficient to convince the Court that the British and the Hurons had entered into a treaty. Thus only by resorting to "extrinsic" evidence (evidence outside of the text of the document in question) of the relevant historical circumstances was the Court able to conclude with assurance that solemn and lasting treaty commitments were intended and were indeed entered into by Great Britain and the Huron Nation.[46]

In other words, the document and its mere 144 words were insufficient to prove definitively that a treaty had been concluded on September 5, 1760. In order to make a clear determination, the Court looked at other materials of historical relevance, such as the journals of British officials. Interestingly, the extrinsic evidence used by the Court did not include additional oral histories beyond the testimony heard in the lower courts. In addition, the only known historical account of the September 5, 1760, meeting from a Huron-Wendat perspective, the Petit-Étienne interview of 1828, was not discovered until ten years after the final ruling.

While clarifying how the courts should use historical materials, the approach used by the Supreme Court created division and criticism within the historical community. At its root was the fact that the now recognized

---

[44] See Chapter 1.
[45] Ibid., 1035.
[46] Gertler and Hutchins, "The Marriage of History and Law," 125.

"Murray Treaty of 1760" was largely unknown to historians prior to the court case in the mid-1980s.[47] While there have been numerous studies and examination of the circumstances of the events of September 5, 1760, since the Supreme Court decision in 1990, there appear to have been little prior to the 1987 Court of Appeal decision first recognizing the treaty's validity. As Jean-François Lozier, French colonial historian at the Canadian Museum of History, notes in his article "History, Historiography, and the Courts," the Court's recognition of the treaty divided the historical community into two camps, each one supporting one of the two positions taken in the courtroom. On the one hand, Denys Delâge and Cornelius Jaenen argued that a treaty had been concluded in large part due to the British "policy of conciliation that characterized the years of the Conquest."[48] On the other, Marcel Trudel, Alain Beaulieu, and Denis Vaugeois replied that there was insufficient historical evidence of protocol and ceremony, specifically the absence of wampum and ceremonial language, to support a valid treaty and that the document should be seen as a "mere certificate of safe-conduct" allowing the Huron-Wendat to return to their village.

In the decades since the *Sioui* ruling, the debate within the historical community about whether the court should have recognized the document as a treaty has not abated. Discoveries of related materials since 1990 have added to the debate, such as in 1996 when another copy of the certificate with slightly different wording was located in the Quebec archives, or the unearthing of the Petit-Étienne oral history of the treaty meeting in 2000. For some, such as Quebec historian Rachel Chagnon, the ruling affected historical approaches, with some historians adopting the Court's rules for "broad and generous interpretation" as part of their historical analysis. Chagnon argues that while the Court's rules of interpretation may create greater fairness, this does not imply a more accurate history of the treaty.[49] While historians continue their debates, the Huron-Wendat have continued to recount their perspective of the treaty. When the Royal Commission on Aboriginal Peoples held its hearings in Wendake, community leaders and Elders saw the treaty as the key to their future: "with the political and economic autonomy of the Hurons-Wendat, with the application of the Murray Treaty, with all the land claims already under way, we hope that one day we will be able to act as kings and masters of our own house."[50]

---

[47] Lozier, "History, Historiography, and the Courts," 120.
[48] Ibid., 122.
[49] Chagnon, "Clio et Thémis," 114.
[50] Testimony of Deputy Chief François Vincent, Council of the Huron-Wendat Nation, November 17, 1992, Wendake, Quebec, *Public Hearings of the Royal Commission on Aboriginal Peoples*, 2047-5, QUE 92-11-17, p. 19.

FURTHER READINGS

Denys Delâge. "Les Premières Nations et la Guerre de la Conquête (1754–1765)." *Les Cahiers des dix* 63 (2009): 1–67.

Serge Goudreau. "Etienne Ondiaraété (1742–1830): un chef huron du village de Lorette." *Mémoire de la Société généalogique canadienne-francaise* 54, no. 4, cahier 238 (2003): 269–88.

L.C. Green and Olive Dickason. *The Law of Nations and the New World.* Edmonton: University of Alberta Press, 1993.

George E. Sioui. *Pour une auto-histoire amérindienne.* Quebec: Presses de l'Université Laval, 1991.

Marguerite Vincent Teharionlina. *La nation huronne: son histoire, sa culture, son esprit.* Quebec: Éditions du Pélican, 1984.

Denis Vaugeois, ed. *Les Hurons de Lorette.* Sillery, QC: Éditions du Septentrion, 1996.

QUESTIONS FOR DISCUSSION

1. In your opinion, what is the meaning of the document issued by General James Murray on September 5, 1760?
2. Read the following extracts of the British and Huron-Wendat accounts of the treaty negotiations and identify where the accounts are similar and where they diverge from one another.

> **Journal of James Murray, *An Historical Journal of the Campaigns in North America for the Years 1757, 1758, 1759 and 1760* by Captain John Knox, vol. III, ed. A.G. Doughty (Toronto: Champlain Society, 1916), 331**
>
> Sepr 5th March'd with them myself and on the road, met the Inhabitants who were coming to deliver their arms, and take the oaths, there two nations of Indians, of Hurons and Iroquois, came in & made their Pace, at the same time Three of Sir William Johnstons Indians came in wth a letter from General Amherst.

> **"Indian of Lorette," *The Star and Commercial Advertiser*, February 27, 1828**
>
> Before many days had passed, we heard that the War was at an end. Our Chiefs immediately on hearing the news mounted their horses and went to LaPrairie where the English General was. Upon their arrival at the quarters of the General, their horses were taken care of by the soldiers; the Officers took our Chiefs by the arm and led them to their General. As soon as he saw them he cried out "These are the Huron! Why did you leave your village? You have

nothing to fear from us, go back to your Village, you are safe" and he turned around to some one near him and gave an order. We received the next morning a paper from him, which we understood to mean that Peace was made.

3. In the absence of records, how can an oral history help us understand what occurred during the meeting between the Huron-Wendat and General Murray?
4. How did the Supreme Court of Canada justify the recognition of the document as a treaty?

DOCUMENTS

Treaty Text: Huron-British Treaty of 1760. As transcribed in the May 24, 1990, *R. v. Sioui* decision of the Supreme Court of Canada, and originating in Archives nationales du Québec, Records of notary Barthélémy Faribault fils, deposited on August 4, 1810, CN301, S99

THESE are to certify that the CHIEF of the HURON tribe of Indians, having come to me in the name of his Nation, to submit to HIS BRITANNICK MAJESTY, and make Peace, has been received under my Protection, with his whole Tribe; and henceforth no English Officer or party is to molest, or interrupt them in returning to their Settlement at LORETTE; and they are receiving upon the same terms with the Canadians, being allowed the free exercise of their Religion; their Customs, and Liberty of trading with the English: – recommending it to the Officers commanding the Posts, to treat them kindly.

Given under my hand at Longueil, this 5th day of September, 1760.
By the Genl's Command,
JOHN COSNAN,
Adjut Genl.
JA. MURRAY.

"Indian of Lorette," *The Star and Commercial Advertiser*, February 27, 1828, AMICUS: 8396067

The story of Oui-ha-ra-lih-te or Petit Etienne
What happened after the Battle of the Plaines?
We hastened to the Village. The French and Canadian army that had fought the battle retreated by St. Foy to Montreal.

The men who had remained at Beauport with Vaudreuil consisted almost entirely of Militia; these were Habitants from the Upper part of the Province, and from the neighbourhood of Quebec. It was between 7 or 8 in the evening when Vaudreuil arrived in the village and gave the orders to our agent and marched forward without stopping. He had marched by the Charlesbourg road, – there were not more than five or six, and twenty regular soldiers with him, the rest were Militia – These were in a very great numbers, I should think that there were many more than 1000; – it took them half the day to pass by the Village as they marched towards Montreal, each man stopped as he came to his own house.

The Agent called a meeting of our Council and told us the orders of the General were that we should follow him; – By 12 o'clock that night we and our women and children had commenced our march; but before doing so, we concealed all that we had in the woods, in the neighbourhood of the Village, taking nothing with us but the ornaments and sacred vessels of our Church. We marched the whole night and reached Capsa, which is just beyond the limits of Old Lorette, about 7 o'clock on the following morning. We passed the whole of that day and the following night there. The next morning as soon as we had boiled our kettles, we again commenced our march, and reached the hither side of Jacques Cartier River that night; and we put up our Cabins on the high lands at its mouth. We crossed this River the next day in the canoes of some of our Hunters and with the assistance of the ferrymen who had received orders to that effect. A store house was erected on the other side, we pitched our cabins here for the Winter, receiving provisions from the King's stores.

...

Had you any thing to do with the English that Winter?

There were two sentries posted at Cap Rouge, our young men sometimes exchanged shots with their piquets.

We were unwilling latterly to take any active part in the War by opposing the English, – our council of Chiefs thought our force too small to effect much for our own safety, they determined upon being neutral. – We knew our weakness and observed that neutrality which did not endanger us with the conquerors.

... When the spring had come we were told from the Commandant that if we expected to get provisions we must follow the French Army to Montreal – This we did, but the English Army had started before us in batteaux, and we travelled with our wives and children in our canoes, and on land; following as close to them as we could, 'till we reached Pointe-du-Lac, where we crossed over to the Islands of Sorrel, and we cabined ourselves. We placed four warriors on the look out; and I remember that in a day or two after, a boat with six men and an officer came near the Island with an intention to land; our warriors shewed themselves at the approach of the boat, which they meant as a sign of peace, for we might have killed them all before they could have seen us. Our Chiefs had ordered us to follow the English army without firing upon them. Those in the boat were very much alarmed when they saw us, and immediately turned about their boat. One of those men however fired at the most advanced of our warriors, who received no injury, but was so exasperated that he returned the fire, and shot the man.

We afterwards found out that the Officer was Major Holland, who was always a very great friend to us, and often spoke to us about this affaire.

We proceeded to Montreal, and soon after were ordered to the Village of the Iroquois at the Sault St. Louis. We went there and found the Village deserted like our own, there was nobody in it. We took possession of the houses; but sent some of our young men in search of the Iroquois.

Before many days had passed, we heard that the War was at an end. Our Chiefs immediately on hearing the news mounted their horses and went to LaPrairie where the English General was. Upon their arrival at the quarters of the General, their horses were taken care of by the soldiers; the Officers took our Chiefs by the arm and led them to their General. As soon as he saw them he cried out "These are the Huron! Why did you leave your village? You have nothing to fear from us, go back to your Village, you are safe" and he turned around to some one near him and gave an order.

We received the next morning a paper from him, which we understood to mean that Peace was made. *Have you that paper?* No – it belongs to the Nation; it is in the house of the second Chief where the Council always meets. *Can you get it for me?* No body can give it but the Council.

Excerpts from the Journal of James Murray (vol. III, p. 331) and the Journal of Captain John Knox, September 6, 1760 (vol. I, p. 516), in *An Historical Journal of the Campaigns in North America for the Years 1757, 1758, 1759 and 1760 by Captain John Knox*, ed. A.G. Doughty (Toronto: Champlain Society, 1916)

Journal of James Murray

Sepr 5th March'd with them myself and on the road, met the Inhabitants who were coming to deliver their arms, and take the oaths, there two nations of Indians, of Hurons and Iroquois, came in & made their Pace, at the same time Three of Sir William Johnstons Indians came in wth a letter from General Amherst ...

Journal of Captain John Knox

Eight Sachems, of different nations, lately in alliance with the enemy, have surrendered, for themselves and their tribes, to General Murray: these fellows, after conferring with his Excellency, and that all matters had been adjusted to their satisfaction, stepped out to the beach opposite to Montreal, flourished their knives and hatchets, and set up the war-shout; intimating to the French, that they are now become our allies and their enemies. While these Chieftains were negociating a peace, two of our Mohawks entered the apartment where they were with the General and Colonel Burton ...

Excerpt from *R. v. Sioui*, [1990] 1 S.C.R. 1025

Both *Simon* and *White and Bob* make it clear that the question of capacity must be seen from the point of view of the Indians at that time, and the Court must ask whether it was reasonable for them to have assumed that the other party they were dealing with had the authority to enter into a valid treaty with them. I conclude without any hesitation that the Hurons could reasonably have believed that the British Crown had the power to enter into a treaty with them that would be in effect as long as the British controlled Canada ... (p. 1038)

In my view ... the respondents are correct in stating that on September 5, 1760, Murray was the highest ranking British officer with whom the Hurons could have conferred. The circumstances prevailing at the time, in my view, thus support the respondents' proposition that Murray in fact had the necessary capacity to enter into a treaty. Furthermore, if there is still any doubt, I think it is clear in any event that Murray had such authority in New France that it was reasonable for the Hurons to believe that he had the power to enter into a treaty with them. (p. 1041)

Without going so far as to suggest that there cannot be treaties other than agreements under which the Indians cede land to the Crown, the appellant argues that a treaty could not confer rights on the Indians unless the latter could claim historical occupation or possession of the lands in question ... In the Court's opinion that [this argument] would limit severely the scope of the word "treaty" and run contrary to the principle that Indians treaties should be liberally construed and uncertainties resolved in favour of the Indians. The argument made here must be rejected in the same way. There is no reason why an agreement concerning something other than a territory, such as an agreement about political or social rights, cannot be a treaty within the meaning of s. 88 of the Indian Act. (p. 1042)

While the analysis thus far seems to suggest that the document of September 5 is not a treaty, the presence of a clause guaranteeing the free exercise of religion, customs and trade with the English cannot but raise serious doubts about this proposition. It seems extremely strange to me that a document which is supposedly only a temporary, unilateral and informal safe conduct should contain a clause guaranteeing rights of such importance. As Bisson J.A. noted in the Court of Appeal judgment, there would have been no necessity to mention the free exercise of religion and customs in a document the effects of which were only to last for a few days. Such a guarantee would definitely have been more natural in a treaty where "the word of the white man" is given. (p. 1048)

... a more flexible approach is necessary as the question of the existence of a treaty within the meaning of s. 88 of the Indian Act is generally closely bound up with the circumstances existing when the document was prepared (*White and Bob, supra*, at pp. 648–49, and *Simon, supra*, at pp. 409–10). In any case, the wording alone will not suffice to determine the legal nature of the document before the Court. On the one hand, we have before us a document the form of which and some of whose subject matter suggest that it is not a treaty, and on the other, we find it to contain protection of fundamental rights which supports the opposite conclusion. (p. 1050)

The foregoing passage [by Knox] shows that the document of September 5 was not simply an expression of General Murray's wishes, but the result of negotiations between the parties. This document was thus not simply a unilateral act, a simple acknowledgment or safe conduct, but the embodiment of an agreement reached between the representative of the British Crown and the representatives of the Indian nations present, including the representative of the Lorette Hurons. (p. 1059)

I am therefore of the view that the document of September 5, 1760 is a treaty within the meaning of s. 88 of the Indian Act. (p. 1060)

The 1760 document is a treaty within the meaning of s. 88 of the Indian Act. Though the wording of the document does not suffice to determine its legal nature, the historical context and evidence relating to facts which occurred shortly before or after the signing of the document indicate that General Murray and the Hurons entered into an agreement to make peace and guarantee it. They entered into this agreement with the intention to create mutually binding obligations that would be solemnly respected. All the parties involved were competent to enter into this treaty. Even if Great Britain was not sovereign in Canada in 1760, the Hurons could reasonably have believed that it had the power to enter into a treaty with them and that this treaty would be in effect as long as the British controlled Canada. The circumstances prevailing at the time indicate that Murray had the necessary capacity to enter into a treaty, or at least that the Hurons could reasonably have assumed he did in view of the importance of his position in Canada at the time. In the case of the Hurons, though they could not claim historical occupation or possession of the lands in question, this did not prevent them from concluding a treaty with the British Crown. A territorial claim is not essential to the existence of a treaty within the meaning of s. 88 of the Indian Act. (p. 1026)

CAST OF CHARACTERS: HURON-BRITISH TREATY OF 1760

Étienne Ondiaraété "Petit-Étienne": b. c. 1737–1742; d. c. April 1830

Étienne Ondiaraété was likely born in the late 1730s or early 1740s in the Huron-Wendat village of la Jeune Lorette near Quebec City. Being in his late teens/early 20s during the Seven Years' War, Ondiaraété witnessed the fall of New France and the establishment of British rule in the St. Lawrence Valley. He, along with other Huron warriors, fought alongside the British during the American War of Independence and the siege of Quebec. By the late 1700s, he was a member of the chiefs' council, where he advocated for the protection of the Huron mission lands from settler encroachment. Ondiaraété was a member of the Huron delegation led by Nicolas Vincent (Tsaouenhohoui), his son-in-law, before the legislative assembly of Lower Canada in 1819 and 1823. In 1828, in his mid-80s, Ondiaraété gave an interview to journalists of the *Star and Commercial Advertiser* newspaper in Quebec, recounting the experiences of his community during the Seven Years' War and the conclusion of the agreement made on September 5, 1760, with General James Murray.

James Murray: b. January 21, 1721/2; d. June 18, 1794

James Murray was born at Ballencrieff, the family home of the Baron of Elibank in Lothian, Scotland. As was the common practice for the sons of the landed nobility, Murray enrolled as a cadet at the age of 15 with the Colyears' Regiment of the Scots Brigade. After a brief period serving in Belgium, Murray joined the British Army in 1739/40 as a second lieutenant, rising to the rank of major-general by 1762. While he served in both Europe and the Americas, he was a significant leader in the British efforts during the Seven Years' War, serving under General Wolfe during the sieges of both Louisbourg (1758) and Quebec (1759). After the death of Wolfe on the Plains of Abraham, Murray assumed command of the British occupation forces and led one of the three columns converging on Montreal, culminating in its capitulation in September 1760. During the siege of Montreal, Murray secretly met with leaders of the Huron-Wendat, allies of the French who were seeking safe passage back to their village at Lorette, near Quebec City, in exchange for their abandonment of the French. After the fall of Montreal, Murray was appointed military governor of New France and, after the signing of the Treaty of Paris in 1763, the first governor of the British Province of Quebec until 1766. During his administration, he sought to maintain a delicate balance between British and French interests in the colony but had little control or influence over the growing administration of Indigenous affairs.

William Johnson: b. c. 1715; d. July 11, 1774

William Johnson was born in Smithtown, Ireland, in a merchant family with ties to the British Navy. After acting for his uncle, British Vice-Admiral Peter Warren in Ireland, Johnson moved to the colony of New York in 1739 to administer one of his uncle's new estates in the Mohawk Valley near Albany. With the financial backing of his uncle, within a decade Johnson became one of the most successful businessmen and merchants in the colony, with substantial land holdings and a busy fur trade with the Mohawk of the Haudenosaunee Confederacy. An active member of colonial society, he became the primary liaison between Albany and the Six Nations, holding the position of "colonel of the Six Nations Indians." Well versed in Indigenous practices, customs, and Iroquoian languages, he proved to be a skillful negotiator for both the colony and his business. His ties to the Haudenosaunee were strengthened by his marriage to Molly (Mary) Brant, a member of an influential Mohawk family. As the conflict with France reached its zenith in the mid-1750s, the British military consolidated the administration of Indigenous affairs and appointed Johnson superintendent of Indian Affairs for the northern colonies in 1755. After an active military role during the Seven Years' War, where he rallied Haudenosaunee and other allied nations to the British, Johnson played a vital role in maintaining the peace between the former allies of the French and the British in the Great Lakes region after the fall of New France and after the issuance of the Royal Proclamation of 1763. He recognized the importance of kinship ties and worked to bridge Indigenous and British perspectives for mutual benefit. Until his death in 1774, Johnson remained in control of Indigenous affairs and set British policy for the decades that followed.

Nicolas Vincent: b. c. April 11, 1769; d. October 31, 1844

Nicolas Vincent (Tsaouenhohoui) was born in the Huron village of Jeune-Lorette near Quebec City, into one of the leading families of the community. By the age of 34, he was appointed war chief for the Huron-Wendat and fought alongside British troops and Canadian militia during the War of 1812. In 1811, Vincent was made grand chief of the Huron-Wendat Nation Council and granted the title of Tsaouenhohoui, "the man who sees clearly" or "the falcon." He quickly became a fierce defender of Huron-Wendat interests, especially defending the land interests and protecting hunting and fishing grounds. A talented diplomat, Vincent urged the British authorities to recognize the promises made in 1760 to protect the lands of the Council of Seven Fires, representing his community before the Assembly of Lower Canada, and bringing these concerns directly to the British Crown during a meeting with George IV in 1825. Vincent was one of the last hereditary chiefs and the last person to bear the name Tsaouenhohoui, since the Indigenous system of choosing chiefs disappeared around the 1880s, after an elective method was instituted by the Canadian government.

Figure 2.1 James Murray, c. 1770. Second in command of the British forces during the Battle of the Plains of Abraham, James Murray had first-hand experience with the military prowess of France's Indigenous allies.

Source: Library and Archives Canada, Acc. No. 1997-227-1, C-002834.

Figure 2.2 Nicolas Vincent (Tsaouenhohoui), c. 1825. By the early nineteenth century, the Huron-Wendat of Lorette no longer held the same influence as they did during the French period. Nicolas Vincent (Tsaouenhohoui) sought to renew that relationship by building on the agreements of the past.

Source: Library and Archives Canada, Acc. No. R9266-3182, e002140054.

Chapter 3
Upper Canada Land Surrenders: Rice Lake Treaty of 1818

In 1763, the territory comprising present-day southern Ontario was inhabited largely by Anishinaabeg peoples. European settlers were occupying sites only in or near the various military posts situated in strategic locations along communication routes through the interior. The end of the Seven Years' War in 1763 marked a new reality for Indigenous peoples in the Great Lakes basin as the European contest for control of North America had come to an end. In and around the lakes, the British now had control of French posts. This caused anxiety among the nations around the Great Lakes and into the Ohio Valley. Many were increasingly fearful of the consequences of the departure of their long-time French allies and the increased British presence.[1] This occupation, combined with the refusal of the British to supply gunpowder or to resume the fur trade, led many Indigenous leaders to believe that the British planned to exterminate their people and occupy their land.[2]

The management of Indigenous affairs in the region was the responsibility of Sir William Johnson. Appointed by the British Crown as the first superintendent of Indian Affairs in the northern colonies, he heeded to the growing apprehension and mistrust between the British and the Indigenous communities due to the British frontier policy preceding the Seven Years' War.[3] The issue of unchecked encroachment of European settlement onto Indigenous lands was a long-standing complaint, and Indigenous peoples feared further displacement, especially in light of the competing colonial

---

[1] Jack Stagg, *Anglo-Indian Relations in North America to 1763 and an Analysis of the Royal Proclamation of 7 October 1763* (Ottawa: Research Branch, Indian and Northern Affairs Canada, 1981), 249.
[2] Ibid., 239–43.
[3] Robert S. Allen, *His Majesty's Indian Allies: British Indian Policy in the Defence of Canada, 1774–1815* (Toronto: Dundurn Press, 1993), 25.

governments' push toward expanding their borders.[4] After the conclusion of a peace treaty with France in 1763, the British imperial government began the process of creating a comprehensive American colonial policy that would better manage the colonies and also promote security and trade with Indigenous peoples.[5] On October 7, 1763, George III issued a Royal Proclamation to firmly announce British plans for North America.

The Proclamation covered several broad topic areas: the administration of new territories, grants of land to decommissioned soldiers, and the management of Indigenous affairs. On this last point, the Proclamation aimed to create a border between settlers and Indigenous peoples, prevent the illegal acquisition of Indigenous lands, and establish protocols and practices to manage future acquisitions by Crown representatives.[6] Holding the responsibility of managing the fragile relationship around the Great Lakes, Johnson quickly circulated copies of the Proclamation in December 1764. Hoping to secure an end to the Indigenous uprising against the British presence in the Great Lakes, Johnson aimed to use the Royal Proclamation to forge a new relationship during a special assembly to be held at Fort Niagara in July 1764. During the conference at Niagara, Indigenous representatives from across the region gathered to meet with Johnson, who extended the Covenant Chain of Friendship to all. This offering was made to renew the relationship with British Indigenous allies and to form new alliances with the former allies of France. Johnson was able to gain the respect of Indigenous leaders by honouring their social conventions and recognizing how First Nations understood their relationship with the Crown.

The first land cession under the protocols of the Royal Proclamation was concluded between Sir William Johnson and the Seneca of the Haudenosaunee Confederacy, when two miles were ceded on either side of the Niagara River for the purposes of communication and travel between Lake Erie and Lake Ontario.[7] In the two decades after the Royal Proclamation, there was little new European settlement in what is now

---

[4] Stagg, *Anglo-Indian Relations*, 29.

[5] John Borrows, "Wampum at Niagara: The Royal Proclamation, Canadian Legal History, and Self-Government," in *Aboriginal and Treaty Rights in Canada: Essays on Law, Equality, and Respect for Difference*, ed. Michael Asch (Vancouver: University of British Columbia Press, 1997), 161.

[6] "By the King, A Proclamation," George III, October 7, 1763. Broadside. Robert Baskett, Printer, 1763. LAC, e010778430, AMICUS no. 7468714.

[7] Articles of Peace Concluded with the Seneca, in *Documents Relating to the Colonial History of New York*, vol. 7, ed. E.B. O'Callaghan (Albany, NY: Weed, Parson and Co. Printers, 1856), 621–3.

Canada but rather around the American colonies. As a result, only three land surrenders were concluded between the Department of Indian Affairs and Indigenous communities between 1764 and 1783: two at Niagara and one at the trading post on St. Joseph's Island, near Sault Ste. Marie. These surrenders covered very small parcels of land and dealt more with security and trade than with settlement.

After the loss of the American colonies in 1783, some 30,000 United Empire Loyalist refugees fled to the remaining British colonies in North America, and treaty making began in earnest. The fear of an American invasion propelled the British goal of establishing a continuous line of settlement between Montreal, Kingston, Niagara, and Detroit to ensure safe and efficient communication between those posts.[8] New agreements were negotiated for the lands extending up the St. Lawrence, across to Detroit, and up to Georgian Bay. Between 1783 and 1812, fifteen land-surrender treaties were concluded in the Upper Canadian peninsula in the hopes that land cessions would precede the arrival of settlers in the area. Until the 1810s, the majority of British settlement was concentrated in small pockets along the St. Lawrence River, at the Toronto Carrying Place, Niagara, and the St. Clair River, and their numbers were dwarfed by the large Indigenous population, making relations fairly easy to maintain. Indigenous signatories received extra payments as well as the yearly presents from the British, and since the settler population grew very slowly and was largely concentrated, hunting and fishing were not severely limited.[9]

The written terms of the agreements, where they have survived, are relatively simple. They describe the groups involved in the surrender, the extent of the lands surrendered, and what Indigenous signatories were to receive in compensation. A few of these treaties also establish reserved lands for the Indigenous signatories, such as in the 1790 McKee Treaty concluded at Detroit.[10] Before 1818, British payments in these agreements were limited to one-time payments in goods or money or both, paid to the signatories at the time of the treaty. The written agreements, while using terms such as "yield" and "cede" in regard to lands, are largely silent on the matter of other rights, such as hunting or fishing. As the British settlements were few,

---

[8] Joan Holmes and Associates, *Land Cession Treaties and Reserves Surrenders in Pre-Confederation Ontario*, vol. II, for Indian Affairs and Northern Development Canada, 2003, p. 36.
[9] Jean-Pierre Morin, "Concepts of Extinguishment in the Upper Canada Land Surrender Treaties, 1764–1862," in *Aboriginal Policy Research, vol. VII: A History of Treaties and Policies*, ed. Jerry P. White, Erik Anderson, Jean-Pierre Morin, and Dan Beavon (Toronto: Thompson, 2010), 24.
[10] R.J. Surtees, *Indian Land Surrenders in Ontario 1763–1867* (Ottawa: Treaties and Historical Research Centre, Indian and Northern Affairs Canada, 1984), 28.

Anishinaabeg, Haudenosaunee, and others continued to use much of the land around the Great Lakes, even those under the treaties.[11]

In the period following the War of 1812, however, the newfound peace between the United States and Britain, as well as waves of new immigrants flocking into Upper Canada to join the earlier Loyalist settlers, brought a new reality to the Anishinaabeg and Haudenosaunee peoples of the Great Lakes. The establishment of a lasting peace between Britain and the United States meant the need to maintain strong military alliances with Indigenous nations lost its significance for British officials, and the arrival of thousands of new immigrants brought renewed pressure to open more land for settlement. Unsurrendered Indigenous hunting grounds were seen as untapped agricultural lands being wasted by underdevelopment.[12] As land acquisition became the primary focus of the Indian Department, Indian agents shifted their roles from solidifying military alliances with Indigenous nations toward encouraging them to abandon their traditional ways of life and to adopt a more agricultural and sedentary lifestyle. In the colonies of Upper and Lower Canada, the Indian Department became the vehicle for the new British plan of "civilization."

After 1818, British administrators opted for a yearly payment, or annuity, in an effort to reduce the initial expense of treaty making. Annuities could be funded by revenue earned from the sale of the surrendered lands to settlers. Annuity monies were used by the Indian Department to build agricultural communities on which they intended to settle Indigenous peoples. The annuity money funded home construction and purchased agricultural implements and livestock. As the rate of treaty making increased, its consequences were increasingly being felt by the region's original inhabitants. By the 1820s, nearly all lands had been covered by one treaty or another, and Indigenous communities were becoming increasingly dispossessed. The growing number of settlers and the push for land cessions led to a rapid decrease in the ability of Indigenous peoples to hunt and fish, as they were limited to the remaining available lands and small reserves set aside by the Crown. In 1820, a Mississauga chief poetically summed up the impact of the treaties in a comment to a British visitor to his community, saying that the British "came as the wind blown across the Great Lake. The wind wafted you to our shores, we received you – we planted you – we

---

[11] Morin, "Concepts of Extinguishment," 26.
[12] Jean-Pierre Morin, "Peace, Order and Good Government: Indian Treaties and Canadian Nation Building," Canadian Studies Conference, "First Nations, First Thoughts," Edinburgh, Scotland, May 6, 2005, p. 8.

nursed you. We protected you till you became mighty trees that spread thro our Hunting Lands. With its branches you now lash us."[13]

There is considerable debate as to whether Indigenous leaders fully understood the British perspective and intent behind these agreements, or even if the concept of a land surrender was understood at all. It is possible that some leaders may have had a better understanding because of their own close contact with administrators, most notably Joseph Brant, leader of the Six Nations. Upon relocating to lands on the Grand River north of Lake Erie, he commented that communities needed to "retain some of their Lands, for unless they do, they certainly will be beggars."[14] Donald Smith suggests, in his study of the alienation of the Mississauga land, that the Anishinaabeg may not have fully understood that the cessions meant the full surrender of their lands and rights.[15] The process of treaty making was closely linked to the long-standing practice of gift giving, a yearly event that aimed to renew alliances – a practice that did not end till 1855. Consequently, these agreements continued the long-standing process of relationship building that had been established since the arrival of Europeans.

Despite these different understandings behind the agreements, more treaties were concluded between 1815 and 1836 covering most of the remaining lands of Upper Canada, from the productive agricultural lands south of Lake Huron to the resource-rich lands around Georgian Bay. Throughout the 1850s, several attempts were made by the Indian Department to secure the sale of the final tracks of land in the province, culminating with the Saugeen Treaty of 1854 and, in 1862, another treaty surrendering the majority of Manitoulin Island. By the time of the Confederation of the new Dominion of Canada in 1867, nearly the entire land mass of the province of Ontario was covered by a treaty.

ORAL AND WRITTEN ACCOUNTS OF RICE LAKE TREATY NO. 20

Prior to the outbreak of the War of 1812, the Indian Department, now under the direction of Sir John Johnson, son of William Johnson, the first superintendent of Indian Affairs, had managed to conclude land cession treaties along the entire waterfront of Upper Canada, from Glengarry County in

---

[13] Donald B. Smith, "The Dispossession of the Mississauga Indians: A Missing Chapter in the Early History of Upper Canada," *Ontario History* 73, no. 2 (1981): 82.
[14] Holmes and Associates, vol. I, p. 36.
[15] Smith, "Dispossession of the Mississauga Indians," 71.

the east to Windsor in the west. While the agreements concluded prior to 1812 were largely one-time payments in goods or money for the surrender of lands, the financial pinch after the war led to a new method of payment: the annuity. As Indigenous warriors had lost their strategic military value in the eyes of British administrators, London no longer wanted to bear the cost of managing Indian Affairs in the colony. Because Upper Canada now assumed the cost of any land purchase, Lieutenant-Governor Peregrine Maitland suggested a new approach. Instead of a large single payment at the time of signing, which was seen as a drain on the cash-strapped treasury of Upper Canada, smaller yearly payments would be made to the signatory communities derived from the sale of the lands covered by the treaty.[16] Armed with new instructions from the colonial leadership to open more land for the expected waves of European immigrants to Upper Canada, William Claus, deputy superintendent general of the Indian Department, concluded three treaties in the fall of 1818, including one at Smith's Creek with the Chippewa (Anishinaabeg), who used and inhabited the lands around Rice Lake. On November 5, 1818, Claus convened a council at what is now Port Hope on Lake Ontario, with the Anishinaabeg leaders "inhabiting the back parts of the New Castle District." A provisional agreement, which became the official treaty, was finalized that same day. The concluded agreement exchanged some 1.9 million acres of land, covering the majority of the Kawartha Lakes, for an annuity of £740 "to be well & truly paid, yearly, and every year."[17]

In addition to the text of that agreement, the archival records of the Indian Department have two other documents recounting the meeting between William Claus and the assembled Anishinaabeg leaders. The first is a letter from Claus to the military secretary to the governor general, Major Bowles, written five days after the treaty signing.[18] The second document, transcribed by Indian agent Alexander McDonnell, records the exchange between Claus and Anishinaabeg chief Buckquaquet during the treaty conference.[19] These documents allow readers to examine not only how the Indian agents understood their Indigenous counterparts but also how the Indian Department reported on its activities.

---

[16] Lillian F. Gates, *Land Policies of Upper Canada* (Toronto: University of Toronto Press, 1968), 158.

[17] Provisional Agreement No. 20, November 5, 1818, Canada, *Indian Treaties and Surrenders*, vol. I (Saskatoon: Fifth House Publishers, 1992), pp. 48–9.

[18] William Claus, Deputy Superintendent General of Indian Affairs, to Major Bowles, Military Secretary, November 10, 1818, LAC, RG10, vol. 489, pp. 29439–41, C-13339.

[19] Minutes of Council Meeting, November 5, 1818, LAC, RG10, vol. 790, pp. 7029–32, C-13499.

In his letter to Major Bowles, Claus reported on the events of the treaty conference as part of a summary of the three agreements concluded in October and November 1818.[20] First stating that the impetus for the treaties was requested by the governor at Quebec and the lieutenant-governor at York, he then provided a short two-paragraph account of the meeting, indicating that "the Chippawa of the Rice Lake ... also agree to surrender to His Majesty, a Tract of Land" totalling some 1.9 million acres for a yearly annuity of £740. Claus also stated that the chiefs asked that the "Islands as may be found in any of the said Waters" would be "reserved to themselves" and that he recommended this addition. As was fairly typical of other reports by Claus and the Indian Department to colonial officials, there are no details of the nature of the discussions or of any possible concerns on the part of Indigenous signatories. It should be noted that the Indian Department's records do not contain any confirmation that islands were set aside as reserves, although a surrender was concluded in the 1850s for those same islands.

If the only record to have survived relating to this treaty had been Claus's letter, there would be little on which to build. Fortunately, the historical record is somewhat more complete than Claus's letter. Alexander McDonnell, an assistant Indian agent, recorded some of the exchanges between Claus and the Indigenous leaders present. McDonnell's account, known as the "Minutes of a Council held at Smiths Creek" in the records of the Indian Department, records the stylized language of the treaty meeting and the way in which Indian agents had adapted their approach to secure deals. Referring to the assembled leaders as "Children" of the Great Father, the king, Claus commenced the discussions by first mentioning how he had convened them to request the surrender of the "back parts of this Country which you seem to think were never disposed of to the King."[21] Specifically, these lands were those to the north of the boundary of a previous treaty concluded in 1787/88 – the so-called "Gunshot Treaty." Citing that the king's "Children" – specifically new settlers to the province – had "no home, & out of pity for them, he wishes to acquire Land to give to them" and that he would pay the Anishinaabeg signatories "as long as any of you remain on the Earth ... every year, besides the presents he now gives you."[22]

---

[20] Claus to Bowles, November 10, 1818.
[21] Minutes of Council Meeting, November 5, 1818.
[22] Ibid.

After a brief meeting of the representatives, Buckquaquet, whom McDonnell indicates was the "principal chief," replied by drawing attention to the destitute nature of his own people:

> Father.
> If I was to refuse what our Father has requested, our Women & Children would be more to be pitied. From our Lands we receive scarcely anything, & if your words are true we will get more by parting with them, than by keeping them – our hunting is destroyed, & we must throw ourselves on the compassion of our Great Father the King.[23]

While agreeing to the requested land surrender, because his "young People & Chief have always thought of not refusing our Father any request he makes to us, & therefore do what he wishes," Buckquaquet added two requests before agreeing: that his people "not be prevented from the right of Fishing, the use of the Waters, and Hunting in where we can find game"; and that the islands "be left for them that when we try to scratch the Earth, as our Brethren the Farmers do." Claus's reply, which also closes off the account of the meeting, agreed with the suggestion of setting the islands as reserves but noted that he would "inform him [the Great Father] of, & have no doubt but that he will accede to your wish." In regard to the issue of hunting and fishing, Claus's answer was somewhat less direct, as he stated that "the Rivers are open to all & you have an equal right to fish & hunt on them," implying that settlers and other newcomers would have the same rights as the treaty signers.[24]

Claus's reply to the question of the island reserves and rights to hunt and fish is interesting because there is no mention of it in the treaty document itself. While it does appear to be a direct promise maintaining these rights, the reference to the "Rivers" also seems to link back to the islands being set aside as reserves. As Peter Schmalz mentions in his study *The Ojibwa of Southern Ontario*, the language used by Claus during the treaty negotiations appears to allow a limited continuance of rights to hunt and fish instead of a complete cession of those rights.[25] On other occasions, Indian Department officials had made direct links between hunting and fishing and reserve land, as was done in the 1796 Chenail Écarté treaty.

---

[23] Ibid.
[24] Ibid.
[25] Peter S. Schmalz, *The Ojibwa of Southern Ontario* (Toronto: University of Toronto Press, 1991), 124.

In other words, hunting and fishing were seen as part of the regular land usage of reserve lands. Despite this inclusion in the treaty discussions noted in McDonnell's account, the Indian Department, and consequently the colonial and later Canadian governments, based their understanding on the limited wording of the treaty document. Since the treaty document did not have any clauses recognizing the island reserves or any specific rights to hunt or fish, the Crown understood the agreement as a straight cession of all Indigenous rights and resources.

Where the government's understanding of the treaty focused on the land cession and viewed any hunting and fishing rights of the signatories as an "equal" right shared by all, the long oral history of the Anishinaabeg of the Kawartha Lakes region, such as Curve Lake and Hiawatha First Nations, sees the treaty in a different light. In the two centuries since the conclusion of the agreement, the Anishinaabeg have shared their understanding, on several occasions, that while the treaty opened the land so that "the Great Father's children" could settle the area, the treaty protected their ongoing right to hunt and fish on the waterways and lakes of the Kawarthas.

One of the earliest Anishinaabeg accounts of the treaty of 1818 was made by Chief George Paudash, one of the treaty signers, and found in the papers of A.E. Williams from the law firm Hunter and Hunter.[26] In a transcript of an account believed to have been made in the mid-1840s,[27] in both Anishinaabeg and English, Chief Paudash described how the Indian Department had come to his people on three separate occasions to negotiate land purchases.[28] The account of the treaties provides a unique glimpse into how the Anishinaabeg saw the treaty-making process. In many ways, this account corroborates the exchanges recorded by Alexander McDonnell. After having described how the British had convened his people in 1787 to purchase lands along the shore of Lake Ontario and again in 1811 for lands along the Moira River near Belleville, Chief Paudash recounted that a third treaty meeting was called at the mouth of Pemetashotiang Creek, described as Smith's Creek in Claus's account – now Port Hope, Ontario. According

---

[26] Account by Chief George Paudash, date unknown, A.E. Williams/United Indian Bands of the Chippewas and the Mississaugas Collection, Provincial Archives of Ontario, F 4337-11-0-8.
[27] J. Michael Thoms, "Ojibwa Fishing Grounds: A History of Ontario Fisheries Law, Science, and the Sportsmen Challenge to Aboriginal Treaty Rights, 1650–1900" (PhD dissertation, University of British Columbia, 2004), 103, n46.
[28] David T. McNab, "The Promise That He Made to My Grand Father Was Very Sweet: The Gun Shot Treaty of 1792 at the Bay of Quinte," *Canadian Journal of Native Studies* 16, no. 2 (1996): 293.

to Paudash, Claus stated that "once more your great father has come to ask you to surrender your land to him, to which the assembled Anishinaabeg all agreed to grant his request, and we said Hurrah. Let us surrender our land to our great father."[29] Paudash's account further places this discussion in the context of the previous treaties where the Anishinaabeg sought to protect some of their interests, saying that they made "the same agreement with him – to Reserve a part of the main land the Points and mouths of Rivers and Islands." Where the Indian Department's account placed caveats around hunting and fishing rights, the Paudash oral history presents a broader understanding of these rights, reporting that Claus promised "that these Islands, Points, Mouths of Rivers, and part of the main land ... shall be reserved for your hunting and fishing purposes."[30] As one of the signers of the treaty and recounting the events of the treaty negotiations, Chief Paudash both confirmed the land cession from the Anishinaabeg to the Crown as in the Indian Department record and reaffirmed the understanding that hunting and fishing rights extend beyond the limited territory of the reserve islands.

As well as repeating many of the elements included in the McDonnell account of the treaty conference, Chief Paudash's account is part of the broader understanding of the treaty. In 1847, the leaders of the Mud Lake (Curve Lake), Rice Lake, and Scugog Lake communities responded to a letter from Indian Department superintendent Thomas G. Anderson confirming that they had not included any islands as part of the surrender of 1818.[31] The efforts of the communities to set aside the island reserves and protect hunting and fishing rights in accordance with the treaty promises have been extensive. In his dissertation examining the impact of fisheries legislation on the Anishinaabeg in Ontario, J. Michael Thoms cites different ways in which the Anishinaabeg put their understanding of treaty terms to the settler state through petitions, letters, and testimony. For example, the Anishinaabeg complained to the lieutenant-governor of Upper Canada in 1829 that the colony's laws were not protecting their fishing grounds from encroachment,[32] and in the 1850s the leaders of the Curve Lake, Hiawatha, and Scugog communities complained in a letter to

---

[29] Account by Chief George Paudash.
[30] Ibid.
[31] Mississaugas of Mud Lake to Thomas G. Anderson, June 5, 1847, LAC, RG10, vol. 165, no. 96185–7; Mississaugas of Rice Lake, June 21, 1847, LAC, RG10, vol. 165, no. 96182–3; and Jacob Crane and William Johnson, Mississaugas of Scugog Lake, to Anderson, June 24, 1847, LAC, RG10, vol. 165, no. 96174, 96175, reel C-11502.
[32] Thoms, *Ojibwa Fishing Grounds*, 178.

the Legislative Assembly of the Province of Canada that while the treaty of 1818 surrendered the land, it reserved the islands for them, and settlers were encroaching upon them.[33]

The continuity and consistency of the Anishinaabeg understanding of the Rice Lake Treaty of 1818 can also be seen in the testimony provided during the 1923 Williams Treaty Commission.[34] Established by the provincial and federal governments to examine outstanding Indigenous land claims in central Ontario, the Williams Commission heard from 17 Elders and community leaders of the Rice Lake Treaty signatories. On several occasions, the Rice Lake Treaty communities reaffirmed that the treaty surrendered land to the Crown but reserved the islands and the right to hunt and fish. One example was provided by Robert Paudash of Hiawatha, the grandson of Chief George Paudash: "they [the Indian Department] make treaty that we should hunt on the creeks, but the land is not ours. The white man has the dry land, but we have the wet land."[35] Other witnesses, such as Johnson Paudash, described the treaty boundaries in great detail, showing which lands were included in or excluded from the 1818 treaty.[36] The Anishinaabeg communities of the Rice Lake Treaty continue to refer to the traditional knowledge of the treaty to this day in both claims of treaty infringement and during consultation processes with government and developers. For example, Curve Lake First Nation provided a written submission to the Ontario Municipal Board in 2016 in relation to a proposed development outlining the proposal's potential impacts on their treaty rights.[37]

RICE LAKE TREATY NO. 20 AND THE COURTS

In June 1977, Wayne Taylor and Douglas Williams were arrested on Crowe Lake near Peterborough, Ontario, for having hunted and taken 65 bullfrogs from the waters of the lake. They were arrested for having violated the *Game and Fisheries Act* of Ontario that imposed a closed hunting season

---

[33] Ibid., 143.
[34] See Chapter 8.
[35] Testimony of Robert Paudash, September 26, 1923, *Bound Volume of Testimony Given to a Commission, Chaired by A.S. Williams, Investigating Claims, by the Chippewas & Mississaugas of the Province of Ontario, to Compensation for Lands Not Surrendered by the Robinson Treaty of 1850*, p. 229, 1923, LAC, RG10, vol. 2332, file 67,071–4C, reel C-11203.
[36] Testimony of Johnson Paudash, September 26, 1923, *Bound Volume of Testimony Given to a Commission*, pp. 234–9.
[37] Written Submission to the Ontario Municipal Board, Curve Lake First Nation, OMB Case no. PL150313, October 18, 2016.

on bullfrogs between October 1976 and July 1977. After their conviction in the lower court, Taylor and Williams appealed to the Divisional Court of Ontario, where they argued successfully that they had a right to hunt on the water of Crowe Lake, as promised by the 1818 Rice Lake Treaty, and that under section 88 of the *Indian Act*, the provincial legislation did not apply to them.

Upon the subsequent appeal by the province, the Provincial Court of Appeal agreed to hear the case.[38] Throughout the proceedings, the Court re-examined the archival and recorded evidence, including the treaty text itself, the "Minutes of a Council held at Smiths Creek" drafted by Alexander McDonnell, and William Claus's letter to Major Bowles reporting on the treaty conference of November 5, 1818. In a ruling written by Associate Chief Justice Bert MacKinnon, the Court of Appeal upheld the divisional court decision. In a period prior to the enshrinement of Aboriginal and treaty rights in the Constitution, the *Taylor and Williams* decision redefined how treaties should be understood. In his analysis, Justice MacKinnon held that "Cases on Indian or aboriginal rights can never be determined in a vacuum. It is of importance to consider the history and oral traditions of the tribes concerned, and the surrounding circumstances at the time of the treaty, relied on by both parties, in determining the treaty's effect."[39] Building on previous rulings such as *White and Bob* of 1969, Justice MacKinnon reinforced that the interpretation of a treaty cannot be limited to the treaty document, but its context must also be considered. By emphasizing the importance of the community's oral history, in this case that bullfrogs had been hunted for food "since earliest memory," oral traditions formed a core element in understanding the context around the treaty text.

While the province's argument was built on the absence of any reference to hunting or fishing in the treaty text, Justice MacKinnon set aside this position by stating that the Minutes of the Council recorded by McDonnell also formed part of the treaty because they represent the transcription of the "oral terms" of the agreement to "preserve the historic right of these Indians to hunt and fish on Crown lands in the lands conveyed."[40] As constitutional legal scholar Thomas Isaac notes in *Aboriginal Law: Commentary and Analysis*, the Court ruled that the "oral portions of

---

[38] *R. v. Taylor and Williams*, [1981] 62 C.C.C. (2d) 227, p. 1.
[39] Ibid., 60.
[40] Ibid., 12.

the treaty were deemed to be as much part of the treaty as the written portions" of the historic record.[41]

Before the Divisional Court, the province of Ontario contended that all rights, whether they be specified or not in the treaty text, were ceded through the words "do freely, fully and voluntarily surrender and convey the same to His Majesty without reservation or limitation in perpetuity." The Divisional Court rejected this position, arguing that "whether or not aboriginal rights were reserved in the treaty, it is also my opinion that even in a situation where there is no treaty, or if a treaty remains silent with respect to aboriginal rights, such as native hunting and fishing, these rights that have existed from the beginning of time continue."[42] At the Court of Appeal, Justice MacKinnon reaffirmed the lower Court's ruling, stating that the issue of hunting and fishing rights had been discussed by the parties:

> Once it is accepted that the Minutes of the Council meeting between the representative of the Crown on the one hand and the Indian Chiefs on the other is part of the treaty, it cannot be successfully argued that Treaty No. 20 is "silent" on the question of the right to hunt and fish.[43]

As a result, the Court of Appeal upheld the earlier ruling, commenting that after 160 years of largely uninterrupted exercise of the right to hunt and fish from the water, it was "too late to deprive these Indians of their historic aboriginal rights."

The *Taylor and Williams* ruling is more than just a decision on whether the Rice Lake Treaty of 1818 recognizes a right of the Anishinaabeg to hunt bullfrogs. It fundamentally changes how the courts, and to a certain degree historians, look at the context surrounding an agreement between Indigenous signatories and the Crown. Readers of treaties must consider how the treaties would have been understood by the parties at the time of signing.[44] The written text of treaties, no matter their reputation or standing, must be placed in a broader contextual frame that is supported by other sources, most especially oral histories and traditions.

---

[41] Thomas Isaac, *Aboriginal Law: Commentary and Analysis*, 4th ed. (Saskatoon: Purich, 2012), 110.
[42] *R. v. Taylor and Williams*, [1980] 1 C.N.L.R. 83 (Ont. Div. Court), p. 90.
[43] *R. v. Taylor and Williams*, [1981] 62 C.C.C. (2d) 227, p. 12.
[44] Thomas Isaac, *Aboriginal Law: Commentary, Cases and Materials*, 3rd ed. (Saskatoon: Purich, 2004), 79.

FURTHER READINGS

Robert Allen. *His Majesty's Indian Allies: British Indian Policy in the Defence of Canada, 1774–1815.* Toronto: Dundurn Press, 1993.

John Borrows. "Wampum at Niagara: The Royal Proclamation, Canadian Legal History, and Self-Government." In *Aboriginal and Treaty Rights in Canada: Essays on Law, Equality, and Respect for Difference*, ed. Michael Asch, 155–72. Vancouver: University of British Columbia Press, 1997.

David McNab. "'The Promise That He Gave to My Grand Father Was Very Sweet': The Gun Shot Treaty of 1792 at the Bay of Quinte." *Canadian Journal of Native Studies* 16, no. 2 (1996): 293–314.

Donald B. Smith. "The Dispossession of the Mississauga Indians: A Missing Chapter in the Early History of Upper Canada." *Ontario History* 73, no 2 (1981): 67–87.

R.J. Surtees. *Indian Land Surrenders in Ontario 1763–1867.* Ottawa: Treaties and Historical Research Centre, Indian and Northern Affairs Canada, 1984.

QUESTIONS FOR DISCUSSION

1. Read the follow excerpts from the three different sources and identify how they present the promises made by William Claus in the treaty negotiations:

   William Claus, Deputy Superintendent General of Indian Affairs, to Major Bowles, Military Secretary, November 10, 1818, LAC, RG10, vol. 489, pp. 29439–41, C-13339
   The third meeting with the Chippawa of the Rice Lake, was held at Smiths Creek, near the said Lake, when they also agree to surrender to His Majesty, a Tract of Land, bordering on the before mentioned Lake, & waters belonging to them & supposed to contain 1,961,200 Acres, for the yearly consideration, in perpetuity of £740 Provincial Currency, reserving to themselves such Islands as may be found in any of the said Waters.

   Minutes of Council Meeting, November 5, 1818, LAC, RG10, vol. 790, pp. 7029–32
   You must perceive the number of your Great Fathers children about here have no home, & out of pity for them, he wishes to acquire Land to give to them – He is charitable to all, does not like to see his Children in distress. Your Land is not all that he has been purchasing, he has looked to the setting of the Sun, as well as to the rising, for places to put his Children, & when he asked your Country from you, he does not mean to do as formerly, to pay you

at once, but as long as any of you remain on the Earth to give you Cloathing [sic] in payment every year, besides the presents he now gives you. You will go to your Camp & consult together & when you have made up your minds come & let me hear what it is.

Account by Chief George Paudash, date unknown, A.E. Williams/ United Indian Bands of the Chippewas and the Mississaugas Collection, Provincial Archives of Ontario, F 4337-11-0-8
This ... was the third time the governor came to us for land. same place. Port Hope ... The meeting was called by Chief ["Ahpishto" stroked out] Ah-pish-ki-yoshk. And Na-si-ge-kahbowh. was the name of the Interpreter that time. And this is what the Governer ... said. My Dear Children. once more your great father has come to ask you to surrender your land to him. We all agreed to grant his request, and we said Hurrah. let us surrender our land to our great father. And again I remembered the promise the Govnmt ... made with ... my Grand father ... which was very sweet. And we again decided to make the same agreement with him – to Reserve a part of the main land the Points and mouths of Rivers and Islands. And this is what the Governor said. Your great father is very glad. And ... I thank you very much. And I promise ... that these Islands. Points. Mouths of Rivers. and part of the main land ... shall be reserved for your hunting and fishing purposes, and that the supplies of Clothing. blankets &&tc. from the Govrnt shall never stop. and that this promise shall be good. as long as the Sun lasts. and Rivers flow and as long as the grass grows.

2. In your opinion, how do the different accounts influence our understanding of the agreements concluded in 1818?
3. How do the courts reconcile the competing perspectives of these treaties?

DOCUMENTS

Treaty Text: Rice Lake Treaty, no. 20, November 5, 1818, LAC, RG10, vol. 1842, IT160, IA 20, T-9938

ARTICLES OF PROVISIONAL AGREEMENT entered into on Thursday, the fifth day of November, 1818, between the Honorable William Claus, Deputy Superintendent General of Indian Affairs on behalf of His Majesty, of the one part, and Buckquaquet, Chief of the Eagle Tribe; Pishikinse,

Chief of the Rein Deer Tribe; Pahtosh, Chief of the Crane Tribe; Cahgogewin of the Snake Tribe; Cahgahkishinse, Chief of the Pike Tribe; and Pininse, of the White Oak Tribe, Principal Men of the Chippewa Nation of Indians inhabiting the back parts of the New Castle District, of the other part, Witnessth: that for and in consideration of the yearly sum of the seven hundred and forty pounds Province currency in goods at the Montreal price to be well and truly paid yearly, and every year, by His said Majesty to the said Chippewa Nation inhabiting and claiming the said tract which may be otherwise known as follows: A tract of land situate between the western boundary line of the Home District, and extending northerly to a bay at the northern entrance of Lake Simcoe, in the Home District, commencing in the western division line of the Midland District at the north-west angle of the Township of Rawdon; then north sixteen degrees west thirty-three miles, or until it strikes the line forty-five; then along said line to a bay at the northern entrance of Lake Simcoe; then southerly along the water's edge to the entrance of Talbot River; then up Talbot River to the eastern boundary line of the Home District; then along said boundary line south sixteen degrees east to the townships of Darlington, Clark, Hope and Hamilton to the Rice Lake; then along the southern shore of the said lake and of the River Trent to the western division line of the Midland District; then north sixteen degrees west to the place of beginning, containing about one million nine hundred and fifty-one thousand acres. And the Buckquaquet, Pishikinse, Pahtosh, Cahgahkishinse, Cahgagewin and Pininse, as well for themselves as for the Chippewa Nation inhabiting and claiming the said tract of land as above described, do freely, fully and voluntarily surrender and convey the same to His Majesty without reservation or limitation in perpetuity. And the said William Claus, in behalf of His Majesty, does hereby promise and agree to pay to the said Nation of Indians inhabiting as above mentioned, yearly, and every year, forever, the said sum of seven hundred and forty pounds currency in goods at the Montreal price, which sum the said Chiefs and Principal People, parties hereunto, acknowledge as a full consideration for the lands hereby sold and conveyed to His Majesty.

IN WITNESS WHEROF, the parties have hereunto set their hands and seals on the day first above mentioned in the Township of Hope, Smith's Creek.

Signed, sealed and delivered in the presence of }
J. GIVINS, S.I.A.
WM. HANDS, Sen., Clerk Ind. Dept.,
WM. GRUET, Interpreter, Ind. Dept.
W. CLAUS, Depy. Supt. Gen. I. A., on behalf of the Crown, [L.S.]

BUCKQUAQUET, (totem) [L.S.]
PISHIKINSE, (totem) [L.S.]
PAHTOSH, (totem) [L.S.]
CAHGAHKISHINSE, (totem) [L.S.]
CAHAGAGEWIN, (totem) [L.S.]
PAHTOSH, (totem) [L.S.]

William Claus, Deputy Superintendent General of Indian Affairs, to Major Bowles, Military Secretary, November 10, 1818, LAC, RG10, vol. 489, pp. 29439–41, C-13339

York, 10th November 1818

Sir,

I have the honor of stating for the information of his Grace, the Commander of the Forces, that in obeisance to His Grace's direction of the 16th of last September, & to the subsequent communication from His Excellency the Lieut. Governor Sir Peregrine Maitland, I met with the Messessague & Chippawa Nations at the respective places to which they have been summoned to assemble … near the Rice Lake, for the purpose of purchasing from them, on behalf of His Majesty, certain tracts of their Country …

…

The third meeting with the Chippawa of the Rice Lake, was held at Smiths Creek, near the said Lake, when they also agree to surrender to His Majesty, a Tract of Land, bordering on the before mentioned Lake, & waters belonging to them & supposed to contain 1,961,200 Acres, for the yearly consideration, in perpetuity of £740 Provincial Currency, reserving to themselves such Islands as may be found in any of the said Waters.

I have, on behalf of His Majesty, entered into a Provisional Agreement, with the Chiefs and Principal men, inhabiting, and claiming the respective Tracts, for the [illeg] payment of the several annuities, or they, on their part, & in behalf of their several Nations & Tribes, have [?] For the surrender of the lands alluded to, with the Islands as above specified & copies of these agreements have been forwarded to His Excellency, Sir Peregrine Maitland.

Not conceiving myself at liberty to accede to the request made, respecting a medical person, I merely replied "that I would communicate their wish … to their Great Father." – Doing so, I beg leave, in the event of His Grace according to their request, to mention the name of Barton Lee, who formerly was [employed?] in the Indian Department at this port, & who is otherwise qualified to fill the appointment, by his speaking their language – I further bet to mention for His Grace's information that Barton Lee has served His Majesty nearly 30 years.

>I have the honor, to be, Sir, your most obedient and most humble servant

>William Claus, Dty Sup Gen, Ind. Aff.

Minutes of Council Meeting, November 5, 1818, LAC, RG10, vol. 790, pp. 7029–32

Minutes of a Council held at Smiths Creek, in the Township of Hope on Thursday the 5th of November 1818, with the Chippewa Nation of Indians, inhabiting & claiming a Tract of Land situate between the Western Boundary Line of the Midland District & the Eastern Boundary Line of the home District, & extending Northerly to a Bay at the Northern Entrance of Lake Simcoe in the Home District

Present
The Honbl W. Claus Dep. Supt. General of Indian Affairs
I. Givins Esq. Supt. of Indian Affairs for the Port of York
W. Hands, Clerk Indn. Dept.
W. Gruet, Interpreter

After the usual ceremonies the Dep. Supt. General addressed the Chiefs as follows:

Children.

I salute you in behalf of your Great Father & condole with you for the loss you have met with since I last met you – it is the will of the Great Spirit to remove our nearest & dearest connexions, we must submit to his will & not repine.

I should have seen you before this, but I have had business with others of your Nation which has kept me until this day. My errand is, to put at rest the doubts with respect to the Lands in the back parts of this Country which you seem to think were never disposed of to the King, & hope that hereafter none of your young men will be so idle as to remove the Posts or marks which will be put up by the Kings Surveyors. Your Great Father has directed me to lay before you a sketch of the Country in the back of this & you will point out to me the Land as far as the last purchase was, from the Waters edge from the Great Lake.

Children.

You must perceive the number of your Great Fathers children about here have no home, & out of pity for them, he wishes to acquire Land to give to them – He is charitable to all, does not like to see his Children in distress. Your Land is not all that he has been purchasing, he has looked to the setting of the Sun, as well as to the rising, for places to put his Children, & when he asked your Country from you, he does not mean to do as formerly, to pay you at once, but as long as any of you remain on the Earth to give you Cloathing [sic] in payment every year, besides the presents he now gives you. You will go to your Camp & consult together & when you have made up your minds come & let me hear what it is.

Buckquaquet, Principal Chief addressing the Dept. Supt. general, said:

Father.

We have heard your words, & will go to our Camp & consult & give you an answer to the request of our Great Father – But, Father, our Women & Children are very hungry, and desired me to ask you to let them taste a little of our Fathers Provisions & Milk –

After their return, Buckquaquet continued

Father.

You see me here, I am to be pitied, I have no old men to instruct me. I am the Head Chief, but a young man. You must pity me, all the old people have gone to the other world. My hands are naked, I cannot speak as our Ancestors were used to.

Father.

If I was to refuse what our Father has requested, our Women & Children would be more to be pitied. From our Lands we receive scarcely anything, & if your words are true we will get more by parting with them, than by keeping them – our hunting is destroyed, & we must throw ourselves on the compassion of our Great Father the King.

Father.

Our young People & Chief have always thought of not refusing our Father any request he makes to us, & therefore do what he wishes.

Father.

If it was not for our Brethren the Farmers about the Country we should near starve for our hunting is destroyed.

Father.

We hope that we shall not be prevented from the right of Fishing, the use of the Waters, and Hunting in where we can find game. We hope that the Whites who are to come among us will not treat us ill, some of our young men are giddy, but we hope they will not hurt them.

Father.

The young men, I hope you will not think it hard at their requesting, that the Islands may be left for them that when we try to scratch the Earth, as our Brethren the Farmers do, & put any thing in that it may come up to help our Women & Children

Father.

We do not say that we must have the Islands, but we hope our Father will think of us & allow us this small request – this is all we have to say –

To which the Dept. Supt. general replied

Children

I have heard your answer, & in the name of your Great Father thank you for the readiness with which you have complied with his desire. Your words shall be communicated to him. The request for the Islands, I shall also inform him of, & have no doubt but that he will accede to your wish. The Rivers are open to all & you have an equal right to fish & hunt on them. I am pleased to learn from you, that your Brothers the Whites have been so kind to you & hope those that will come among you will be as charitable. Keep from Liquor, & your young men will not be giddy. It is the ruin of your Nation. As soon as I get your Numbers you shall get something to eat, & some Liquor. Do not expect much, for I have so great a dread of it that I am at all times disinclined to give you any. We will now sign the Paper, it is merely to shew your Great Father our work, & when he agrees to our proceeding, you will then have to sign another Paper which Conveys the Country we now talk about to him, & the first payment will be made, an equal quantity of which you will receive every year.

Account by Chief George Paudash, date unknown, A.E. Williams/United Indian Bands of the Chippewas and the Mississaugas Collection, Provincial Archives of Ontario, F 4337-11-0-8

… another time. This ["is" stroked out] was the third time the governor came to us for land. same place. Port Hope. ["Kah dab" stroked out] The meeting was called by Chief ["Ahpishto" stroked out] Ah-pish-ki-yoshk. And Na-si-ge-kahbowh. was the name of the Interpreter that time. And this is what the Governer [Governor] said. My Dear Children. once more your great father has come to ask you to surrender your land to him. We all agreed to grant his request, and we said Hurrah. let us surrender our land to our great father. And again I remembered the promise the Govnmt. [Government] made with ["our" stroked out] my Grand father ["long ago" stroked out]. which was very sweet. And we again decided to make the same agreement with him – to Reserve a part of the main land the Points and mouths of Rivers and Islands. And this is what the Governor said.

Your great father is very glad. And ["he" stroked out] I thank you very much. And I promise to ["Reserve" stroked out] that these Islands. Points. Mouths of Rivers. and part of the main land. ["and that" stroked out] shall be reserved for your hunting and fishing purposes, and that the supplies of Clothing. blankets &&tc. from the Govrnt [Government]. shall never stop. and that this promise shall be good. as long as the Sun lasts. and Rivers flow and as long as the grass grows. And that was the last time that the Govrnt [Government]. asked for land. that was in the winter of 1818.

... At that time he did not give me any writing to keep in my hands but I know all. and now you ask me what I am always talking about: These are the things I ment [meant] viz. Islands. and all points, and mouths of Rivers and part of the main land. that are Reserved for our hunting and fishing purposes.

... Last Treaty at Port Hope. this is the last time we met at Port Hope. and I was the one that made that bargain that [that is] why you often here [hear] me say that I own all the Islands. – And they were pretty well satisfied with the bargain. Colonel [William] Claus and Coil [Colonel] Gibbins [Givins] and this is what they said. Your Great father will be very well satisfied with the bargain. And they mentioned the promise viz. the Rivers. ["Points." stroked out] grass, and the Sun. as long as you see these, you shall enjoy that blessing.

Excerpt from *R. v. Taylor and Williams*, 1981, CARSWELLONT 641, 62 C.C.C. (2d) 227 (Ont. C.A.). Reproduced by permission of Thomson Reuters Canada Limited.

Cases on Indian or aboriginal rights can never be determined in a vacuum. It is of importance to consider the history and oral traditions of the tribes concerned, and the surrounding circumstances at the time of the treaty, relied on by both parties, in determining the treaty's effect. (p. 6)

... the tribes who were parties to the treaty had hunted and fished in the area covered by the treaty, and had taken bullfrogs for food there since earliest memory. It is part of the oral tradition of the tribes that this right was not only recognized at the time of the treaty, but that they continued to exercise the right without interruption up until the present. The respondents' evidence as to the oral traditions of the Indian tribes concerned was accepted by the trial judge and was not disputed by the Crown. (p. 7)

In my view, all the principles recited lead to the conclusion that the terms of the treaty, which include the oral terms recorded in the Minutes, preserve the historic right of these Indians to hunt and fish on Crown lands in the lands conveyed and fall under the exception established by the opening words of s.88 of the Indian Act.

The Crown's position was simply that "the terms of the treaty" did not preserve or grant the right to fish and hunt on Crown lands inconsistent with the application of provincial laws. The surrender of the Indian lands to the Crown, counsel submitted, included a surrender of their aboriginal hunting and fishing rights. Once it is accepted that the Minutes of the Council meeting between the representative of the Crown on the one hand and the Indian Chiefs on the other is part of the treaty, it cannot be successfully argued that Treaty No. 20 is "silent" on the question of the right to hunt and fish. (p. 12)

The transcript of the Minutes cannot and should not be analyzed in minute detail. The use of certain words and their conciliatory tone only serve to emphasize the disparity in the positions of the two parties to the treaty, but do not lessen the force of the request nor the right to be attached to the assurance – quite the contrary.

The Indians' request for the continued right to hunt and fish was put on a higher plane than their request for the Islands ... No such qualification or limitation was put on their request that their traditional and historic right to hunt and fish for food continue. The representative of the Crown was clearly not intending to put any limitation on the rights of the Indians by saying that the rivers were open to "all" and that the Indians had an "equal" right to fish and hunt. These words immediately follow his dealing with the Indians' request for the Islands to which he replied that no doubt "[your Great Father] will accede to your wish." It seems to me that rather than putting a limitation on the Indians' ancient right, William Claus, whose integrity was respected by the Indians, was emphasizing that that right would continue. The accepted evidence was that this understanding of the treaty has been accepted and acted on for some 160 years without interruption. In my view, it is too late now to deprive these Indians of their historic aboriginal rights. (p. 13)

CAST OF CHARACTERS: RICE LAKE TREATY NO. 20, 1818

George Cheneebeesh Paudash: b. c. 1765; d. c. 1869

A member of the Crane (Passinassi) clan of the Anishinaabeg, commonly known as the Mississauga in historical records, George Cheneebeesh Paudash was a prominent leader in the Kawartha Lakes region. Although few details remain describing his early life, he was a recognized chief by the late 1780s and his name appears on several treaty documents, including the 1792 "Gunshot Treaty" and the 1818 Rice Lake Treaty. As one of the last hereditary chiefs in the Kawartha region, Chief Paudash often represented and advocated for his people to government officials. Between 1825 and 1842, he kept records of the various Mississauga and Chippewa (Anishinaabeg) council meetings that provide insights into Anishinaabeg political organization and strategies to protect lands and Indigenous rights.

William Claus: b. September 8, 1765; d. November 11, 1826

William Claus was born in Williamsburg, New York, in one of the most influential families of the colony. His father, Daniel Claus, was a son-in-law to William Johnson and a senior official in the Indian Department. Due to their loyalist positions during the American War of Independence, the Claus family relocated to the province of Quebec. Joining the fight in 1777 as a volunteer in the King's Royal Regiment under the command of his uncle Sir John Johnson, Claus participated in several raids alongside Mohawk leader Joseph Brant. Remaining in the army after the war and rising to the rank of captain by 1795, he joined the Indian Department in 1796 as deputy superintendent of the Six Nations at Niagara. Remaining in the department for the rest of his career, Claus worked closely with Indigenous communities seeking to avoid conflicts with the growing number of settlers. By 1800, he became deputy superintendent for Upper Canada, the second highest position in the Indian Department at the time. In the years prior to the War of 1812, Claus worked to maintain the often tense relationship between the Six Nations and the British administration of Upper Canada, as well as to negotiate some of the land cession treaties along the north shore of Lake Ontario and along the Thames River. With the shift toward opening the colony to increased settlement, Claus led the activities of the Indian Department in Upper Canada through a new series of land cessions around Rice Lake, the Rideau River, and Carleton County. He also redirected the first efforts of the Indian Department to bring British agrarian settlement to Indigenous communities. Along with his duties with the Indian Department, Claus was also appointed to the executive council and the legislative council of the province of Upper Canada until his death in 1826.

Figure 3.1 Treaty no. 20, "Lake Rice Purchase," 1818. Throughout the southern Great Lakes region, Indian Department officials argued that the documents signed during the treaty meetings encapsulated all possible terms of the agreement, despite the contrary statements of Indigenous signatories.

Source: Library and Archives Canada, e011198146.

Chapter 4
The Making of the Robinson-Huron Treaty, 1850

Prior to the 1850s and driven by the need to claim more land for agricultural settlement, the majority of treaty making in what is now Ontario focused exclusively on the lands of the southern Great Lakes and the St. Lawrence River, since the primary driver was opening up new land for agricultural settlement. Since the end of the War of 1812, the agents of the Indian Department had focused their treaty-making efforts in the more southern regions of the colony, eventually securing the near totality of the lower Great Lakes and St. Lawrence Valley in Upper Canada.[1] As the non-Indigenous population grew through increased European immigration, new interests and industries began to develop, requiring new resources. After the *Act of Union* merged Upper and Lower Canada into the new Province of Canada in 1841, the new government sought to expand its development by tapping into the colony's resource wealth.[2] Although unilaterally determined to be part of Upper Canada since 1791, the lands of the upper Great Lakes, poorly known to non-Indigenous settlers, began drawing the attention of those seeking those resources.

Long part of the fur trade routes, the watershed of lakes Huron and Superior had witnessed over two centuries of interaction and relationship building between the Anishinabek and European traders. The area had been part of the network that linked the western end of Lake Superior to Montreal, first for the French, then for the English traders of the Northwest Company. After 1821, the Hudson's Bay Company assumed full control over the fur trade, centring its operations around Sault Ste. Marie at the

---

[1] See Chapter 3.
[2] Douglas Leighton, "The Historical Significance of the Robinson Treaties of 1850," paper presented to the Annual Meeting of the Canadian Historical Association, Ottawa, 1982, p. 6.

narrows between the lakes and interior posts.[3] The region's Indigenous peoples were active participants in the fur trade. Relatively undisturbed by the fur traders, they continued to occupy and use their lands as they had done for centuries, with different communities using defined areas for summer and winter village sites.[4]

While the lands of the Canadian Shield were not seen as suitable agricultural lands, the development of mining and other extraction activities in the Upper Michigan peninsula by the early 1840s drew the attention of prospectors to the eastern shores of lakes Huron and Superior.[5] One resource that was known in the vicinity of Sault Ste. Marie was copper, exploited by Indigenous nations for centuries and first mentioned in European records by French missionary Father Alouez in the seventeenth century.[6] Although it was technically within Upper Canada, there was little government presence in the northern region and therefore no regulating of prospecting or mining. As Rhonda Telford notes in her study of the Indigenous mineral resources in Ontario, prospectors and miners were causing disruptions throughout the region, prompting Indigenous leaders to complain to the colonial government.[7] These leaders pointed out that prospecting and extraction of resources constituted trespassing, because the lands had never been sold, as Garden River chief Shingwaukonse indicated in a letter of August 1840. Despite the petitions and complaints, the new Union government of the Province of Canada paid little attention and proceeded to open the region to development. By 1841, it was issuing licences and "location tickets" to prospectors and mining companies, flexing its growing independence from British authority as it proceeded against the advice of the governor general, Lord Elgin, who recommended preceding development with a treaty.[8] Importantly, the Province of Canada was acting in contradiction of the long-standing practices established by the Royal Proclamation of 1763 to conclude treaties prior to settler exploitation of lands and resources. The successful mining operations on the American

---

[3] "Competition and Consolidation, 1760–1825," Plate 61, *Historical Atlas of Canada*, vol. 1, ed. R. Cole Harris (Toronto: University of Toronto Press, 1987).
[4] Robert Surtees, *Treaty Research Report: Robinson Treaties (1850)* (Ottawa: Indian and Northern Affairs Canada, 1986), 3.
[5] J.R. Miller, *Compact, Contract, Covenant: Aboriginal Treaty-Making in Canada* (Toronto: University of Toronto Press, 2009), 110.
[6] Surtees, *Treaty Research Report*, 3.
[7] Rhonda Telford, "'The Sound of the Rustling of the Gold Is Under My Feet Where I Stand; We Have a Rich Country': A History of Aboriginal Mineral Resources in Ontario" (PhD dissertation, University of Toronto, 1996), 122.
[8] Miller, *Compact, Contract, Covenant*, 110.

side of the border, well known to the communities on the Canadian side of the lakes, were not immediately replicated on the Canadian side despite attempts to exploit silver, lead, and copper throughout the region. It was not until the Bruce Copper Mine began its operations in the mid-1840s, on the north shore of Lake Huron, that mining became truly profitable.[9] By 1845, mining operations such as the Lake Superior Company and the Montreal Mining Company were staking claims throughout the region as far north as Batchawana Bay on Lake Superior.[10]

As historian James Morrison recounts in his study *The Robinson Treaties of 1850: A Case Study* for the Royal Commission on Aboriginal Peoples, leaders took every opportunity to express their displeasure at the increased trespassing. When provincial surveyor Alexander Vidal arrived in Sault Ste. Marie in 1846, he was confronted by chiefs such as Shingwaukonse and Nebenagoching, who were "claiming all the land here as their own" and argued that Vidal had no right to survey the land as it had never been purchased by the Crown, nor should licences have been issued without their consultation.[11] Community leaders continued to push government officials to recognize their claim to both the lands and the resources. Indian Affairs superintendent George Ironside reported in 1846 that the Anishinabek "had a very high idea of the value" of the region's mineral wealth and that they wanted a part of the benefits of extraction.[12] The Crown Lands Department of the Province of Canada did nothing to appease Indigenous concerns but rather worked to assist mining companies, leading to complaints of patronage and corruption.[13] The commissioner of crown lands, Denis-Benjamin Papineau, even rejected the idea that the Anishinabek had any kind of claim upon the region, arguing that they were "American Indians" and that they were too poorly organized. As Telford points out, ignoring Indigenous claims was financially profitable for the cash-strapped colony, as hundreds of thousands of dollars would flow into government coffers through licensing fees.[14]

Anishinabek were increasingly frustrated with both the incursions into their lands and the silence of government officials. Tensions grew on the

---

[9] Surtees, *Treaty Research Report*, 4.
[10] Telford, "'The Sound of the Rustling of the Gold,'" 123.
[11] James Morrison, *The Robinson Treaties of 1850: A Case Study*, report for the Royal Commission on Aboriginal Peoples, 1996, p. 36.
[12] George Ironside to Deputy Superintendent-General George Vardon, September 29, 1846, LAC, RG10, vol. 160, part 2, pp. 92149–51.
[13] Morrison, *The Robinson Treaties of 1850*, 35.
[14] Telford, "'The Sound of the Rustling of the Gold,'" 127.

ground as surveyors were either blocked from their work or threatened with violence. Dozens of petitions were sent to Indian Affairs and the governor general. In June 1846, Shingwaukonse again tried to secure recognition of his people's claim in a letter to the governor general. Recalling his participation in the War of 1812 in service of the British Crown, Shingwaukonse reminded the "Great Father" that his people had been promised that they would be "unmolested forever" in their lands. Despite that promise, he reported that there were "men with large hammers coming to break open my treasures to make themselves rich."[15] Calling on the "Great Father" to take pity on his people, Shingwaukonse sought to convince him, not only that he was aware of the value of the mineral wealth in his territories but that his people deserved to be compensated for its exploitation. The following year, the leaders of four separate communities together again petitioned the governor general, informing him that the "whitemen came stealing along our shores" and used their communities' traditional knowledge to find sources of minerals and ore.[16] They also complained that the surveyors continued to come to their communities despite any surrender of their lands.

While colonial officials continued to deny or ignore Anishinabek claims, the arrival of James Bruce, Earl of Elgin, as governor general in 1847 brought new attention to the issue.[17] Unlike his predecessors, Lord Elgin showed considerable interest toward Indigenous peoples and actively pushed the colonial government to change its course and attitude toward the Anishinabek of the upper Great Lakes. Highly critical of the activities of the Crown Lands Department, Elgin, responsible for Indian policy in the colony, sent Thomas G. Anderson, Indian superintendent and a long-standing employee of the Department, to the upper Great Lakes to investigate Anishinabek claims throughout the area. Holding a series of meetings and a general council at Sault Ste. Marie in August 1848, Anderson heard from numerous leaders, including Shingwaukonse, who argued that copper and other resources were placed in these lands for their use by the Creator. Chief Peau-de-Chat from Fort William on Lake Superior reminded Anderson that the Anishinabek had been there long before the arrival of Europeans.[18]

---

[15] Chinguak (Shingwaukonse) to Governor General, June 10, 1846, LAC, RG10, vol. 612, p. 117, reel C-13385.
[16] Telford, "'The Sound of the Rustling of the Gold,'" 131.
[17] Morrison, *The Robinson Treaties of 1850*, 42.
[18] Janet Chute, "A Unifying Vision: Shingwaukonse's Plan for the Future of the Great Lakes Ojibwa," *Journal of the Canadian Historical Association* 7 (1996): 69.

At the conclusion of his investigation, Anderson recommended that the Crown recognize the Indigenous claims throughout the upper Great Lakes region as no cession or sale had been made with the Crown. He further recommended that a limited treaty be concluded for the areas covered by the mining licences.[19] As Morrison notes, Anderson's report was not viewed favourably. The commissioner of crown lands would agree only to the setting aside of reserve lands at village sites, while the governor general felt that the report was not sufficiently detailed to resolve all Indigenous claims in the region, especially those on Lake Superior.[20]

In order to fully resolve the extent of possible claims, Anderson was again sent out to investigate, but this time accompanied by provincial surveyor Alexander Vidal. Heading out late in the season of 1849, Anderson and Vidal met with Indigenous leaders at Fort William on the western shore of Lake Superior on September 25, St. Ignace Island on September 29, Michipicoten on October 9, and Sault Ste. Marie on October 13.[21] Due to the lateness of the season, many communities were unable to participate in the gatherings as they were out on the land. Despite the sparse attendance at the meetings, government officials viewed them as successful for helping them understand the extent of Indigenous claims. Anderson and Vidal concluded that the treaty covering the entire north shores of lakes Huron and Superior could be successfully concluded if it was done quickly and fairly.[22] Their report even included a list of potential reserve lands for signatory communities. For the Anishinabek, the outcome of the meetings was less than desirable, since they expected Anderson and Vidal to negotiate a treaty, not to seek greater clarity of their claims. The dissatisfaction with the meetings resulted in several tense encounters, especially between Garden River chief Shingwaukonse and Alexander Vidal.[23]

Colonial officials moved quickly to address the claim after a violent clash erupted between the First Nations and Métis warriors and miners at Batchawana Bay in November 1849.[24] The Executive Council instructed William Benjamin Robinson, former fur trader in the Muskokas and member of the colonial legislature, to negotiate a treaty.[25] Robinson was

---

[19] T.G. Anderson to Civil Secretary, August 26, 1848, LAC, RG10, vol. 179, pp. 100436–7.
[20] Morrison, *The Robinson Treaties of 1850*, 53.
[21] Surtees, *Treaty Research Report*, 8.
[22] Ibid., 12.
[23] Chute, "A Unifying Vision," 73.
[24] Ibid., 74.
[25] Telford, "'The Sound of the Rustling of the Gold,'" 166.

issued a budget of £7,500 to buy as much land as possible.[26] The Council expected Robinson to obtain the rights to a considerable amount of land in the upper lakes' watershed and to settle for no less than "the north shore of Lake Huron and the mining sites along the eastern shore of Lake Superior." During the spring of 1850, Robinson made an exploratory trip through the proposed surrender lands around lakes Huron and Superior.

Just as Lord Elgin left the region as part of a provincial tour in late August 1850, Robinson started the process toward a new treaty by visiting several Anishinabek communities in the Sault Ste. Marie area. Representatives of nations living along the north shores of lakes Superior and Huron gathered to meet him, and treaty discussions began on September 4 at the Hudson's Bay Company's warehouse in Sault Ste. Marie.[27] Robinson told the gathered Indigenous leaders that he was prepared to offer a one-time payment of £4,000 and £1,000 per annum thereafter for the territory around the lakes. The leaders of Indigenous communities living north of Lake Superior agreed to these terms.[28] After those leaders from around Lake Huron requested a $10-per-person annuity and also larger reserve tracts, Robinson negotiated a separate treaty with the Lake Superior nations on September 7. The treaty included lands along the north shore of Lake Superior, from Batchawana Bay west to Pigeon River and north to the height of the land.[29] Robinson then leveraged the fact that he had negotiated a treaty with the Lake Superior nations to reopen negotiations with the Lake Huron nations, stating that he would leave the other nations empty-handed.[30] On September 9, the Lake Huron Indigenous leaders acquiesced, and a second treaty, now referred to as the Robinson-Huron Treaty, was signed. The surrender covered land along the shore of Lake Superior between Batchawana Bay and Sault Ste. Marie, and the Lake Huron shore between Sault Ste. Marie and Penetanguishene, back from the lakeshore to the height of the land. In both treaties, the region's Indigenous inhabitants retained hunting and fishing rights in the territory until the lands were taken up for development or settlement, and the lands would be set aside for each group as a reserve, although the specific amount of land was not clearly defined in the treaties.[31]

---

[26] Leighton, "Historical Significance," 10.
[27] Surtees, *Treaty Research Report*, 17.
[28] Morrison, *The Robinson Treaties of 1850*, 113.
[29] Surtees, *Treaty Research Report*, 18.
[30] Morrison, *The Robinson Treaties of 1850*, 121.
[31] Robinson-Huron Treaty, September 9, 1850, LAC, RG10, vol. 1844, IT no. 148, IA 61, reel T-9938.

While Robinson stated in his report that the Superior and Huron treaties were "based on the same conditions as all preceding ones," in reality they are rather different. As had become the practice in the land cessions in Upper Canada since the 1820s, the two treaties formalized the setting aside of reserve lands for each individual signing group. Instead of negotiating for relatively small and compact parcels of land, similar to the preceding land cessions in Upper Canada, the 1850 agreements included the surrender of huge tracts of land with different and disparate Indigenous groups. Also, the Robinson treaties changed the way in which annuity monies, that is, obligatory yearly payments, were issued; cash payments went to individual band members instead of payment to the band in either goods or cash. Finally, the Robinson Superior and Huron Treaties maintained an ongoing right to hunt and fish throughout the treaty territory, as long as those lands are not "taken up" – set aside for mining and resource development or for settlement. While some earlier Upper Canada land-surrender treaties did include some of these elements, the Robinson treaties were the first to bundle them all together. This model was deemed to be so effective that the Robinson treaties became the model for subsequent treaties conducted in the post-Confederation period.

ORAL AND WRITTEN ACCOUNTS OF THE ROBINSON-HURON TREATY, 1850

Previous Upper Canada agreements had been negotiated by Indian Department officials, but the 1850 treaties were concluded by a specifically appointed treaty commissioner, William Benjamin Robinson, a member of one of the most influential Tory families in colonial Canada, where his brother, John Beverly, was the colony's chief justice and his brother-in-law, Samuel P. Jarvis, had served as chief superintendent of Indian Affairs. Robinson, himself, had run the family's fur trade operations in the Muskokas and had served as a commissioner of public works.[32] A sitting member of the legislature in 1849, he offered his services to help "expedite the settlement of existing difficulties" on the upper Great Lakes to the Indian Department.[33] In a decision that prompted accusations of patronage, the Executive Council recommended Robinson's appointment on January 11.[34] As Morrison reports in his study of the 1850 treaties,

---

[32] Surtees, *Treaty Research Report*, 16.
[33] William Benjamin Robinson to Colonel Bruce, January 10, 1850, LAC, RG1, E7, vol. 34.
[34] Minutes of the Executive Council, January 11, 1850, Canada State Minute Book J, LAC, RG1, E1, p. 590, reel C-114.

Robinson was a highly political choice for treaty commissioner. Well connected with the higher echelons of Upper Canadian society, he was also involved in the mining developments of the region, having received a mining licence and having worked for the Montreal Mining Company at the Bruce Copper Mine, a company with two shareholders sitting on the Executive Council.[35] Robinson was also very familiar with Indigenous issues in the region, having had numerous meetings and encounters with Shingwaukonse of Garden River as well as the leadership on St. Joseph's Island and at Thessalon.

Another significant difference with earlier treaties was that Robinson received specific instructions to guide the negotiation of the treaty, although only after he requested them. In an April 16 Order-in-Council, he was tasked "to negotiate for the extinction of the Indian title to the whole territory on the north and North Eastern Coasts of Lakes Huron and Superior," but if that was not possible, to at least secure a land cession for the areas being considered for mining along "the North Eastern Coast of Lake Huron and such portion of the Lake Superior Coast as embraces the location at Mica Bay and Michipicoton."[36] The Executive Council also informed Robinson that payment for the cession should be done in cash and not exceed £5,000, and that an annuity of £1,500, divided among a maximum of 600 claimants, be offered. With his instructions and commission from the governor general in hand, Robinson headed up to Sault Ste. Marie in May for initial meetings that would set the date for the formal treaty conference in the fall.

The official account of the treaty conference held on September 5–9, 1850, was drafted by Robinson upon his return to Toronto, two weeks after the treaty signing. Despite having held several weeks of meetings and discussions prior to the treaty signing, as noted in his diary, Robinson's report presents a relatively short account of the negotiations themselves; he spent considerably more time justifying the clauses that went beyond his instructions. Reporting that there were "twenty-one chiefs present, about the same number of principal men, and a large number of their Indians, belonging to the different bands," Robinson offered a cash payment of £4,000 and an annuity of £1,000 divided among the signatories – a full £1,500 less than the maximum allowed by his instructions.[37] Robinson's account also confirms that hunting and fishing would continue, since the land use

---

[35] Morrison, *The Robinson Treaties of 1850*, 89.
[36] Minutes of the Executive Council, April 16, 1850, Canada State Minute Book K, LAC, RG1, E1, pp. 180–2, reel C-115.
[37] William Benjamin Robinson, Treaty Commissioner's Report, September 24, 1850, LAC, RG10, vol. 191, no 54001–5500, p. 111709, reel C-11513.

by settlers or miners would not prevent their continued rights. He notes that there was some initial resistance to his offer, with comparisons being made to American treaties in the Michigan peninsula and other treaties in Upper Canada. Some Indigenous leaders, such as Shingwaukonse and Nebenaigoching, considered the terms to be insufficient and demanded $10 annuities per individual.

Although mandated to conclude a single treaty, Robinson informed the Crown that he was required to conclude two separate agreements, as the "Chiefs from Lake Superior desired to treat separately for their territory." He provides no details about why this was the case. The Lake Superior leaders agreed to the treaty terms on September 7, and then Robinson held a specific meeting with the "Lake Huron" leaders on the 9th. He offered the same terms as the treaty concluded two days earlier, arguing that larger annuities or "free grants of land" would not be acceptable.[38] After some debate, the terms were accepted by the Anishinabek chiefs. The treaties concluded were somewhat different from his instructions. In his report, Robinson states he believed that the government wanted as clear and extensive a surrender as possible, but he needed to include "small reservations made by the Indians" to secure agreements. Interestingly, he reports that he modified the annuity to reflect a suggestion made by Alexander Vidal in 1849 so that it could be increased in the future if the government was able to do so "without loss," but does not mention that the term written in the treaty text limits the amount of the increase to a maximum of £1 per individual.[39] He also reported that the location of reserves was also determined at that time, and these were the lands "they had heretofore been in the habit of using for purposes of residence and cultivation." He also guaranteed continued hunting and fishing on surrendered lands because the Anishinabek did not want the Government to take "from them their usual means of subsistence."

While the accounts of previous treaties negotiated between the Crown's representatives and Indigenous communities in the Great Lakes region tend to have little information relating to the preparations leading up to the treaty conferences, the same cannot be said for the 1850 Robinson treaties. In the five years leading up to the treaty meeting at Sault Ste. Marie, there were two official government investigations into Indigenous claims, and Robinson, upon being appointed treaty commissioner,

---

[38] Ibid.
[39] Janet Chute, "Moving on Up: The Rationale for, and Consequence of, the Escalation Clause in the Robinson Treaties," *Native Studies Review* 18, no 1 (2009): 56.

undertook a preliminary trip through the region in the spring of 1850. These records provide rich sources for readers seeking to understand the Crown's intentions, as well as its perspective of the agreements concluded in early September. Where his official report provides few details as to the discussions leading up to the conclusion of the treaties, Robinson's diary, held by the Archives of Ontario, provides a day to day account of both his spring trip to set a treaty conference and the September negotiations.[40] In reality, the treaty negotiations started unofficially during the initial spring visit, as Robinson visited communities from Manitoulin Island to as far north as Michipicoten on Lake Superior. For example, his diary recounts his May 1 stop at Garden River near Sault Ste. Marie, where Robinson met with local leaders such as Shingwaukonse and Nebenaigoching to discuss a future treaty meeting. He also had them all sign a notice indicating "that the Chiefs interested in surrender of the Lands on the Northern side of Lakes Huron and Superior and the Islands therein shall meet the Agents on the part of the Government" after the annual distribution of presents at Manitoulin.[41] The next day's entry informs the reader that he used this notice as the announcement for the treaty conference, as he sent copies to the various Hudson's Bay Company posts for distribution among the communities.

As both Morrison and Surtees note, the diary entries indicate how Robinson used Lord Elgin's visit to Sault Ste. Marie to bolster his credibility in the days leading up to the September treaty meetings.[42] In the last days of August, the entries recount how Robinson arranged meetings between the gathering Anishinabek leaders and Colonel Bruce, the superintendent general of Indian Affairs and Lord Elgin's secretary. On September 3, a meeting was held with the governor general prior to his departure from Sault Ste. Marie, where he expressed his confidence in Robinson.[43] His entries relating to the treaty discussions of September 5 and 6 provide more detail than the official report, as Robinson also discusses the advantages of "reservations for their own use for farming &c. &c., &, that they would still have the free use of all the territory ceded to H.M. [Her Majesty], to hunt & fish over as heretofore, except such places as were sold to white people and others by the Gov't. & occupied in a manner to prevent such hunting."

---

[40] William Benjamin Robinson, "Journal of W.B. Robinson on a visit to the Indians to make a treaty 1850," May 1, 1850, J.B. Robinson Papers, AO, F44, MS 4, reel 5.
[41] William Benjamin Robinson to Colonel Bruce, May 13, 1850, LAC, RG1, E5, vol. 13, file 162.
[42] Morrison, *The Robinson Treaties of 1850*, 107–8; Surtees, *Treaty Research Report*, 17.
[43] Robinson, "Journal of W.B. Robinson."

Robinson also shows the divisions between the communities, recording that Peau-de-Chat from the Fort William region was agreeable to the terms and that he "asked for ½ of the money for Lake Superior & might do what his Great Father pleased with the rest," while Shingwaukonse argued that the annuities were insufficient and should be $10 per head as well as needing a larger reserve. Once a treaty was signed with the Lake Superior chiefs, Robinson then used that first agreement to pressure the remaining leaders to make an agreement. Ultimately, Robinson presented a "take it or leave it" scenario, as his September 7 entry states:

> I sh'd prepare the Treaty &, bring it over on Monday, that those who choosed might sign it. I wd. not press anyone to sign. Those who signed wd. get the money for their tribes & those who did not sign wd. get none, & I shd. take the remainder of the money back to Toronto, give it to the Gov't, to take no further trouble about the treaty matter.[44]

Robinson was very much aware that the treaty conference did not encompass all communities that inhabited the Huron and Superior watersheds. Building on the Anderson and Vidal report, Robinson attempted to get a better sense of the region's Indigenous population when he "took measures for ascertaining as nearly as possible the number of Indians inhabiting the north shore of the two lakes." He acknowledged that those assembled at Sault Ste. Marie did not represent all of the possible communities in the treaty area, especially for those inland from Lake Huron. Consequently, Robinson recommended that George Ironside, Indian superintendent at Manitoulin, "be furnished with copies of that document and also of the paylists, in order that he may correct, in time, any errors that are found to exist."[45] This later process would have serious consequences for some communities, such as Teme-Augama Anishnabai, who would never formally adhere to the 1850 treaty.[46]

Robinson's diary provides a view of his tactics for concluding the agreements, from getting the "Crown's" declaration of confidence prior to the meetings to dealing first with the more seemingly unified leaders from Lake Superior. These leaders represented communities who were less

---

[44] Ibid.
[45] Ibid.
[46] David T. McNab, "Who Is on Trial? Teme-Augama Anishnabai Land Rights and George Ironside, Junior: Re-considering Oral Tradition," *Canadian Journal of Native Studies* 18, no. 1 (1998): 121.

affected by the mining exploitation in and around Sault Ste. Marie. He then used the lack of unity among the Anishinabek communities of Lake Huron to make a deal with the willing and threatened to exclude those who would not sign on to the treaty. While, compared to his official report, Robinson's diary does provide more information on how the treaty was explained to the Indigenous party, as Rhonda Telford mentions this still does not provide a complete account of the negotiations, as it is unclear why he signed two treaties instead of an adherence of the Lake Huron chiefs to the agreement concluded two days earlier, or why Shingwaukonse changed his mind and agreed to sign the treaty after holding out for better terms.[47] Unfortunately, no written settler records of speeches mentioned in the diary have ever been found, although James Morrison does note that John William Keating, an employee of the Indian Department who spoke Anishinaabemowin, had been tasked to record the speeches.

Armed with the two signed treaty documents and Robinson's report of the treaty conference, the colonial administration, both the Indian Department and the government of the Province of Canada, were confident that it now held all lands and titles to the Huron and Superior watersheds. Unencumbered by Indigenous claims, the full resources development plans for the region could go forward. Over the course of the following decades, however, Anishinabek understanding of the agreements was frequently expressed in letters and petitions to the Crown, especially those who signed the Robinson-Huron Treaty. In all cases, their perspective went beyond the limited scope of the Crown's understanding of the treaty as a land sale with a limited annuity.

The difference between these perspectives came to light almost immediately after the conclusion of the treaties. Less than a year after the treaty conference at Sault Ste. Marie, chiefs Wagemake and Papaseance of Henvey Inlet wrote to the governor general to complain that the extent of land surrendered was unclear. Specifically, they argued that "no inquiry as to the actual extent owned by each Chief and Band was made," and therefore the amount of payment and annuity did not correspond with the value of the land sold.[48] They argued that there appeared to be two different "rules," one for settlers and one for treaty signatories. They further elaborated that the terminology used by Robinson to describe the size of reserve lands also created confusion, as they did not understand "miles" as a measure

---

[47] Telford, "'The Sound of the Rustling of the Gold,'" 170–2.
[48] Wa-ge-ma-ke and Pa-pa-seance to Governor General, August 17, 1851, LAC, RG10, vol. 572, reel C-13373.

of distance, relying instead on descriptions of "certain points" to delineate desired reserve lands. As Morrison notes in his submission to the Royal Commission on Aboriginal Peoples, Wagemake and Papaseance's letter shows that there were definite misunderstandings during the treaty conference, contrary to Robinson's statement that he "had no difficulty in making them comprehend" the extent of land surrendered or the value of the land.[49] The Anishinabek signatories also expressed concern that despite the assurance of the treaty, their remaining lands were being threatened by development. In a letter to the Marquis of Lorne, the governor general, Chief Dokis, who signed the Huron Treaty in 1850, expressed his concern over proposed rail-line development through his community's reserve.

The question of the amount of land covered by the treaty and its value has been a constant thread in different Anishinabek accounts of the treaty. Just as Wagemake and Papaseance had stated that "in proportion to the quantity of land owned and possessed by each Band should be [the] proportion of the annuity it receives," other accounts also questioned the amount of the annuity payment.[50] In 1887, the chiefs and councillors of Parry Island informed the Department of Indian Affairs that promises made by Robinson were not being upheld, specifically that the amount of the annuity had never been increased up by $1 a year to a maximum of $10.[51] Ten years later, John Mashekyash, who had signed the Robinson-Huron Treaty as a headman for the community at Batchewana Bay, recounted a similar understanding of further increases to the value of the annuity. In this report, part of the papers held by Aemilius Irving, counsel to the province of Ontario at the end of the nineteenth century, Mashekyash stated that Robinson said,

> When you get the four dollars per head per year I now promise you then the government which I here represent will have fulfilled my promise I am now making to you. But if your great Mother the queen should think it right to give you more it will only be by her most gracious goodness towards you to do so.[52]

In the decades following the signing, the communities clearly expressed an understanding that the annuity they were to receive was not supposed

---

[49] Morrison, *The Robinson Treaties of 1850*, 143.
[50] Wa-ge-ma-ke and Pa-pa-seance to Governor General, August 17, 1851.
[51] Chiefs and Councillors, Parry Island, to Department of Indian Affairs, March 25, 1887, LAC, RG10, vol. 2369, file 74,634, p. 75579, reel C-11209.
[52] Information of John Mashekyash, June 1, 1893, AO, Irving Papers F1027–1.

to be static but was tied to the value of the land as it increased with development. This understanding of an increasing annuity points directly to the wording of the treaty text: "should the Territory ... produce such an amount as will enable the Government of this Province, without incurring loss, to increase the annuity hereby secured to them, then and in that case the same shall be augmented from time to time."[53] It also reflects Robinson's official report on the clause, in which he reported on "prospective advantages should the lands in question prove sufficiently productive at any future period to enable the Government without loss to increase the annuity."[54] In other words, when the province accumulated revenue from the development of resources, the annuity would be increased up to a maximum of £1, an increase that did not happen for another 25 years, when it was increased and fixed at $4 in 1875.[55] This position remains constant today, as the communities continue to argue that the treaty annuity clause has not been properly interpreted by the Crown. They commenced legal action on the matter in 2014.[56]

THE ROBINSON-HURON TREATY AND THE COURTS

As William Benjamin Robinson notes in his report to the governor general, efforts had been made to ascertain which Anishinabek should be included in a treaty for the lands of the upper Great Lakes. His diary also records his efforts to announce the upcoming treaty conference at Sault Ste. Marie by asking the Hudson's Bay Company to announce and promote the meeting at all trading posts throughout the region.[57] When the treaty conference started in early September, Robinson reported that there were "twenty-one chiefs present, about the same number of principal men, and a large number of their Indians."[58] Despite the presence of over forty Anishinabek leaders, Robinson was well aware that not all of the communities inhabiting the watersheds of lakes Superior and Huron had attended the treaty council; he recommended that George Ironside "be furnished with copies of that document and also of the paylists, in order

---

[53] Robinson-Huron Treaty, September 9, 1850.
[54] Robinson, Treaty Commissioner's Report, September 24, 1850, pp. 111709–17.
[55] Chute, "Moving on Up," 63.
[56] Ontario, Superior Court of Justice, Statement of Claim, *Mike Restoule, Patsy Corbiere, et al., v. the Queen, AG of Canada, and AG of Ontario*, court file no. C-3512-14.
[57] Robinson, "Journal of W.B. Robinson."
[58] Robinson, Treaty Commissioner's Report, September 24, 1850, p. 111710.

that he may correct, in time, any errors that are found to exist." As many historians of the Robinson treaties, such as Morrison and McNab, have noted, there were at least four absent communities: Pic River and Long Lake for the Robinson-Superior Treaty, and "Green Lake" and Temagami (Teme-Augama Anishnabai) for the Robinson-Huron Treaty.[59]

The Anishinabek presence at Lake Temagami, just to the north of Lake Nipissing in Central Ontario, had long been known to European settlers and colonial administrators.[60] Despite an awareness of the community, there were no recorded participants from Teme-Augama Anishnabai present during the treaty meetings in September 1850. Some 50 years later, Chief Michel Dokis, one of the treaty signatories from the Lake Nipissing region, indicated that no invitation had even been sent to Nebenegwune, the community's chief prior to the conference.[61] Even though there is no mention of a Teme-Augama Anishnabai presence at Sault Ste. Marie, George Ironside did include the name "Naibanagonai of Temaguming" as a recipient of a treaty annuity on September 13, 1850, at Manitowaning, although the oral history of Teme-Augama Anishnabai indicates that Nebenegwune had not participated in this event on Manitoulin Island.[62] In an 1857 letter to Richard Pennefather, the superintendent general of Indian Affairs, George Ironside, who had been responsible for paying annuities, reported that several chiefs had complained that "many of the people justly entitled" had not been included in the 1850 treaty. He stated that in the days following the treaty signing, an agreement had been made to allow the "absent parties who reside about and beyond Lake Nipissing to come and supply the information required" to receive annuities under the treaty.[63] As McNab notes, steps to secure a formal adherence to the treaty do not seem to have occurred.[64] In the 150 years since the treaty signing, the issue of the Teme-Augama Anishnabai's adherence to the Robinson-Huron Treaty has not been fully resolved. Between the 1880s and the 1920s, questions regarding this community were openly discussed between the provincial and the federal governments, focusing

---

[59] Morrison, *The Robinson Treaties of 1850*, 97 and 100; McNab, "Who Is on Trial?," 119.
[60] Toby Morantz, "The Judiciary as Anthropologists: New Insights into Social Organization: The Teme-Augama Anishnabay Case," *Papers of the Algonquian Conference* 23 (1992): 288.
[61] Morrison, *The Robinson Treaties of 1850*, 100.
[62] McNab, "Who Is on Trial?," 123.
[63] George Ironside to Richard Pennefather, February 2, 1857, LAC, RG10, vol. 573, pp. 154–6, reel C-13374.
[64] McNab, "Who Is on Trial?," 124.

more on allocation of a reserve than treaty adherence.[65] The case of the Teme-Augama Anishnabai is of particular note, since it culminated in the Supreme Court's *Bear Island* decisions in 1991.

In 1973, three legal notices were made by the Teme-Augama Anishnabai regarding a possible development on Lake Temagami. Specifically, the legal notices were to stop the province of Ontario developing some 10,000 square kilometres of land in and around the lake. This action would eventually escalate between the province and the community into a full court case brought forward by the province against the Teme-Augama Anishnabai's Bear Island Foundation.[66] The central question of the case, commonly known as *Bear Island*, was whether the province had ownership of the lands clear of Indigenous claim, or whether the Teme-Augama Anishnabai have unextinguished rights that could prevent development.[67] The Teme-Augama Anishnabai had never signed any treaty with the Crown surrendering their rights or title, had received a reserve only in the 1970s after a century of requests, and therefore still had full Indigenous rights and title to the lands of the n'Daki Mena ("our land"). In his factum and testimony before the court, Gary Potts, chief of the Teme-Augama Anishnabai, shared his community's oral history of their exclusion from the treaty signing. Arguing that the government officials such as Anderson, Vidal, and Robinson were unfamiliar with the higher lands of the Lake Huron watershed, Potts asserted that the lands north of Lake Nipissing were never truly considered to be part of the land cession. Furthermore, the Teme-Augama Anishnabai were unaware of the treaty meeting, as no one had come to inform them of the treaty conference of 1850.[68] As a consequence, all Indigenous rights and title were unaffected because no representative participated in the treaty signing, nor was there a later attempt to secure their treaty adherence.

The province of Ontario presented two central arguments that the community had indeed adhered to the Robinson-Huron Treaty. The first concerned the participation of an individual named Tawagaiwene, who was a treaty signatory. The province argued that Tawagaiwene had the "authority" to act for other Anishinabek communities, and that he

---

[65] Bruce Hodgins, "The Temagami Indians and Canadian Federalism: 1867–1943," *Laurentian University Review* 11, no. 2 (1979): 95.
[66] Jocelyn Thorpe, *Temagami's Tangled Wild: Race, Gender, and the Making of Canadian Nature* (Vancouver: University of British Columbia Press, 2011), 93.
[67] *Ontario (Attorney General) v. Bear Island Foundation*, [1991] 2 S.C.R., 571.
[68] *Ontario (Attorney General) v. Bear Island Foundation*, Appellant's Factum, vol. III, History of the Teme-Agama Anishnabay and Land Use.

had some connection to Nebenegwune, the actual chief of the Teme-Augama Anishnabai.[69] Second, the province further argued that since Nebenegwune's name appeared on the 1850 list of those who received a payment at Manitoulin on September 13, 1850, his action constituted an acceptance of the 1850 treaty.[70] Over the course of three separate court processes over an eight-year period, the arguments of the province proved to be the most convincing to the courts.

In 1984, Justice Donald Steele ruled that the province of Ontario held the rights to the lands in question and that the defendants had not properly demonstrated that they held Indigenous land rights.[71] He also determined that the Teme-Augama Anishnabai did not constitute an "organized band level of society in 1763" and therefore "could not exclusively occupy and make aboriginal use of the land claim area."[72] In regard to the adherence to the treaty, Justice Steele argued that the record of the September 13 meeting at Manitowaning was sufficient evidence to conclude that Nebenegwune had agreed to the treaty. He added, just as Ontario had argued, that Tawagaiwene was the overall chief of Lake Wanapitei, that "Nebenegwune was merely a principal man or headman ... and the Temagami Indians ... were included as part of Tawgaiwene's band," and "that no contemporary evidence of Nebenegwune or any members of the Temagami Band attempting to disassociate themselves from Tawgaiwene's actions."[73] In effect, the Teme-Augama Anishnabai were never an independent Indigenous community.

As a final commentary on the nature of the Teme-Augama Anishnabai claim, Steele also took the opportunity to severely criticize the community's oral history, stating that he was disappointed "that there was so little evidence given by Indians themselves. Chief Potts was the principal Indian witness to give oral history ... The knowledge of these Indian witnesses was generally limited in time to their immediate grandparents." After losing its appeal at the Ontario Court of Appeal, the Teme-Augama Anishnabai pushed the case up to the Supreme Court of Canada. In a short ruling rendered in 1991, the Supreme Court dismissed the appeal, agreeing that the community's Indigenous rights had "been extinguished either by the Robinson-Huron Treaty or by the subsequent adherence

---

[69] Morantz, "The Judiciary as Anthropologists," 294.
[70] Thorpe, *Temagami's Tangled Wild*, 113.
[71] *Ontario (Attorney General) v. Bear Island Foundation*, [1984] O.J. No. 3432.
[72] Ibid., para. 35.
[73] Ibid.

to that treaty by the Indians."[74] While disagreeing with some elements of the Justice Steele decision at the trial level with respect to the existence of Indigenous rights prior to 1850, the Supreme Court Justices determined that the community's "right was in any event surrendered by arrangements subsequent to that treaty by which the Indians adhered to the treaty in exchange for treaty annuities and a reserve."[75] In essence, because Teme-Augama Anishnabai had requested and received a reserve and, at some point in time, accepted treaty annuities, it should be considered a treaty adherent.

The courts' various decisions in *Bear Island* are interesting additions to the study and understanding of treaties, especially the ruling that the community had adhered to the Robinson-Huron Treaty of 1850. In the 25 years since the final ruling, dozens of articles and several books have been published discussing, debating, and largely criticizing its impact.[76] As legal scholar Kent McNeil comments in his article "Temagami Indian Land Claim," Justice Steele, by deciding that Tawagaiwene had signed the treaty for the Teme-Augama Anishnabai, made a number of inferences that were contrary to the community's understanding of the treaty and its own history.[77] This approach is in contradiction to one of the legal principles of treaty interpretation, specifically that "[i]n determining the signatories' respective understanding and intentions, the court must be sensitive to the unique cultural and linguistic differences between the parties."[78] McNeil further criticizes the rulings that the community adhered to the treaty by accepting annuities. As he points out, adherence to other treaties, such as those in Western Canada, required a formal signature by a community leader to be accepted; in the *Bear Island* case, the requirement was far lower, namely the simple acceptance of benefits.[79]

Similarly, anthropologist Toby Morantz was highly critical of the Court's historical and anthropological interpretations: on the one hand it denied that the Teme-Augama Anishnabai held Indigenous rights as an

---

[74] *Ontario (Attorney General) v. Bear Island Foundation*, [1991] 2 S.C.R., 571.
[75] Ibid., 575.
[76] B.W. Hodgins, U. Lischke, and D.T. McNab, eds., *Blockades & Resistance: Studies in Actions of Peace and the Temagami Blockades of 1988–89* (Kitchener, ON: Wilfrid Laurier University Press, 2003).
[77] Kent McNeil, "The Temagami Indian Land Claim: Loosening the Judicial Strait-jacket," in *Temagami: A Debate on Wilderness*, eds. Matt Bray and Ashley Thomson (Toronto: Dundurn Press, 1990), 191.
[78] *R. v. Marshall*, [1999] 3 S.C.R. 456, para. 78.
[79] McNeil, "Temagami Indian Land Claim," 194.

"organized society" under the Supreme Court's *Baker Lake* test, while on the other hand it stripped the community of its agency and ability to recognize its own leadership at the time of treaty making.[80] Of particular note, Bruce Granville Miller, in his examination of the use of oral history in the judicial system, sees the comments made by Justice Steele regarding the nature and significance of oral history in the case as highly problematic. By criticizing the quality of the oral understanding of the community's history presented by Chief Gary Potts and others, the *Bear Island* decision made "unwarranted assumptions about the nature of the transmission of oral history," thus reinforcing the dominance of the written record over oral history.[81] The trial court's comments on the matter again appear to contradict treaty interpretation principles, where the goal is to reconcile "the interests of both parties at the time the treaty was signed" and not discount one interpretation over another.[82]

FURTHER READINGS

Janet Chute. "A Unifying Vision: Shingwaukonse's Plan for the Future of the Great Lakes Ojibwa." *Journal of the Canadian Historical Association* 7 (1996): 55–80.

David McNab. "Who Is on Trial? Teme-Augama Anishnabai Land Rights and George Ironside, Junior: Re-considering Oral Tradition." *Canadian Journal of Native Studies* 18, no. 1 (1998): 117–33.

James Morrison. *The Robinson Treaties of 1850: A Case Study*. Report for the Royal Commission on Aboriginal Peoples, 1996.

Robert Surtees. *Treaty Research Report: Robinson Treaties (1850)*. Ottawa: Indian and Northern Affairs Canada, 1986.

Rhonda Telford. "'The Sound of the Rustling of the Gold Is Under My Feet Where I Stand; We Have a Rich Country': A History of Aboriginal Mineral Resources in Ontario." PhD dissertation, University of Toronto, 1996.

QUESTIONS FOR DISCUSSION

1. According to the treaty text, why were treaties concluded in 1850?
2. Based on the following excerpts, how does the oral history describe the impact of the treaty on the community's ability to control their lands?

---

[80] Morantz, "The Judiciary as Anthropologists," 291.
[81] Bruce Granville Miller, *Oral History on Trial: Recognizing Aboriginal Narratives in the Courts* (Vancouver: University of British Columbia Press, 2011), 107.
[82] *R. v. Marshall*, para. 78.

Wa-ge-ma-ke and Pa-pa-seance to Governor General, August 17, 1851, LAC, RG10, vol. 572, reel C-13373

Great Father,
When the Treaty was made, no enquiry was made as to the actual extent owned by each Chief and Band.

Great Father,
We think that in proportion to the quantity of land owned and possessed by each Band should be proportion of the annuity it receives.

Great Father,
If the white man owns little and sells he receives little. If he holds much and sells he receives much – it is right. It is just – shall then be one rule for the White Man and another for the Red Man. Numbers are the test of right.

Michel Le Aigle Dokis to Governor General, Marquis of Lorne, 1878, LAC, RG10, vol. 2067, file 10,307, pt. 1, pp. 21762–3, reel C-11149
We now find that the above promises are not being carried out with us, there are preparations being made to run a Railroad track through our Reserve, and we are not willing to give up our permission to have it done, and we do not which to have any further surveying done on our Reserve, and we wish to have the promises Mr. Robinson made to us carried out that is to leave our Reserves for our Children and their Children.

Chiefs of Parry Island to Department of Indian Affairs, 1887, LAC, RG10, vol. 2369, file 74,634, p. 75579, reel C-11209
Now about eight years after the treaty at Penetanguishene, I went to the city of Toronto, and said to Mr. Robinson, I come to see you. He said "Why do you come to see me, for anything?" I said, what you said to the Indians when you asked them for their land does not come to pass. Then he, Mr. Robinson, took up a paper and asked me, "what did I say." I then repeated as above stated. Then Mr. Robinson said "I did say so. Why does not the Governor do it. Do not let him alone till he does it all." … therefore believe that there is a written treaty made at Penetanguishene recording to the above, because I was present also, and saw and heard as above stated what took place at Penetanguishene between Robinson, Esq. and the two chiefs.

3. What does the official report of the treaty meetings say about the various clauses of the treaties?
4. In your opinion, what does the Court say about the manner in which Indigenous communities adhered to the treaty?

DOCUMENTS

Treaty Text: Robinson Treaty Made in the Year 1850 with the Ojibewa Indians of Lake Huron Conveying Certain Lands to the Crown, September 9, 1850, LAC, RG10, vol. 1844, IT 148, IA 61, T-9938

THIS AGREEMENT, made and entered into this ninth day of September, in the year of our Lord one thousand eight hundred and fifty, at Sault Ste. Marie, in the Province of Canada, between the Honorable WILLIAM BENJAMIN ROBINSON, of the one part, on behalf of HER MAJESTY THE QUEEN, and SHINGUACOUSE NEBENAIGOCHING, KEOKOUSE, MISHEQUONGA, TAGAWININI, SHABOKISHICK, DOKIS, PONEKEOSH, WINDAWTEGOWININI, SHAWENAKESHICK, NAMASSIN, NAOQUAGABO, WWBEKEKIK, KITCHEPOSSIGYN by PAPASAINSE, WAGEMAKI, PAMEQUONAISHEUG, Chiefs; and John Bell, PAQWATCHININI, MASHEKYASH, IDOWEKESIS, WAQUACOMICK, OCHEEK, METIGOMIN, WATACHEWANA, MINWAPAPENASSE, SHENAOQUOM, ONINGEGUN, PANAISSY, PAPASAINSE, ASHEWASEGA, KAGESHEWAWETUNG, SHAWONEBIN; and also Chief MAISQUASO (also Chiefs MUCKATA, MISHOQUET, and MEKIS), and MISHOQUETTO and ASA WASWANAY and PAWISS, principal men of the OJIBEWA INDIANS, inhabiting and claiming the Eastern and Northern Shores of Lake Huron, from Penetanguishine to Sault Ste. Marie, and thence to Batchewanaung Bay, on the Northern Shore of Lake Superior; together with the Islands in the said Lakes, opposite to the Shores thereof, and inland to the Height of land which separates the Territory covered by the charter of the Honorable Hudson Bay Company from Canada; as well as all unconceded lands within the limits of Canada West to which they have any just claim, of the other part, witnesseth:

THAT for, and in consideration of the sum of two thousand pounds of good and lawful money of Upper Canada, to them in hand paid, and for the further perpetual annuity of six hundred pounds of like money, the same to be paid and delivered to the said Chiefs and their Tribes at a convenient season of each year, of which due notice will be given, at such places as may be appointed for that purpose, they the said Chiefs and Principal men, on behalf of their respective Tribes or Bands, do hereby fully, freely, and voluntarily surrender, cede, grant, and convey unto Her Majesty, her heirs and successors for ever, all their right, title, and interest to, and in the whole of, the territory above described, save and except the reservations set forth in the schedule hereunto annexed; which reservations shall be held and occupied by the said Chiefs and their Tribes in common, for their own use and benefit.

And should the said Chiefs and their respective Tribes at any time desire to dispose of any part of such reservations, or of any mineral or other valuable productions thereon, the same will be sold or leased at their request by the Superintendent-General of Indian Affairs for the time being, or other officer having authority so to do, for their sole benefit, and to the best advantage.

And the said William Benjamin Robinson of the first part, on behalf of Her Majesty and the Government of this Province, hereby promises and agrees to make, or cause to be made, the payments as before mentioned; and further to allow the said Chiefs and their Tribes the full and free privilege to hunt over the Territory now ceded by them, and to fish in the waters thereof, as they have heretofore been in the habit of doing; saving and excepting such portions of the said Territory as may from time to time be sold or leased to individuals or companies of individuals, and occupied by them with the consent of the Provincial Government.

The parties of the second part further promise and agree that they will not sell, lease, or otherwise dispose of any portion of their Reservations without the consent of the Superintendent-General of Indian Affairs, or other officer of like authority, being first had and obtained. Nor will they at any time hinder or prevent persons from exploring or searching for minerals, or other valuable productions, in any part of the Territory hereby ceded to Her Majesty, as before mentioned. The parties of the second part also agree, that in case the Government of this Province should before the date of this agreement have sold, or bargained to sell, any mining locations, or other property, on the portions of the Territory hereby reserved for their use; then and in that case such sale, or promise of sale, shall be perfected by the Government, if the parties claiming it shall have fulfilled all the conditions upon which such locations were made, and the amount accruing therefrom shall be paid to the Tribe to whom the Reservation belongs.

The said William Benjamin Robinson, on behalf of Her Majesty, who desires to deal liberally and justly with all her subjects, further promises and agrees, that should the Territory hereby ceded by the parties of the second part at any future period produce such an amount as will enable the Government of this Province, without incurring loss, to increase the annuity hereby secured to them, then and in that case the same shall be augmented from time to time, provided that the amount paid to each individual shall not exceed the sum of one pound Provincial Currency in any one year, or such further sum as Her Majesty may be graciously pleased to order; and provided further that the number of Indians entitled to the benefit of this treaty shall amount to two-thirds of their present number, which is fourteen hundred and twenty-two, to entitle them to claim the full benefit thereof. And should they not at any future period amount to two-thirds of fourteen hundred and twenty-two, then the said annuity shall be diminished in proportion to their actual numbers.

The said William Benjamin Robinson of the first part further agrees, on the part of Her Majesty and the Government of this Province, that in consequence of the Indians inhabiting French River and Lake Nipissing having become parties to this treaty, the further sum of one hundred and sixty pounds Provincial Currency shall be paid in addition to the two thousand pounds above mentioned.

William Benjamin Robinson, Treaty Commissioner's Report, September 24, 1850, LAC, RG10, vol. 191, no. 54001–5500, pp. 111709–17, reel C-11513

I have the honor herewith to transmit the Treaty which on the part of the Government I was commissioned to negotiate with the tribes of Indians inhabiting the northern shore of Lake Huron and Superior; and I trust that the terms on which I succeeded in obtaining the surrender of all the lands in question, with the exception of some small reservations made by the Indians, may be considered satisfactory. They were such as I thought it advisable to offer, in order that the matter might be finally settled, without having any just grounds of complaint on the part of the Indians.

The Indians had been advised by certain interested parties to insist on some extravagant terms as I felt it quite impossible to grant; and from the fact that the American Government had paid very liberally for the land surrendered by their Indians on the south side of Lake Superior, and that our own in other parts of the country were in receipt of annuities much larger than I offered, I had some difficulty in obtaining the assent of a few of the chiefs to my propositions.

I explained to the Chiefs in council the differences between the lands ceded heretofore in this Province and those then under consideration; they were of good quality and sold readily at prices which enabled the Government to be more liberal. They were also occupied by the whites in such a manner as to preclude the possibility of the Indians hunting over or having access to them; whereas the lands now ceded are notoriously barren and sterile, and will in all probability never be settled except in a few localities by Mining companies; whose establishment among the Indians instead of being prejudicial would prove of great benefit, as they would afford a market for any thing they may have to sell & bring provisions & stores of all kinds among them at reasonable prices.

Neither did the British Government contemplate the removal of the Indians from their present haunts to some (to them) unknown region in the far west, as had been the case with their brethren on the American side.

I told them that the two chiefs who were in Toronto last winter (Shinguacouse and Nebenaigoching) only asked the amount which the Government had received for Mining locations, after deducting the expenses attending their sale. That amount was about Eight thousand pounds which the Gov't would pay them without annuity or certainty of further benefit; or one half of it down, and an annuity of about one thousand pounds. There were twenty-one chiefs present, about the same number of principal men, and a large number of their Indians, belonging to the different bands, and they all preferred the latter proposition, though two of them (Shinguacouse and Nebenaigoching) insisted on receiving an annuity equal to ten dollars per head.

The Chiefs from Lake Superior desired to treat separately for their territory &, said at once in Council that they accepted my offer. I told them I would have the Treaty ready on the following morning, & I immediately proceeded to prepare it. And as agreed upon, they signed it cheerfully at the time appointed: I then told the Chiefs from Lake Huron (who were all present when the others signed) that I should have a similar treaty ready for their signature the next morning, when those who signed it would receive their money; and that as a large majority of them had agreed to my terms & should abide by them.

I accordingly prepared the treaty and proceeded on the morning of the 9th instant to the council room to have it formally executed in the presence of proper witnesses – all the Chiefs and others were present. I told them I was then ready to receive their signatures; the two Chiefs Shinguacouse and Nebenaigoching, repeated their demand of ten dollars a head by way of annuity, and also insisted that I should insert in the treaty a condition securing to some sixty half-breeds a free grant of one hundred acres of land each. I told them they already had my answer as to larger annuity, and that I had no power to give them free grants of land. The other Chiefs came forward to sign the treaty and seeing this the two who had resisted up to this time also came to the table and signed first, the next immediately following.

I trust His Excellency will approve of my having concluded the treaty on the basis of a small annuity and the immediate and final settlement of the matter, rather than paying the Indians the full amount of all moneys on hand, and a promise of accounting to them for future sales. The latter course would have entailed much trouble on the government, besides giving the opportunity to evil disposed persons to make the Indians suspicious of any accounts that might be furnished.

Believing that His Excellency and the Government were desirous of leaving the Indians no just cause of complaint on their surrendering the extensive territory embraced in the treaty; and knowing there were individuals who most assiduously endeavoured to create dissatisfaction among them, I inserted a clause securing to them certain prospective advantages should the lands in question prove sufficiently productive at any future period to enable the Government without loss to increase the annuity.

This was so reasonable and just that I had no difficulty in making them comprehend it, and it in a great measure silenced the clamor raised by their evil advisers.

In allowing the Indians to retain reservations of land for their own use I was governed by the fact that they in most cases asked for such tracts as they had heretofore been in the habit of using for purposes of residence and cultivation, and by securing these to them and the rights of hunting and fishing over the ceded territory, they cannot say that the Government takes from them their usual means of subsistence and therefore have no claims for support, which no doubt they would have preferred, had this not been done. The reservation at Garden River is the largest and perhaps of most value, but as it is occupied by the most numerous band of Indians, and from its locality (nine miles from the Sault) is likely to attract others to it, I think it was right to grant what they expressed a desire to retain. There are two mining locations at this place, which should not be finally disposed of unless by the full consent of Shinguacouse and his band; they are in the heart of the village, and show no indication of mineral wealth, they), are numbered 14 and 15 on the small map appended to Messrs. Anderson and Vidal's report. I pledged my Word on the part of the Government that the sale of these locations should not be completed, as the locatees have not, I believe, complied with the conditions of the Crown Lands Department there can be no difficulty in cancelling the transaction.

The Chiefs are desirous that their several reservations should be marked by proper posts or monuments, and I have told them the Government would probably send someone next spring for that purpose. As I know many of the localities I shall be able to give the necessary information required.

When at Sault Ste. Marie last May, I took measures for ascertaining as nearly as possible the numbers of Indians inhabiting the north shore of the two lakes; and was fortunate enough to get a very correct census particularly of Lake Superior. I found this information very useful at the council as it enabled me successfully to contradict, the assertion (made by those who were inciting the Chiefs to resist my offers) that there are on Lake Superior alone, eight thousand Indians. The number on that lake, including eighty-four half-breeds, is only twelve hundred and forty and on Lake Huron, about fourteen hundred and twenty two, including probably two hundred half-breeds, and when I paid the Indians they acknowledged they know of no other families than those on my list.

The number paid, as appears on the pay-list, does not show the whole strength of the different bands, as I was obliged at their own request to omit some members of the very large families. I have annexed to this Report the names of the Chiefs, their localities, and number of souls in each band as recognized by me in apportioning the money, thinking it will be useful when paying the annuity hereafter.

This information may I believe be fully relied on for Lake Superior, but the census for Lake Huron is not as perfect; and I would suggest that Captain Ironside should be furnished with copies of that document and also of the paylists, in order that he may correct, in time, any errors that are found to exist.

...

The Canadians resident on the lands just surrendered at Sault Ste. Marie are very anxious to obtain titles to the land on which they have long resided and made improvements; they applied to me after the treaty and I advised them to memorialize the Government the usual way, setting forth the manner in which they were put in possession by the military authorities of the time, and that I had little doubt that the Government would do them justice. I think the survey of the tract should be made so as to interfere as little as possible with their respective clearings and that those who can show a fair claim to the favourable consideration of the Government should be liberally dealt with.

It will be seen on referring to the Treaty that I have kept within the amount at my disposal; of the £4,160 agreed by me to be paid to the Indians of both Lakes, there remains £75 unexpended. I could not from the information I possessed tell exactly the number of families I should have to pay, and thought it prudent to reserve a small sum to make good any omissions; there may still be a few who will prefer claims, though I know of none at present. If not the amount can be paid next year with the annuity to such families as are most deserving; or it may be properly applied in extinguishing the claims made by the Lake Simcoe Indians, should it appear on enquiry to be just.

The whole amount given to me in August was £5,033.6s.8d; of this sum there remains £800, which I have placed in the Bank of Upper Canada to the Credit of the Receiver General, and I have prepared a detailed account of the whole, which, with the proper vouchers, I shall deliver to the Accountant of the Crown Land Department.

I will thank you to lay the two treaties accompanying this Report before His Excellency and trust they may meet with his approval.

Wa-ge-ma-ke and Pa-pa-seance to Governor General, August 17, 1851, LAC, RG10, vol. 572, reel C-13373

Great Father

We salute you, our Warriors our Women our Children salute you and offer you the hands of friendship.

Great Father,

We are of the tribes who signed the treaty last summer & we are perfectly satisfied with it. Its provisions were wise and good.

Great Father,

We thank you for the promise it contained that our annuities shall increase as our lands are sold or leased, & that the contents of each Bands Reserve shall if valuable be for its Sole and individual benefit.

Great Father,

The timber of no value to us on our Reason we shall be glad to sell to those who come to live among us, & we feel assured that we shall derive benefit from it.

Great Father,

There is one thing however that we think not right and we come to you to tell you of it sure of redress.

Great Father,

When the Treaty was made, no enquiry was made as to the actual extent owned by each Chief and Band.

Great Father,

We think that in proportion to the quantity of land owned and possessed by each Band should be proportion of the annuity it receives.

Great Father,

If the white man owns little and sells he receives little. If he holds much and sells he receives much – it is right. It is just – shall then be one rule for the White Man and another for the Red Man. Numbers are the test of right.

Great Father,
We do not wish our words only to be believed – we wish that you should employ one of our own Chiefs to ascertain in the next Council at Manitowamining when it can be done open by and in the face of all the extent of each Band's right and then distribution the annuity accordingly ...

Great Father,
In describing our reserves, we did not understand the distances of miles; but we gave certain points and we hope that in the survey these boundaries will be adhered to and not the imagined space which a term conveys to this tho well known to you.

Great Father,
We will point out to the surveyor the Lake we mentioned and which from inquiry of the Whites, we find would be further then we said.

Great Father,
We also wish to know if we have not the exclusive right to the fisheries immediately adjoining and opposite our reserves.

Great Father,
This is all we have to say – again we salute you and beg you to listen to our words.

Great Father,
Please to take from my hands in the name of my people the pouch which is to contain the pipe of peace and plenty.

Signed, Wa-ge-ma-ke
Signed, Pa-pa-sense

Michel Le Aigle Dokis to Governor General, Marquis of Lorne, 1878, LAC, RG10, vol. 2067, file 10,307, pt. 1, pp. 21762–3, reel C-11149

When Mr. Robinson came to the Indians to make a Treaty for their lands, they were not willing to give up their lands and would not sign a Treaty – He told them they need not be afraid to give up their rights because the Government would never do any thing to make them suffer, he said you know yourselves where you have the best lands and there is where you can have your Reserves for yourselves and your children and their children ever after – He also said if at any time you have any grievance you can go to the Governor and he will see that you get all your rights or whatever you may ask ...

We now find that the above promises are not being carried out with us, there are preparations being made to run a Railroad track through our Reserve, and we are not willing to give up our permission to have it done, and we do not which [sic] to have any further surveying done on our Reserve, and we wish to have the promises Mr. Robinson made to us carried out that is to leave our Reserves for our Children and their Children –

We find already that a great deal of our valuable timber has been destroyed by cutting out a line for the Railroad – We think we have already signed away the most of our rights when we gave up nearly all our lands, and we think there should be some [next line illegible] going through our small Reserve –

We have come to you to ask you to see that we get our rights and beg of you to put a stop to the Railroad running through our Reserves.

We feel that after having given over so much of our lands to the government, they will now look after us and agree to our requests – And we hope you will not allow any one to interfere with our Reserves, as we have [?] to do as Mr. Robinson told us, that is to hand it down to our Children and their Children and others coming after them. –

Our Grandfathers told us, and we suppose the white people know that us well as we did when they asked us to sign away our rights to all lands as far as the Red River –

I Chief Dokis have been sent here by the Nippissing Bands of Indians to lay this matter before you, and I beg you will give me a friendly answer to that back to my people.

Chiefs of Parry Island to Department of Indian Affairs, 1887, LAC, RG10, vol. 2369, file 74,634, p. 75579, reel C-11209

We the undersigned send you the following statements of William King and Chief Papabahmowadung which causes us to believe that there must be a different record of a Treaty made with Mukudameshuguod and Mekis, than that made at Sault St-Marie where they were not present, and it is that that we ask for.

Viz – Robinson Esq, said at Penetanguishene "The Governor also the Queen ask you for your land." Chiefs Mukudameshuguod and Mekis sat quietly for a long time. Mr. Robinson then said, "if you do not give up your land the Big Knife will take your land from you then you will get nothing for it. But if you give up your land to me, I will pay you well. You will not be in want for clothing and what you will eat on account of the money I will give you. The money you will now receive at this time Four Dollars each is thanking you for giving up your land to me. The money you will get at the end of the year will be $1.50 for each, Second year $2.00 each, third year $3.00 each, tc. up to the tenth year $10 each, then it would not increase. The Queen does not ask you for your Islands, but only for the main land."

The chiefs spoke and answered Mr. Robinson. "What my fellow Indians have done at Sault St. Marie, we do also, because you would not stop asking us. You asked us to sell our land to you, so we sell you our land. We now tell you what we want as long as Indians live their pay must never cease." Mr. Robinson asked chief Mukudameshuguod how much land he wished to reserve. The chief answered "ten miles square." Mr. Robinson wrote it down. Chief Mekis was also asked the same and he answered "the same quantity, ten miles square."

Now about eight years after the treaty at Penetanguishene, I went to the city of Toronto, and said to Mr. Robinson, I come to see you. He said "Why do you come to see me, for anything?" I said, what you said to the Indians when you asked them for their land does not come to pass. Then he, Mr. Robinson, took up a paper and asked me, "what did I say." I then repeated as above stated. Then Mr. Robinson said "I did say so. Why does not the Governor do it. Do not let him alone till he does it all."

I therefore believe that there is a written treaty made at Penetanguishene recording to the above, because I was present also, and saw and heard as above stated what took place at Penetanguishene between Robinson, Esq. and the two chiefs.

Information of John Mashekyash – Batchewana Bay, Archives of Ontario, Irving Papers 20/36/3(3), June 1, 1893

Mr. Robinson said that we would get five dollars per head. Mr. Robinson then also told us all that next year that we would get one dollar and a half per head and that for four years; and at the end of the four years when the government will have sold enough of the land you now have ceded to them to enable them to give you four dollars per head you will get that every year as an annuity. When you get the four dollars per head per year I now promise you then the government which I here represent will have fulfilled my promise I am now making to you. But if your great Mother the queen should think it right to give you more it will only be by her most gracious goodness towards you to do so. Then we all thanked Mr. Robinson, we got the five dollars and we were all pleased and satisfied. But the present government has not dealt with us Indians as Mr. Robinson promised they would do.

Excerpt from *Ontario (Attorney General) v. Bear Island Foundation*, [1991] 2 S.C.R., 570

Respondent Attorney General for Ontario brought action against appellant Bear Island Foundation after the latter had registered cautions against tracts of unceded land on behalf of the Temagami Band of Indians. Respondent sought a declaration that the Crown in right of Ontario has clear title and that the appellants have no interest therein, and further sought certain injunctive relief. The Foundation counterclaimed and sought a declaration of quiet title on the ground that the Temagami have a better right to possession of all the lands by virtue of their aboriginal rights in the land. Ontario claimed that the Temagami had no aboriginal right in relation to the land, or that any right they might have had has been extinguished, either by treaty or unilateral act of the sovereign.

The trial judge found that the appellants had no aboriginal right to the land, and that even if such a right had existed, it had been extinguished by the Robinson-Huron Treaty of 1850, to which the Temagami band was originally a party or to which it had subsequently adhered. These findings were essentially factual, and were drawn from the mass of historical documentary evidence. The counterclaim was dismissed. An appeal to the Court of Appeal was dismissed. On the assumption that an aboriginal right existed, that court held that that right had been extinguished either by the Robinson-Huron Treaty or by the subsequent adherence to that treaty by the Indians, or because the treaty constituted a unilateral extinguishment by the sovereign.

Held: The appeal should be dismissed.

This case raised for the most part essentially factual issues on which the courts below were in agreement. On such issues, the rule is that an appellate court should not reverse the trial judge absent palpable and overriding error which affected his or her assessment of the facts. The rule is all the stronger in the face of concurrent findings of both courts below. A detailed examination of the facts was undertaken by this Court and no issue is taken with the numerous specific findings of fact in the courts below. There was not agreement, however, with all the legal findings based on those facts. In particular, the Indians exercised sufficient occupation of the lands in question throughout the relevant period to establish an aboriginal right.

It is unnecessary, however, to examine the specific nature of the aboriginal right because, in our view, whatever may have been the situation upon the signing of the Robinson-Huron Treaty, that right was in any event surrendered by arrangements subsequent to that treaty by which the Indians adhered to the treaty in exchange for treaty annuities and a reserve. It is conceded that the Crown has failed to comply with some of its obligations under this agreement, and thereby breached its fiduciary obligations to the Indians. These matters currently form the subject of negotiations between the parties. It does not alter the fact, however, that the aboriginal right has been extinguished. (pp. 570–2)

CAST OF CHARACTERS: ROBINSON-HURON TREATY, 1850

Shingwaukonse: b. 1773; d. 1854

Shingwaukonse (Shingwauk, The Pine) was born near Sault Ste. Marie in 1773 of an Anishinaabe mother and English father. Raised in the community of Garden River, Shingwaukonse was a noted member of the Midewiwin (medicine society) who attained great influence as a spiritual leader throughout the central Great Lakes region. With the outbreak of the War of 1812, Shingwaukonse maintained the long-standing alliance of his people and the British, leading some 700 warriors into battle. After the war, and as the British Indian Department was changing its policies toward encouraging a transition to European ways of life, Shingwaukonse became one of the leading voices for the protection of Indigenous rights and self-determination. Seeing the potential benefits of using British education to improve and strengthen his community, he petitioned Lieutenant-Governor Colborne in 1832 that a teacher be sent to Garden River and, in 1847, tentatively supported the establishment of school to teach "industrial vocations" to Indigenous children, a precursor to residential schools. In 1849, he participated in a confrontation with prospectors at Mica Bay, north of Sault Ste. Marie, a confrontation that solidified the government's goal to conclude a treaty for the area. During the treaty meetings in 1850, Shingwaukonse was one of the leading opponents to the terms of the treaty being proposed but eventually agreed to sign it when other chiefs agreed to the government's term. Shingwaukonse died at Garden River four years later in 1854.

William Benjamin Robinson: b. December 22, 1797; d. July 18, 1873

William Benjamin Robinson was born in 1797 into a United Empire Loyalist family in Kingston but was raised in York. His two older brothers, Peter and John Beverly Robinson, would become some of the leading figures in Upper Canadian society and the development of York. Working with his brother Peter, Robinson was an active member of the fur trade throughout the Muskokas and the northern Great Lakes, and he had a reputation for fair dealing. As well as being a merchant, Robinson was elected to the colonial legislature in 1830 and again from 1844 until 1857. Through his strong Tory positions and family connections, Robinson held several different government appointments, such as commissioner of canals and inspector general of Canada West. Due to his long experience with Indigenous relations through the fur trade, Robinson was commissioned in 1850 to negotiate a treaty for the lands around lakes Superior and Huron, as a response to the growing desire for natural resources development and Indigenous resistance to the development. After an initial consultation in May, Robinson met with a number of representatives from Indigenous communities from the upper Great Lakes to conclude an agreement at Sault Ste. Marie in September 1850. After his defeat in the election of 1857, he left public life to focus on his role as commissioner of the Canada Company. Having never gained the prominence of his siblings, Robinson died in Toronto in 1873.

Migisi, "Michel D'Aigle Dokis": b. c. 1818; d. April 25, 1906

Migisi is reported to have been born in 1818, the son of an Anishinaabe woman, Louise Obtagashio, and a French-Canadian fur trader, Michel d'Aigle. Raised as a Anishinaabe by his mother's family, he rose to prominence throughout the central Great Lakes region, establishing a trading post on Lake Nipissing with his half-brothers, Francis and Joseph Washusk, and eventually forming a distinct Anishinaabe community with them around the post, commonly known as the "Dokis band," after the name Migisi used in signing documents. When William Benjamin Robinson organized a treaty meeting in Sault Ste. Marie in 1850, Migisi was chosen to represent his community. Despite some early concerns with the extent of the promises being made by the government, Migisi agreed to the treaty terms and selected some islands on the French River as the reserve lands for his community. In the decades that followed the treaty signing, Migisi fought against encroachment onto his community's lands, which were rich with prime timber, continuing to reject all offers to sell the lands until his death in 1906.

Thomas Gummersall Anderson: b. November 12, 1779; d. February 10, 1875

Thomas G. Anderson was born in November 1779 in Sorel, Quebec, but was raised among the United Empire Loyalists settled at New Johnston

(Cornwall), along the St. Lawrence River. After a short apprenticeship with a merchant in Kingston, in 1800 Anderson became a merchant in the fur trade around Mackinac Island, the central Great Lakes, and the upper Mississippi. After volunteering during the War of 1812, Anderson joined the Indian Department in 1815, where he would spend the remainder of his career. With the change in policies of the Indian Department after the war to encourage the settlement of Indigenous peoples, Anderson was tasked with establishing a model community in 1829 at Coldwater-Narrows, which was deemed a failure in 1837 due to lack of funding and support. In 1845, he relocated from Manitoulin Island in Georgian Bay to York, where he assumed the position of chief superintendent of Indian Affairs for Upper Canada, continuing to encourage the transition of Indigenous communities and education for First Nations children. In 1848–9, he and Alexander Vidal travelled along the coast of lakes Huron and Superior to gauge interest in a possible treaty for the area, and later to organize the treaty meeting. In 1858, after a 43-year career in the Indian Department, Anderson retired to Port Hope and died in 1875.

Figure 4.1 William B. Robinson, Chief Shingwauk, and Chief Nenaigooching, 1850. Although William Robinson tried to use his experiences as a former fur trader to help guide the treaty negotiations, in the end he was unable to convince chiefs such as Shingwaukonse and resorted to threats to get a final agreement with all communities in the region.
Source: Shingwauk Residential Schools Centre, Algoma University.

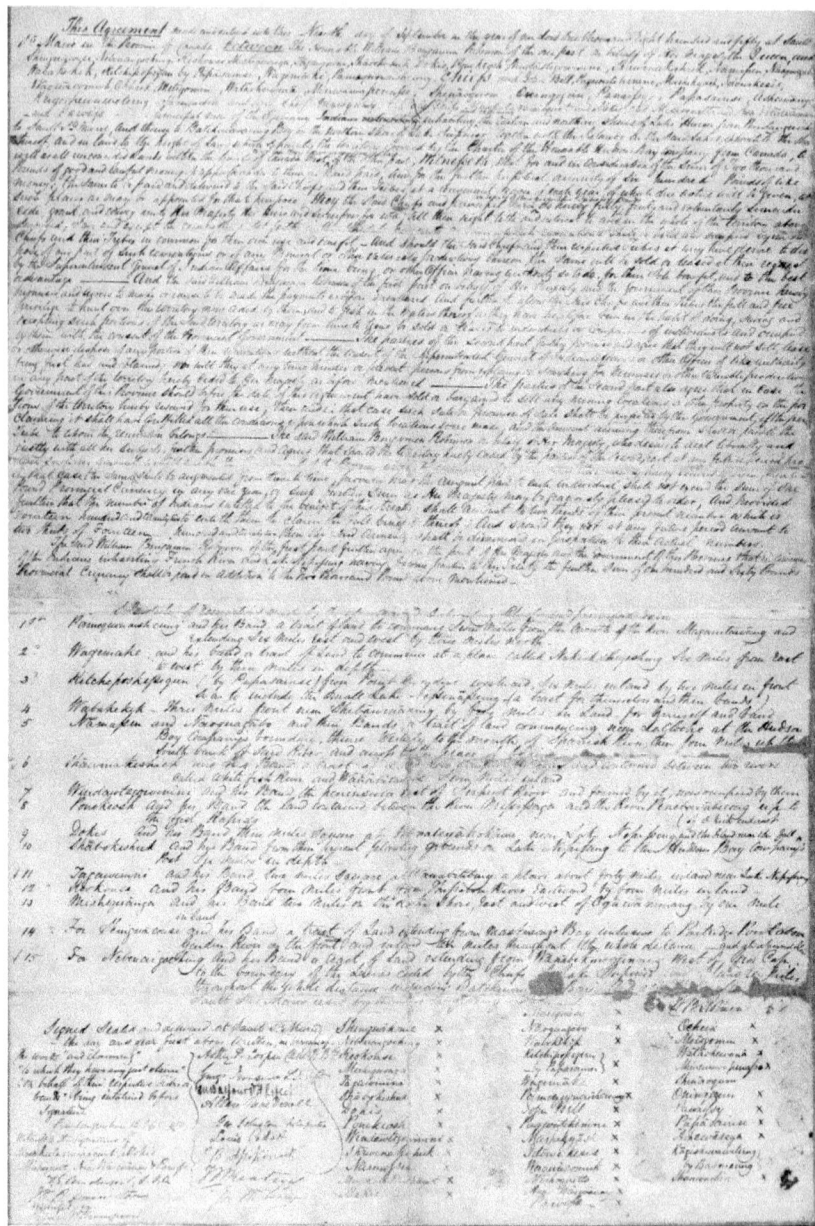

Figure 4.2 Robinson-Huron Treaty, September 9, 1850. The treaties concluded in 1850 included more detailed terms than those signed in the southern regions of the province. Despite this extra information, the written terms fell short of representing a complete Indigenous perspective of the treaties.

Source: Library and Archives Canada, e002994518.

Chapter 5
The Making of the Vancouver Island Treaties: Saanich Treaties, 1852

By the first decades of the nineteenth century, the Hudson's Bay Company's (HBC) operations stretched across the breadth of the North American continent. By the 1810s, HBC explorers and merchants had crossed the Rocky Mountains and were dealing directly with the Indigenous nations of the British Columbia interior. In 1821, the Company received an exclusive licence from the British Crown to exploit and trade in the unsettled parts of British North America, mostly down the Mackenzie River. It was extended in 1838 to include lands west of Rupert's Land, the British Columbia interior, and again in 1849 to bring Vancouver Island under its authority.[1] The inclusion of Vancouver Island under the HBC's licence in 1849 had a very specific clause attached to it: the Company was obligated to establish a Crown colony on the island if it wanted to maintain its monopoly.[2] Fort Victoria, established in 1843, became the new capital of the colony. This requirement was a reaction by the British to the increasing settlement in Oregon and concerns of American expansion northwards, as well as growing British concerns relating to the cost of colonial administration. As Barry Gough, a maritime historian based in British Columbia, mentions in his examination of the early administration of the colony, the British government "could not invest even a farthing in colonial development: it

---

[1] British Foreign Office to [None], 1849, National Archives of the UK, CO 305/1. *The Colonial Despatches of Vancouver Island and British Columbia 1846–1871*, ed. James Hendrickson and the Colonial Despatches project (Victoria: University of Victoria), http://bcgenesis.uvic.ca/getDoc.htm?id=V495PA03.scx. Accessed September 28, 2016.
[2] Wilson Duff, "The Fort Victoria Treaties," *BC Studies* 3 (1969): 6.

had to be self-sustaining in every sense other than naval protection."[3] The financial burden of the colony would be carried by the Company.

Despite the extension of the Company's charter by the British Crown, the legal ownership of the land remained uncertain. As had been the practice in other parts of British North America, it was considered necessary to address the question of the proprietary rights of the colony's Indigenous population. British instructions were clear that questions relating to the extinguishment of any "Indian title are equally obligatory on the Company."[4] Because of their admitted ignorance of the circumstances relating to the region's Indigenous peoples, the Colonial Office and the Committee of the HBC relied upon James Douglas, the chief factor at Victoria and governor of the colony from 1851 to 1864. He had considerable experience with Vancouver Island's Indigenous peoples. A Company man since the merger of the Northwest Company and the HBC in 1821, Douglas had been posted to the Pacific coast in 1830 at Fort Vancouver (near present-day Portland, Oregon). By 1839, he had risen to chief factor of the Columbia District, overseeing the HBC's operations in the region.[5] He was also well acquainted with Vancouver Island, as he had made the recommendation for the establishment of Fort Victoria in 1842, having described the area as "a perfect 'Eden,' in the midst of the dreary wilderness of the Northwest coast."[6]

Douglas was quick to realize that if the colony was to succeed, he needed to secure lands from the local Salish communities. In an 1849 dispatch to Archibald Barclay, secretary of the Company, he stated that "some arrangements should be made as soon as possible with the native Tribes for the purchase of their lands." He also recommended that village, fishing, and agricultural sites "be reserved for their benifit [sic] and fully secured to them by law."[7] In London, Barclay responded, anticipating Douglas's questions by outlining general principles of treaty making and granting him authority to negotiate treaties. Referencing the varying practices among the other colonies, such as the recent conclusion of the Treaty of Waitangi

---

[3] Barry Gough, "Crown, Company, and Charter: Founding Vancouver Island Colony – A Chapter in Victorian Empire Making," *BC Studies* 176 (2012/13): 13.
[4] British Foreign Office to [None], 1849.
[5] Margaret A. Ormsby, "DOUGLAS, Sir JAMES," in *Dictionary of Canadian Biography*, vol. 10, University of Toronto/Université Laval, 2003–, accessed October 5, 2016, http://www.biographi.ca/en/bio/douglas_james_10E.html.
[6] James Douglas to James Hargrave, February 5, 1843, in *The Hargrave Correspondence, 1821–1845*, ed. George P. de T. Glazebrook (Toronto: Champlain Society, 1938), 420–1.
[7] James Douglas to Archibald Barclay, September 3, 1849, in *Fort Victoria Letters 1846–1851*, ed. Hartwell Bowsfield (Winnipeg: Hudson's Bay Record Society, 1979).

by the New Zealand Company in 1840, Barclay provided some parameters but left the specifics largely to Douglas's experience and discretion:

> The Governor and Committee authorize you to adopt in treating with the natives of Vancouver Island but the extent to which it is to be acted upon must be left to your own discretion and will depend upon the character of the tribes and other circumstances. The natives will be confirmed in the possession of their lands as long as they occupy and cultivate them themselves, but will not be allowed to sell or dispose of them to any private person, the right to the entire soil having been granted to the Company by the Crown. The right of fishing and hunting will be continued to them, and when their lands are registered, and they conform to the same conditions with which other settlers are required to comply, they will enjoy the same rights and privileges.[8]

With those instructions, Douglas was largely free to establish his own policies for dealing with the colony's Indigenous peoples.

Left to his own devices, Douglas undertook to secure the lands around the vital posts of the HBC on Vancouver Island and the lands between the Haro and Juan de Fuca straits. These lands were required for the development of the colony and the economic interests of the Company. He negotiated his "deeds of conveyance" around Victoria by negotiating with the specific groups he believed held ownership of those areas; as Wilson Duff, former curator of anthropology at the British Columbia Provincial Museum, noted, the treaties corresponded to different families or "septs."[9] Douglas concluded nine agreements in 1850, which subdivided all the lands between Cadboro Bay and Sheringham Point, with the six Songhees, two Klallam, and one T'souk groups.

Interestingly, these first agreements were concluded with the Indigenous representatives by their signing (or rather making their mark) on a blank sheet of paper where the terms of the agreement would only later be added. The specific language for the treaty was finalized by the HBC and conveyed to Douglas through a letter from Barclay only in August 1850, a few months after the initial treaties were concluded.[10] The diversifying commercial

---

[8] Archibald Barclay to James Douglas, December 17, 1849, London Correspondence Books Outwards, BC Archives, A, C, 20, v.7.
[9] Duff, "Fort Victoria Treaties," 43.
[10] Archibald Barclay to James Douglas, August 16, 1850, London Correspondence Books Outwards, BC Archives, A, C, 20, v.i7.

interests of the Company led to the signing of two more agreements in 1851, negotiated in two parts with the Kwakiutl around Fort Rupert. Douglas wanted to secure access to the coal deposits in the area and prevent any further conflict between the Company miners and the Indigenous population who claimed the land around the deposits. In 1852, more treaties were concluded to cover the Saanich Peninsula in response to Indigenous demands for compensation after the opening of a saw mill. The final treaty was concluded two years later at Nanaimo to secure another coal deposit. The fourteen "deeds of conveyance" were almost all identical in nature.

ORAL AND WRITTEN ACCOUNTS OF THE 1852 SAANICH TREATIES

The presence of the WSÀNEC, historically known as Saanich, throughout the peninsula and on the islands in the Haro Strait was well known to the HBC. The arrival of European explorers and fur traders in the region transformed the various relationships there. As Elder Dave Elliott notes in *Saltwater People*, the WSÀNEC were in constant conflict with Haida and Kwagulths peoples, who were armed with European weapons.[11] By the early nineteenth century, WSÀNEC winter villages from the Gulf Islands had relocated to the peninsula, most likely as a means of protection from attacks by marauding northern Indigenous peoples.[12] As attacks persisted even on the peninsula itself, the WSÀNEC had formed three distinctive villages by the time of the establishment of Fort Victoria in 1843: Tsartlip in Brentwood Bay, Tsawout in Saanichton Bay, and Tseycum in Patricia Bay. The name "Saanich" has been attributed to this specific peninsula since the time of some of the first European records for the region. The Hudson's Bay Company records for Fort Langley record the presence of "Sanch," "Sanatch," and "Sandish" Indians in the southeastern portions of Vancouver Island. The Company's records also show the first census of the WSÀNEC in 1830, conducted by Archibald McDonald, with a population of 60 men listed under the name "Sanutch."[13]

Today the Vancouver Island Treaties (long known as the "Douglas Treaties" by the HBC and the Crown), including the treaties with the

---

[11] *Saltwater People, as told by Dave Elliott Sr.: A Resource Book for the Saanich Native Studies Program*, ed. Janet Poth (Saanich, BC: Native Education, School District 63, 1990), 62.

[12] Wayne P. Suttles, "The Economic Life of the Coast Salish of Haro and Rosario Straits," in *Coast Salish and Western Washington Indians*, vol. II (New York: Garland, 1974), 21.

[13] Archibald McDonald, "Indian Census, Letter and Reports from Sundry Persons to Governor George Simpson and Council from June 1828 to August 1830," HBC Archives, Ms.D.4/123, pp. 66–72.

WSÀNEC, are the source of considerable discussion and debate. While the clauses of the treaties appear simple, the interpretation of their terms is complex, especially when one considers what the different parties understood as the spirit and the intent of the treaties. Essentially, were they land purchases or treaties establishing formal relations between two parties? The 1852 "Deed of conveyance" found in the archives of the Hudson's Bay Company shows the Company's perspective. It states that the Indigenous signatories "do consent to surrender, entirely and for ever, to James Douglas, the agent of the Hudson's Bay Company in Vancouver Island, that is to say, for the Governor, Deputy Governor, and Committee of the same, the whole of the lands."[14] A straight reading of both this text and Douglas's May 1852 report informs us that, from the European context, there was a transfer of land title from one group, the assembled WSÀNEC of the region, to another, the Hudson's Bay Company acting on behalf of the British Crown by right of their charter. For the WSÀNEC there was no transfer of land but an agreement for peaceful relations and sharing of land.

While there are no contemporary records showing the Indigenous perspective of these events, oral history and tradition in the WSÀNEC communities present a different understanding of the treaty negotiations. Most notably, in 1934, the *Victoria Daily Times* published an interview with WSÀNEC Chief Daniel Latasse, a prominent hereditary chief who strove to protect the WSÀNEC communities from the ever-growing spread of settlement and government interference. Although the article stated that the account was of Chief Latasse's experiences, the journalist's lack of familiarity with oral traditions makes it unclear whether Latasse was recalling stories from his own observations or those of his father's experience. Starting with the initial arrival of the HBC men to the region in the 1840s, Chief Latasse recounts the early relationship between the first settlers and the region's original inhabitants: "In the years around 1850 the Indians considered that there was lots of land and had no thought of or fear of extensive settlement by white men. The whites were welcomed, they provided a fine market for the large amount of fur which the tribesmen annually collected."[15] For Latasse, the relationships between the WSÀNEC and

---

[14] "Conveyance of Land to Hudson's Bay Company by Indian Tribes," in *Papers Connected with the Indian Land Question, 1850–1875* (Victoria: R. Wolfenden, 1875).

[15] "105 Years in Victoria and Saanich!" *Victoria Daily Times*, July 4, 1934. It should be noted that Pagett may have inflated Chief Latasse's age to 105. See http://staff.royalbcmuseum.bc.ca/2016/11/03/david-latasse-of-saanich-and-songhees-heritage.

the settlers was largely focused on trade with little interference or impact on the lands occupied by the WSÀNEC who were to the north of Fort Victoria.

As will be seen, Douglas's report referred simply to the establishment of the saw mill as the instigator for the treaties, but Chief Latasse provided a more rounded picture of the events leading up to them: "For some time after the whites commenced building their settlement they ferried their supplies ashore. Then they desired to build a dock, where ships could be tied up close to shore. Explorers found suitable timbers could be obtained at Cordova Bay, and a gang of whites, Frenchmen and Kanakas [Hawaiians] were sent there to cut piles." As a result, a group of warriors, led by chiefs Hotutstun and Whutsaymullet, "manned two big canoes and came down the coast to see what damage was being done and to demand pay from Douglas," but their presence frightened the lumbermen into believing they were about to be attacked, so they spread "the cry that the Indians were on the warpath."

Chief Latasse's account provides many details about the discussions and agreements made during the first encounter at the mill site and subsequent meetings. During the first meeting in early February 1852, Douglas arrived from Fort Victoria to hear the complaints of the chiefs concerning the lack of compensation for the harvesting of lumber on their lands. Latasse relates that the governor promptly agreed to their request for compensation and "ordered two bales of blankets brought from the fort and gave each chief one of them. There was no suggestion that the compensation was for anything other than the timber, no suggestion of title to any land was involved in that matter." According to Latasse, it was the second meeting that focused on the broader issue of the relationship, with Douglas saying that "lands not needed by the natives might be occupied by the whites. The Indians were to have reserved to their use some choice camping sites, were to have hunting rights everywhere and fishing privileges in all waters, with certain water areas exclusively reserved to the use of the tribes."

Latasse's account provides unique insight into how the language used by colonial officials during treaty making was understood. With respect to the need for a written document, Douglas explained through his translator, HBC clerk Joseph Mackay, that the "object of the writing was to assure the Hudson's Bay Company peaceful and continued use of land tracts suitable for cultivation." For the WSÀNEC, this wording implied that the agreement with Douglas was one of peace and friendship, as well as an agreement to share the land according to WSÀNEC conditions. Latasse recounted Douglas's agreement to these conditions, stating, "I heard him give his personal word that, if we agreed to let the white man use parts of our land to grow food, all would be to the satisfaction of the

Indian peoples. Blankets and trade were to be paid. We, knowing a crop grows each year, looked for gifts each year." Latasse's understanding of the agreement made in February 1852 was clear: it was an agreement to restore the peace and compensate the WSÀNEC for settler usage of the land, but they had "sold no part of Saanich" to the HBC.[16]

The oral history of the 1852 agreements is not limited to Chief Latasse's account. In her study of the oral history of the treaties at the University of Victoria, Janice Knighton documents how the knowledge of the treaties was transmitted within WSÀNEC communities. Knighton notes that accounts such as those by Latasse were part of the community's teachings. WSÀNEC Elder Gabriel Bartleman, a key leader in the region, recounted that community meetings often turned to the matter of the treaty, commonly known as "Douglas's word":

> meetings usually were on weekends, and whenever my father was called to sit in at a meeting I went along with him, and [that's] how I happened to hear whatever was discussed. I was told to be quiet and sit down and listen. Many of our older people were very disciplined people, and we were told that when there was something especially good to listen to that we should do so ... Usually that was about "Douglas'[s] word." The understanding that he gave the people at home was that their way of life was never ever going to be disturbed, that they would always be able to take their food and travel as they did before, that nothing would ever be taken away from them.[17]

Just as in the account presented by Chief Latasse, Elder Bartleman presents a broader understanding of the WSÀNEC perspective on the treaty than is found in the historical record left by James Douglas. In addition, the oral account is a clear indication of how this important moment was transmitted through the years.[18] In his *Saltwater People* booklet, Dave Elliott shares his teachings on the treaties with editor Janet Poth. In an account similar to the wording of Latasse in 1934, Elder Elliott reflects the clear transmission of the WSÀNEC understanding of the treaties as agreements for peaceful relations and sharing. In discussing the actual signing of the treaty documents, Elliott recounts how the WSÀNEC viewed the

---

[16] "105 Years in Victoria and Saanich!"
[17] Janice Knighton, "Oral History of the 1852 Saanich Treaty" (MA thesis, University of Victoria, 2004), 9–10.
[18] Ibid., 29.

items being offered by the HBC to sign the treaties: "I think these are peace offerings. I think Douglas means to keep the peace. I think these are the signs of the cross ... This means Douglas is sincere."[19] While Latasse made little reference to the content of the treaty texts, Elder Elliott presents a comparison between them and his community's teachings: "They thought it was just a sign of sincerity and honesty. This was the sign of their God. It was the highest order of honesty. It wasn't much later they found out actually they were signing their land away by putting those crosses out there. They didn't know what it said on that paper."[20] This oral history also shows the dissatisfaction felt by the WSÀNEC communities in the years that followed, as Elder Elliott lists how their lands were lost and their hunting and fishing grounds were encroached upon. In his final words, Elliott sums up his view of the treaties: "The treaty with James Douglas said we could hunt and fish as formerly. We can't. It doesn't live up to its promises."[21]

Turning to the account written by James Douglas, we find a much less detailed report than the oral history of the WSÀNEC. It fell to Douglas, as colonial governor in 1852, to execute and document the required land purchase. As a consequence of the nascent development of the colony, there is only one contemporary account of the conclusion of the 1852 agreements: the one written by Douglas himself reporting on the transaction. In a letter of March 18, 1852, to Archibald Barclay on the activities of the colony, Douglas tersely described the reason for the treaty, the details of the sale and the extent of land it surrendered.[22]

In 1852, interest in establishing a saw mill in the lands north of the burgeoning settlement around the fort led Douglas to conclude two more "deeds of conveyance." He stated that these purchases were required because the WSÀNEC wanted compensation for a proposed saw mill being built. He further reported that he sought to purchase the entire region in two blocks: the South and North Saanich lands. The southern purchase, listed as "South Saanich" in the HBC records, was concluded on February 7 and covers the lands from the northern limit of the Chekonen Songhees purchase of 1850 to Cowichan Head and was signed by ten representatives

---

[19] *Saltwater People*, 72.
[20] Ibid.
[21] Ibid, 73.
[22] James Douglas to Archibald Barclay, March 18, 1852, HBC Archives, Correspondence Outward to HBC on Affairs of Vancouver Island Colony, A.11/73 fos 299–501.

of that "tribe."[23] Four days later, Douglas reported that he signed a second treaty, the "North Saanich" deed, for the lands encompassing the entire Saanich Peninsula north of a line drawn from Cowichan Head to the source of Saanich Inlet. As had been his manner with the other purchases, Douglas wanted to conclude specific purchases with the individual groups holding those lands. He stated, however, that "finding it impossible to discover among the numerous claimants, the real owners of the land in question, and there being much difficulty in adjusting such claims, I thought it advisable to purchase the whole of the Sanitch [sic] country, as a measure that would save much future trouble and expense."[24] Because of this different approach to the treaty, 118 names appear (according to Douglas, the entire adult male population) on the final deed. When Douglas was negotiating the South and North Saanich treaties, he also undertook a census for the lands in question. He recognized a split between the group into those around Mount Douglas – corresponding to the signatories of the South Saanich treaty – with 56 people, and those of the "Saanich Arm" – the signatories of the North Saanich deed – with 683 people.

Based on Douglas's 193 words, the entire transaction was undertaken with the clear intent of securing a full cession of lands from the area's Indigenous population. He provided no context has to how the WSÁNEC came to demand compensation. He did not even reference the fact that he had a stake in the mill itself as an investor. His account of the proceedings was also very straightforward. He stated that he tried to discern which individual community would have specific ownership of the mill site, but being unable to do so, he decided to include all the communities and therefore conclude an agreement for the entire region. In his account, reaching an agreement was quick and not difficult; he stated that he "succeeded in effecting that purchase in a general convention of the Tribe." From his perspective, he had no doubt that those attending the negotiations were fully aware and accepting of the land cession, as shown by their receiving payment for the transaction. His written record has no further information as to how the concept of the land cession was presented or what sort of questions the 128 Indigenous signatories may have had in response to the governor's request for a treaty. For Douglas, Barclay, and the rest of the colonial administration, this brief account was all that was required to confirm the permanent transfer of the title to all the lands in the Saanich Peninsula to the Company, and therefore to the Crown.

---

[23] Duff, "Fort Victoria Treaties," 20.
[24] Douglas to Barclay, March 18, 1852.

THE SAANICH TREATIES AND THE COURTS

While the understanding that the 1852 agreements were purchases of Indigenous lands by representatives of the settler state has remained constant from the HBC period to that of the Colony of British Columbia and the Dominion of Canada, the differing understanding that the 1852 agreements were treaties establishing new relationships continues to be part of WSÁNEC oral tradition. The legal decisions surrounding the Vancouver Island Treaties, largely due to the simple and limited treaty text and the availability of oral history, are good examples of the application of the courts' principles of treaty interpretation. Most notably, the decisions confirm that treaties should be given fair, large, and liberal interpretation in a manner most likely to have been understood by Indigenous signatories. In addition, ambiguity in treaty text must be interpreted in a way that does not prejudice Indigenous understandings at the time of treaty making.

In 1964, the first case regarding the treaties on Vancouver Island made its way to the Supreme Court. The "deeds of conveyance" negotiated by Douglas in the 1850s were not considered by the Crown as "treaties." The Crown argued that as the texts did not include the word "treaty," the deeds were merely land acquisitions and not formal treaties with prescribed terms, and, further, the Crown was not a party to the agreement. In its *White and Bob* decision, with respect to the last treaty concluded in 1854 at Nanaimo, the Supreme Court held that a "deed of conveyance" of the HBC was "more than a mere agreement for the sale of land made between a private vendor and a private purchaser"; it was a treaty between the Crown and Indigenous nations because the HBC was the Imperial Crown's representative on Vancouver Island at the time.[25] Despite the rather definitive nature of this ruling, there was no blanket recognition of the treaties concluded on Vancouver Island in the 1850s. Each one had to be considered individually. Such was the case in the *Saanichton Marina Ltd v. Claxton* decision rendered in 1987.[26] The case revolved around a proposal to redevelop a marina at Saanichton Bay on the western shore of the Saanich Peninsula, next to the Tsawout Reserve. In addition to increasing the marina's capacity, a breakwater was proposed that would shelter the harbour. The Tsawout First Nation saw the proposal as an infringement of their treaty-protected fishing rights, blockaded the bay, and then started a legal challenge.[27]

---

[25] *R. v. White and Bob*, [1965] 52 D.L.R. (2d) 481.
[26] *Saanichton Marina Ltd v. Claxton*, [1987] 2 CNLR 48 (BCSC).
[27] Hamar Foster, "The Saanichton Bay Marina Case: Imperial Law, Colonial History and Competing Theories of Aboriginal Title," *UBC Law Review* 23, no. 3 (1989): 637.

After a long and wide-ranging series of rulings and appeals, where government representatives argued that the 1852 treaty was not binding on the Crown but only on the HBC and that the signatory First Nations did not have a right to fish in the bay because it was not geographically defined in the agreement, the Supreme Court of British Columbia reaffirmed the 1964 *White and Bob* decision that the Saanich Treaties were legally binding on the Crown because the HBC had been an "instrument of imperial policy and a trustee of the Imperial government."[28] By doing so, the Court confirmed that both Douglas and the ancestors of the Tsawout First Nation were competent to conclude a mutually binding treaty. Addressing the Crown's argument that the treaty did not recognize a right to a fishery, Justice Meredith referred to cases such as the 1985 *Simon* decision relating to the Peace and Friendship Treaties of the Atlantic region, and to the language of the treaty that the Indigenous fishery would continue "as formerly." He recognized the right embedded in the treaty, which stated that "it is clear that the word 'fishery' may be used to denote not only the right to catch fish but also the place where the right can be exercised. The Indians do not claim in this case any proprietary interest in the sea bed of the bay or a right, contractual or otherwise, to a fishing ground in the bay. The *sui generis* right they claim is to carry on the fishery as formerly in the bay."

The ruling of the Court of Appeal in the *Saanichton Marina* case is a direct application of the legal principles for treaty interpretation. Where the Crown sought to limit the scope of the agreement to the specific settler signatory, namely the Hudson's Bay Company, the Tsawout First Nation argued that Canada was the successor state to the original colony and bound by the terms of the treaty. By agreeing with the First Nation position, Justice Meredith reconciles the notion that the members of the WSÀNEC people who concluded an agreement with James Douglas saw him as the representative of the ultimate settler authority, the Imperial Crown, just as Douglas's commission as colonial governor affirms. The ruling's statements regarding the fishery rights stemming from the treaty also build on the rules of treaty interpretation. The fishery's "as formerly" clause is clearly difficult to interpret, and again Justice Meredith broadens the Crown's interpretation of the treaty right to bring it more in line with the understanding of the Tsawout First Nation. By doing so, he reaffirms the legitimacy of the oral history of the 1852 treaty, where "Douglas's word" was seen as protecting the interest of the WSÀNEC.

---

[28] *Saanichton Marina Ltd v. Claxton*.

FURTHER READINGS

Wilson Duff. "The Fort Victoria Treaties." *BC Studies* 3 (1969): 3–57.

Raymond Frogner. "'Innocent Legal Fictions': Archival Convention and the North Saanich Treaty of 1852." *Archivaria* 70 (2010): 45–94.

Stephen Royle. *Company, Crown and Colony: The Hudson's Bay Company and Territorial Endeavour in Western Canada.* London: I.B. Tauris, 2011.

Saltwater People, as told by Dave Elliott Sr.: A Resource Book for the Saanich Native Studies Program. Ed. Janet Poth. Saanich, BC: Native Education, School District 63, 1990.

QUESTIONS FOR DISCUSSION

1. Read the following excerpts and identify how the understandings of the two parties differ or are similar on what was agreed to in the meetings of February 1852:

   Chief David Latasse, interviewed by Frank Pagett, "105 Years in Victoria and Saanich!," *Victoria Daily Times,* **July 4, 1934**
   When Douglas met with Chief Hotutston in 1852, and discussed with him and his sub-chiefs the allotment of lands to the Hudson's Bay Company, it was arranged that lands not needed by the natives might be occupied by the whites. The Indians were to have reserved to their use some choice camping sites, were to have hunting rights everywhere and fishing privileges in all waters, with certain water areas exclusively reserved to the use of the tribes ... In return for the use of meadow lands and open prairie tracts of Saanich, the white people would pay to the tribal chieftains a fee in blankets and goods. That was understood by us all to be payable each year.

   Letter from James Douglas to Archibald Barclay, March 18, 1852
   I succeeded in effecting that purchase in a general convention of the Tribe; who individually subscribed the Deed of Sale, reserving for their use, only the village sites and potatoe patches, and I caused them to be paid the sum of £109.7.6 in woollen goods which they preferred to money. That purchase includes all the land north of a line extending from Mount Douglas, to the south end of the Sanitch Inlet, bounded by that Inlet and the Canal de Arro, as traced on the map, and contains nearly 50 square miles or 32,000 statute acres of land.

2. How does the historical record limit our understanding of these events of 1852?
3. Why does the WSÀNEC oral history provide more context of the 1852 event than Douglas's account?
4. How do the courts reconcile the competing perspectives of these treaties?

DOCUMENTS

Treaty Text: Treaties with Saanich Tribe, 1852, "Conveyance of Land to Hudson's Bay Company by Indian Tribes," in *Papers Connected with the Indian Land Question, 1850–1875* (Victoria: R. Wolfenden, 1875)

Saanich Tribe – South Saanich

Know all men that we, the chiefs and people of the Saanich Tribe, who have signed our names and made our marks to this deed on the sixth day of February, one thousand eight hundred and fifty-two, do consent to surrender, entirely and for ever, to James Douglas, the agent of the Hudson's Bay Company in Vancouver Island, that is to say, for the Governor, Deputy Governor, and Committee of the same, the whole of the lands situated and lying between Mount Douglas and Cowichan Head, on the Canal de Haro, and extending Thence to the line running through the centre of Vancouver Island, north and South.

The conditions of our understanding of this sale is this, that our village sites and enclosed fields are to be kept for our own use, for the use of our children, and for those who may follow after us and the land shall be properly surveyed hereafter. It is understood, however, that the land itself, with these small exceptions, becomes the entire property of the white people for ever; it is also understood that we are at liberty to hunt over the unoccupied lands, and to carry on our fisheries as formerly.

We have received, as payment, Forty-one pounds thirteen shillings and four pence.

In token whereof, we have signed our names and made our marks at Fort Victoria, on the 7th day of February, one thousand eight hundred and fifty-two.

(Signed)
Whut-Say-Mullet his X mark and 9 others
Witness to signatures, (signed)
Joseph William McKay, Clerk H.B. Co's service
Richd. Golledge, Clerk

Saanich Tribe – North Saanich

Know all men, that we the chiefs and people of the Saanich Tribe, who have signed our names and made our marks to this deed on the eleventh day of February, one thousand eight hundred and fifty-two, do consent to surrender, entirely and for ever, to James Douglas, the agent of the Hudson's Bay Company in Vancouver Island, that is to say, for the Governor, Deputy Governor, and Committee of the same, the whole of the lands situated and lying as follows, viz: – commencing at Cowichan Head and following the coast of the Canal de Haro North-west nearly to Saanich Point, or Quana-sung; from thence following the course of the Saanich Arm to the point where it terminates; and from thence by a straight line across country to said Cowichan Head, the point of commencement, so as to include all the country and lands, with the exceptions hereafter named, within those boundaries.

The conditions of our understanding of this sale is this, that our village sites and enclosed fields are to be kept for our own use, for the use of our children, and for those who may follow after us and the land shall be properly surveyed hereafter. It is understood, however, that the land itself, with these small exceptions, becomes the entire property of the white people for ever; it is also understood that we are at liberty to hunt over the unoccupied lands, and to carry on our fisheries as formerly.

We have received, as payment [*amount not stated*]

(Signed)
Hotutstun his X mark and 117 others.
Witness to signatures, (signed)
Joseph William McKay, Clerk H.B. Co's service
Richd. Golledge, Clerk

Excerpt from an interview with Chief David Latasse, conducted by Frank Pagett, "105 Years in Victoria and Saanich!," *Victoria Daily Times*, July 4, 1934, AMICUS: 7727707

In the years around 1850 the Indians considered that there was lots of land and had no thought of or fear of extensive settlement by white men. The whites were welcomed, they provided a fine market for the large amount of fur which the tribesmen annually collected. The trade goods the whites gave in return for the furs were highly regarded. The whites at that time also had no idea of asking the Indians to give up their lands. Areas proposed to be used by whites were limited and the gifts of blankets and trade goods were nominal annual dues ...

For some time after the whites commenced building their settlement they ferried their supplies ashore. Then they desired to build a dock, where ships could be tied up close to shore. Explorers found suitable timbers could be obtained at Cordova Bay, and a gang of whites, Frenchmen and Kanakas [Hawaiians] were sent there to cut piles. The first thing they did was set a fire which nearly got out of hand, making such smoke as to attract attention of the Indians for forty miles around.

Chief Hotutstun of Salt Spring sent messengers to Chief Whutsaymullet of the Saanich tribes, telling him that the white men were destroying his heritage and would frighten away fur and game animals. They met and jointly manned two big canoes and came down the coast to see what damage was being done and to demand pay from Douglas. Hututstun was interested by the prospect of sharing in any gifts made to Whutsaymullet but also, indirectly, as the Chief Paramount of all the Indians of Saanich.

... As the two canoes rounded the point and paddled into Cordova Bay they were seen by camp cooks of the logging party, who became panic stricken. Rushing into the woods they yelled the alarm of Indians on the warpath. Every Frenchman and Kanaka dropped his tool and took to his heels, fleeing through the woods to Victoria. As they ran they spread the cry that the Indians were on the warpath.

Douglas hastened to meet the two chieftains and found that the party, with scarcely a weapon other than a few fish spears, were camping in harmony with the white members of the logging detachment. All that was asked was pay for trees cut and damage wrought, which Douglas promptly agreed was right and proper. He ordered two bales of blankets brought from the fort and gave each chief one of them. There was no suggestion that the compensation was for anything other than the timber, no suggestion of title to any land was involved in that matter. That fact is important in view of claims made later, that other big talks for use of land, in which similar small payments of goods and trade were made to Indians to pay for title to land given by the Indian chieftains.

It is in this matter that the Indians claim they have been unjustly treated. When Douglas met with Chief Hotutston in 1852, and discussed with him and his sub-chiefs the allotment of lands to the Hudson's Bay Company, it was arranged that lands not needed by the natives might be occupied by the whites. The Indians were to have reserved to their use some choice camping sites, were to have hunting rights everywhere and fishing privileges in all waters, with certain water areas exclusively reserved to the use of the tribes.

In return for the use of meadow lands and open prairie tracts of Saanich, the white people would pay to the tribal chieftains a fee in blankets and goods. That was understood by us all to be payable each year. It was so explained to us by Joseph MacKay, the interpreter for Governor Douglas. The governor himself solemnly assured us that all asked to be ratified would be entirely to the satisfaction of the Indians. He also stated that the only object of the writing was to assure the Hudson's Bay Company peaceful and continued use of land tracts suitable for cultivation. That was accompanied by [a] gift of a few blankets. We all understood that similar gifts would be made each year, what is now called rent.

More than eighty years ago I saw James Douglas, at the place now called Beacon Hill, stand before the assembled chiefs of the Saanich Indians with uplifted hand ... I heard him give his personal word that, if we agreed to let the white man use parts of our land to grow food, all would be to the satisfaction of the Indian peoples. Blankets and trade were to be paid. We, knowing a crop grows each year, looked for gifts each year, what is now called rent. Our chiefs then sold no part of Saanich.

Excerpt from letter from James Douglas to Archibald Barclay, March 18, 1852, HBC Archives reel 1M11.G1/140 / BC Archives A/C/20/Vi2

The steam saw Mill Company having selected as the site of their operations, the section of land marked upon the accompanying map north of Mount Douglas, which being within the limits of the Sanitch Country, those Indians came forward with a demand for payment, and finding it impossible, to discover among the numerous claimants, the real owners of the land in question, and there being much difficulty in adjusting such claims, I thought it advisable to purchase the whole of the Sanitch Country, as a measure that would save much future trouble and expense. I succeeded in effecting that purchase in a general convention of the Tribe; who individually subscribed the Deed of Sale, reserving for their use, only the village sites and potatoe patches, and I caused them to be paid the sum of £109.7.6 in woollen goods which they preferred to money. That purchase includes all the land north of a line extending from Mount Douglas, to the south end of the Sanitch Inlet, bounded by that Inlet and the Canal de Arro, as traced on the map, and contains nearly 50 square miles or 32,000 statute acres of land.

Excerpt from *Saanichton Marina Ltd. v. Claxton*, British Columbia Court of Appeal, March 30, 1989 (*Saanichton Marina Ltd. v. Claxton*, 1989 CanLII 2721 (BC CA)). Reprinted with permission of the Court of Appeal for British Columbia.

WAS THE 1852 AGREEMENT "A TREATY"?

[10] At trial, the Crown sought to contend that the treaty in question was not binding on the Crown upon the basis that James Douglas, in concluding agreements with the Indians, was implementing Hudson Bay Company policy and not Imperial government policy. Upon the basis of the reasoning in *R. v. White* (1964), 1964 CanLII 452 (BC CA), 52 W.W.R. 193, 50 D.L.R. (2d) 613, affirmed 1965 CanLII 591 (FC), 52 D.L.R. (2d) 48 In (S.C.C.) [B.C.], that position is untenable. Davey J.A. expressed his view at p. 197 as follows:

In the Charter granting Vancouver Island to the Hudson's Bay Company, it was charged with the settlement and colonization of that island. That was clearly part of the Imperial policy to head off American settlement of and claims to the territory. In that sense the Hudson's Bay Company was an instrument of Imperial policy. It was also the long-standing policy of the Imperial government and of the Hudson's Bay Company that the crown or the company should buy from the Indians their land for settlement by white colonists. In pursuance of that policy many agreements, some very formal, others informal, were made with various bands and tribes of Indians for the purchase of their lands. These agreements frequently conferred upon the grantors hunting rights over the unoccupied lands so sold. Considering the relationship between the crown and the Hudson's Bay Company in the colonization of this country, and the Imperial and corporate policies reflected in those agreements, I cannot regard Ex.8 as a mere agreement for the sale of land made between a private vendor and a private purchaser.

[11] In *R. v. Bartleman*, 1984 CanLII 547 (BC CA), 55 B.C.L.R. 78, [1984] 3 C.N.L.R. 114, 13 C.C.C. (3d) 488, 12 D.L.R. (4th) 73 (C.A.), Lambert J.A. in considering the same treaty as in the case at bar concluded that the agreement that was made between the Saanich people, on the one hand, and James Douglas on behalf of the Hudson's Bay Company, on the other hand, was a treaty for the purposes of s. 88 of the *Indian Act*. He referred to the earlier decision of this court in *R. v. White in* reaching that conclusion.

[12] I conclude the 1852 agreement was a treaty.

THE EFFECT OF THE TREATY

(a) The claims of the parties

[13] The Crown contended that it holds a proprietary right to the sea bed of Saanichton Bay and that the claim of the Indians sought to establish a competing proprietary right over the sea bed of Saanichton Bay. Objection was taken to any claim of a proprietary right for the following reasons:

(i) Such a claim is not supported by the ordinary grammatical meaning of the words of the agreement;
(ii) Such a claim would be inconsistent with the purpose of the agreement;
(iii) The Indians could not have understood the treaty to establish a proprietary right; and
(iv) Similarly worded treaties have not been held to create any proprietary right to "fishing grounds."

[14] The Crown contended that all the Indians received by the terms of the treaty was a right held in common with all other members of the public, to fish in Saanichton Bay.

[15] Counsel for the Tsawout Band replied that they do not seek to establish a proprietary interest in the sea bed of the bay. Rather, they claim the right to continue their fishing activities in this particular location, as provided in the treaty.

(b) Interpretation of Indian treaties – general principles

[16] In approaching the interpretation of Indian treaties the courts in Canada have developed certain principles which have been enunciated as follows:

(a) The treaty should be given a fair, large and liberal construction in favour of the Indians;
(b) Treaties must be construed not according to the technical meaning of their words, but in the sense that they would naturally be understood by the Indians;
(c) As the honour of the Crown is always involved, no appearance of "sharp dealing" should be sanctioned;
(d) Any ambiguity in wording should be interpreted as against the drafters and should not be interpreted to the prejudice of the Indians if another construction is reasonably possible;
(e) Evidence by conduct or otherwise as to how the parties understood the treaty is of assistance in giving it content.

...

[18] In *R. v. Fowler*, 1980 CanLII 201 (SCC), [1980] 2 S.C.R. 213, [1980] 5 W.W.R. 511, 53 C.C.C. (2d) 97, 9 C.E.L.R. 115, 113 D.L.R. (3d) 513, 32 N.R. 230 [B.C.], the Supreme Court of Canada had occasion to make

reference to the meaning of the word "fishery." Martland J. delivering the judgment of the court said at p. 223:

The meaning of the word "fishery" was considered by Newcombe J. in this Court in Reference as to the Constitutional Validity of Certain Sections of the Fisheries Act, 1914 [1928 CanLII 82 (SCC), [1928] S.C.R. 457], at p. 472:

"In Patterson on the Fishery Laws (1863) p. 1, the definition of a fishery is given as follows:

'A Fishery is properly defined as the right of catching fish in the sea, or in a particular stream of water; and it is also frequently used to denote the locality where such right is exercised.'

In Dr. Murray's New English Dictionary, the leading definition is:

'The business, occupation or industry of catching fish or of taking other products of the sea or rivers from the water.'"

The above definitions were quoted and followed by Chief Justice Davey in Mark Fishing v. United Fishermen & Allied Workers Union [(1972), 1972 CanLII 1016 (BC CA), 24 D.L.R. (3d) 585], at pp. 591 and 592. Chief Justice Davey at p. 592 added the words:

"The point of Patterson's definition is the natural resource, and the right to exploit it, and the place where the resource is found and the right is exercised."

[19] On the basis of these authorities it is clear that the word "fishery" may be used to denote not only the right to catch fish but also the place where the right can be exercised. The Indians do not claim in this case any proprietary interest in the sea bed of the bay or a right, contractual or otherwise, to a fishing ground in the bay. The sui generis right they claim is to carry on the fishery as formerly in the bay.

CAST OF CHARACTERS: 1852 SAANICH TREATIES

James Douglas: b. June 5/August, 1803; d. August 2, 1877

James Douglas was born in British Guyana in 1803 into a Scottish merchant family. After preparatory education in Scotland, Douglas joined the Northwest Company as an apprentice in the fur trade at the age of 16. After the merger of the Northwest and Hudson's Bay companies in 1821, he remained with the HBC and was regarded as a skilled trader. In 1826, he was sent by the Company to the Pacific coast operations, where he would remain for the rest of his career. In 1827, he married Amelia Connolly, the Métis daughter of HBC chief factor William Connolly. By 1839, Douglas had risen to the rank of chief factor at Fort Vancouver, the primary trading post in the Oregon Territory. His role and influence grew on the coast, as he coordinated most HBC activities in the region, exploring new regions, establishing new posts, such as Fort Victoria in 1843, and leading negotiations with Indigenous trade partners. After the relocation of the HBC to Vancouver Island after the signing of the Oregon Treaty in 1846 and the charter obligation to establish a colony in 1849, Douglas recognized the need to negotiate agreements with the region's Coast Salish, concluding 14 separate agreements, mostly near Victoria, between 1850 and 1854. Douglas was appointed governor of Vancouver Island in 1851, a position he held until his retirement in 1864.

David Latasse: b. c. 1858–63; d. May 2, 1936

David Latasse was a member and hereditary chief of the Tsartlip First Nation, which is part of the Saanich peoples, whose territory is centred on the Saanich Peninsula and southern Gulf Islands. Latasse advocated for the rights of his community and the Saanich against settler incursions into traditional lands. In the last decade of his life, he gained notoriety as a speaker in his native language at ceremonies, as the subject of an early film, and as a source of information via translators for newspaper reporters and at least one anthropologist.

THE MAKING OF THE VANCOUVER ISLAND TREATIES 155

Figure 5.1 Chief David Latasse, 1932. A prominent member and leader of the Tsartlip First Nation, David Latasse was considered to be a fount of traditional knowledge and an advocate for WSÀNEC rights and interests.
Source: Image PN 11781 courtesy of the Royal BC Museum and Archives.

Figure 5.2 James Douglas. As governor of Vancouver Island, James Douglas played a direct role in shaping Indigenous-settler relations in the new colony, although his more conciliatory approach was later rejected by the colonial assembly and his successors.

Source: Library and Archives Canada, C-003316.

Chapter 6
The Early Numbered Treaties: Treaty no. 6, 1876

On July 1, 1867, the *British North America Act* created the Dominion of Canada, and as part of the act, provisions were included to facilitate the admission of other British colonies to Canada, including Rupert's Land.[1] Much like its southern neighbour, the United States, the new Dominion of Canada believed that its future lay in its expansion across North America. As historian Gerald Friesen notes, "the main purpose of Canada was to achieve a separate political existence on the North American continent."[2] While the unification of the British colonies of Canada, New Brunswick, and Nova Scotia created a single block under the banner of the new Dominion of Canada in 1867, both of the major political parties had expansionist views. Prior to Confederation, the Liberal Party had long called for the annexation of Rupert's Land, the huge territory covering lands draining into Hudson Bay. And during the first session of the new Dominion Parliament, Conservative MP William McDougall called for the acquisition of Rupert's Land to be a government priority.

The rapid expansion of the United States across the west alarmed many Canadian politicians and citizens, who feared that the United States would attempt to take Rupert's Land as well. In the early years of the new Dominion of Canada, Canadian policy was largely reactionary to American expansionism, and the acquisition of western lands was seen as a vital part of Canada's economic future.[3] Without Rupert's Land, Canada would be hemmed into the northeast corner of the continent, unable to tap

---

[1] *Constitution Act*, 1867, 30 & 31 Victoria, c. 3 (U.K.), section 146.
[2] Gerald Friesen, *The Canadian Prairies: A History* (Toronto: University of Toronto Press, 2002), 171.
[3] J.R. Miller, *Compact, Contract, Covenant: Aboriginal Treaty-Making in Canada* (Toronto: University of Toronto Press, 2009), 129.

into the resources and riches of the Prairies, limited to the narrow strip of arable land between the Great Lakes, and unable to attract new immigrants to boost the population and drive commerce. The west was a necessary part of both the Conservative and Liberal parties' platforms, which both called for western settlement and the expansion of a working railway network allowing for access to greater markets and resources.[4] Settlement and railways became vital elements of the National Policy, an economic policy meant to encourage industry through high tariffs and the development of western resources, and were prominent in both the 1878 Conservative and 1896 Liberal platforms.

Immediately following the proclamation of Confederation, the Dominion began negotiations with Britain and the Hudson's Bay Company for the acquisition of the Company's charter to Rupert's Land.[5] The charter was secured and full control transferred by the British to the Dominion under the *Rupert's Land Act* of 1868 and the *Northwest Territories Transfer Order* in 1870. After the creation of Manitoba in 1870, the Macdonald Government proceeded to establish the administrative structure of the Northwest Territories. The *Northwest Territories Act* extended Canada's legal jurisdiction over the territories outside of Manitoba and made provisions for an administrative structure and application of Canadian law throughout those territories.[6] In an effort to induce more immigrants to the northwest, the 1872 *Dominion Lands Act*, also known as the *Homestead Act*, was introduced. The Act emulated a US initiative and provided settlers with "one-quarter section, or 160 acres, of free Government land for a 10 dollar registration fee with title conditional upon three years residency."[7]

Regardless of the newly acquired legal status of the Northwest Territories, the territories were devoid of any Canadian authority and were still the domain of Indigenous peoples. Canadian officials feared that the growing violence between the United States and its Indigenous populations in the so-called "Indian Wars" could spread north and incite communities on the Canadian side of the 49th parallel.[8] The Dominion of Canada had also inherited British colonial policies, grounded in the

---

[4] Friesen, *Canadian Prairies*, 175.
[5] Arthur J. Ray, Jim Miller, and Frank Tough, *Bounty and Benevolence: A History of Saskatchewan Treaties* (Montreal & Kingston: McGill-Queen's University Press, 2000), 49.
[6] *An Act to make further provision for the government of the Northwest Territories*, 1871, Chapter 16 (34 Victoria).
[7] P.B. Waite, *Canada 1874–1896: Arduous Destiny* (Toronto: McClelland & Stewart, 1977), 63.
[8] John Leonard Taylor, "Two Views on the Meaning of Treaties Six and Seven," in *The Spirit of the Alberta Indian Treaties*, ed. Richard Price (Edmonton: University of Alberta Press, 1999), 12.

1763 Royal Proclamation that aimed to conclude treaties with Indigenous nations, preferably in advance of the arrival of settlers.[9] While it was the Government's intent to conclude treaties from Lake Superior to the Rocky Mountains, Canada's approach was to proceed to conclude treaties when new lands were required. Partially a reflection of the economic situation of the new Dominion, this plan did not take into consideration the interests and circumstances of the Indigenous nations of the western Prairies.

By 1870, the year the Dominion of Canada formally became an actor on the western stage, the different Indigenous peoples of the prairie and parkland were in a complete state of social and economic transformation. Since the arrival of the first Europeans to the region in the mid-1700s, the way of life of the Saulteaux, Cree, Assiniboine, Blackfoot, and Dene, to name but a few, had been radically altered. The traditional cycle of hunting, trade, and diplomacy had been upended by the European fur trade, the spread of new diseases, and the arrival of settlers. As James Daschuk discusses in *Clearing of the Plains: Disease, Politics of Starvation, and the Loss of Aboriginal Life*, while the new trade with companies such as the HBC brought some material wealth to Indigenous communities, it also brought smallpox, measles, influenza, and scarlet fever, which decimated, in some cases, up to 75 per cent of communities.[10] At the same time, the movement of settlers into the American plains and the growing bison-robe market led to a highly commercialized hunt and a rapid decline in bison stock. With Indigenous communities being long dependent on bison for food, materials, and spirituality, internecine conflicts erupted over the dwindling resources, most notably between the Blackfoot Confederacy and a Cree and Assiniboine alliance in the early 1860s.[11] As treaty historian J.R. Miller indicates in his study of Indigenous-Crown treaties in Canada, on the eve of Canada's takeover of the western prairie from the HBC,

> there was great uneasiness among Native peoples in the region about their future with Canada. Inter-tribal war and epidemic disease had taken their toll among First Nations. The shrinkage of the bison resource, on which western Aboriginal peoples relied, was a cause of worry about the sustainability of their way of life.[12]

---

[9] Ibid., 13.
[10] James Daschuk, *Clearing the Plains: Disease, Politics of Starvation, and the Loss of Aboriginal Life* (Regina: University of Regina Press, 2013), 64–7.
[11] John Milloy, *The Plains Cree: Trade, Diplomacy and War, 1790 to 1870* (Winnipeg: University of Manitoba Press, 1988), 116.
[12] Miller, *Compact, Contract, Covenant*, 149.

Well aware of the growing agricultural settlement in American territories, Indigenous leaders feared dispossession and wanted to conclude treaties that would protect the bison herds and maintain their way of life, thus ensuring their survival.

As part of the obligations created by the transfer of the HBC charter, the *Rupert's Land and Northwest Territory Order* stated in paragraph 14 that "any claims of Indians to compensation for lands required for purposes of settlement shall be disposed of by the Canadian government."[13] Taking the form established by the 1850 Robinson Treaties,[14] the Crown negotiated 11 treaties between 1871 and 1921, covering the former lands controlled by the HBC. The first seven treaties, concluded between 1871 and 1877, covered the more southern regions of the Northwest Territories, what is today the southern half of Manitoba, Saskatchewan, and Alberta.[15] Similar to their model, the "Numbered Treaties" – as they were numbered 1 through 11 – promised reserve lands, annuities, and the continued right to hunt and fish on unoccupied Crown lands in exchange for Indigenous rights and interests in land.[16] However, these treaties also held clauses that were very similar to many of the civilization programs undertaken in central Canada for settlers. All treaties included clauses for schools or teachers to educate children, and agricultural implements were promised to assist Indigenous signatories in their transition toward an agricultural lifestyle.[17] Indigenous signatories were encouraged to settle on reserve lands in sedentary communities, learn agriculture, and receive settler education. The treaty commissioners explained that reserves were to assist Indigenous nations in adapting to a life without the bison hunt and that the government would assist them in the transition to agriculture by providing tools and other farming implements.

Not all Indigenous leaders in the Northwest Territories were comfortable or satisfied with the treaty terms being offered by the Crown's representatives, however. One such example was that of the influential Cree chief Mistahimaswka, often called Big Bear, who was displeased with the agreed

---

[13] *Order of Her Majesty in Council Admitting Rupert's Land and the North-Western Territory into the Union*, June 23, 1870, para. 14.

[14] See Chapter 4.

[15] Olive Dickason, *Canada's First Nations: A History of Founding Peoples from Earliest Times* (Don Mills, ON: Oxford University Press, 2002), 253.

[16] Ibid., 255.

[17] Sarah Carter, *Lost Harvests: Prairie Indian Reserve Farmers and Government Policy* (Montreal & Kingston: McGill-Queen's University Press, 1990), 56.

terms of Treaty 6 and did not adhere to it.[18] Refusing to sign the treaty for another seven years, Mistahimaswka and his followers moved freely across the prairie in an attempt to pressure the Crown to live up to the treaty terms as they were understood by First Nation signatories. After years of hardship due to disappearing bison, occasionally living off North-West Mounted Police rations, and with the numbers of his followers dwindling, Mistahimaswka finally agreed to sign an adherence to Treaty 6 in August 1883 and settle on a reserve, but only after government-supplied rations were denied them, causing starvation.[19] Mistahimaswka and his followers were one of the last major non-treaty First Nation groups in the Prairies.

While the treaties negotiated between 1871 and 1877 are based largely on the model of the 1850 Robinson Treaties, they are not all identical. The general form and scope of the agreements are similar, but the individual circumstances of the treaty signings led each agreement to have unique clauses.[20] The first of the treaties negotiated in Western Canada, Treaties 1 and 2, concluded in close succession in 1871, have fewer clauses than the treaties that would follow. For example, Treaties 1 and 2 are the only ones that do not specify that the First Nation signatories maintain an ongoing right to hunt and fish in the treaty area, or that smaller reserves are set aside for each community.[21] These treaties set aside 160 acres per family of five as reserve lands.

Treaty 3, covering the vital lands between Lake Superior and the Red River, was concluded in 1873, and heavy bargaining between the First Nations and the Crown reflected the strategic importance of the lands in question. The result was significant adjustments to treaty clauses, including larger reserve-land allocation, with 640 acres of land per family of five, guaranteed rights to hunt and fish on unoccupied Crown lands, and an annuity of $5 per person.[22] This treaty agreement effectively became the model for later agreements, such as Treaty 4, negotiated at Fort Qu'Appelle the following year. The terms of Treaty 4 used Treaty 3 as the starting point, and the differences were relatively minor.[23] This was again the case

---

[18] Alexander Morris, *The Treaties of Canada with the Indians of Manitoba and the North-West Territories* (Toronto: Belfords, Clarke and Co., 1880), 192.
[19] Hugh A. Dempsey, *Big Bear: The End of Freedom* (Toronto: Douglas and McIntyre, 1984), 91.
[20] Miller, *Compact, Contract, Covenant*, 183.
[21] Treaty 1, August 3, 1871, LAC, RG10, vol. 1846, D-10-a, IT-255, DIA no. 124, reel T-9939; Treaty 2, August 21, 1871, LAC, RG10, vol. 1846, D-10-a, IT-263, DIA no. 125, reel T-9939.
[22] Treaty 3, October 3, 1873, LAC, RG10, vol. 1846, D-10-a, IT-266, DIA no. 131, reel T-9939.
[23] Treaty 4, September 15, 1874, LAC, RG10, vol. 1846, D-10-a, IT-272, DIA no. 135, reel T-9939.

in 1875 during the negotiations for the lands around Lake Winnipeg in Treaty 5, except that the reserve-land allocation was 160 acres of reserve lands per family of five, as in Treaties 1 and 2, and the amounts for benefits were reduced.[24]

The treaty process continued the following year, when Treaty 6 was concluded at forts Carlton and Pitt. While Treaty 6 comprises all the basic terms from Treaty 3, it also has three unique terms: the inclusion of a medicine chest clause,[25] assistance in times of famine, and additional financial support once reserves were established.[26] When the final southern treaty was concluded in 1877, these three clauses of Treaty 6 were not repeated. Treaty 7 does have its own distinctive clauses, such as an allotment of guns, reduced numbers of agricultural implements, and seed stock in exchange for an increased number of cattle.[27] Another significant difference compared to the preceding treaties is that Treaty 7 states that the Crown will pay for teachers' salaries instead of the maintenance of school buildings.

While the Indigenous communities from the different treaty territories discussed and negotiated with the representatives of the Crown, the parties did not come away with the same understanding of what had transpired or been agreed to. As Jean Friesen notes in her article "Magnificent Gifts: The Treaties of Canada with the Indians of the Northwest 1869–76," the goal of Indigenous signatories was to ensure social and economic security for their people in an arrangement that balanced their need for lands, resources, and assistance with those of the Crown.[28] For the Crown, the treaties were land surrenders on a huge scale. Furthermore, in the eyes of the federal government, the treaties were needed to secure its authority over the west and to ensure peaceful relations as the lands filled with settlers. Once the treaties were signed, however, the government's focus was on the interests

---

[24] Treaty 5, September 20, 1875, LAC, RG10, vol. 1847, D-10-a, IT-285, DIA no. 149A, reel T-9939.

[25] In his study of medical services provided to western First Nations in the nineteenth century, Peter Naylor described a medicine chest as "a medical or pharmaceutical dispensary. The medicines which these chests held were contemporary to their period." These chests were used to treat injury and illness by serving as a pharmaceutical dispensary in more remote locations. They were commonly used by the military, the North-West Mounted Police, and country doctors. Peter Naylor, *An Examination of the Use of the Medicine Chest Among the Indians of British North America and Canada* (Ottawa: Department of National Health and Welfare, 1996), 2.

[26] Treaty 6, August 23, 1876, LAC, RG10, vol. 1847, D-10-a, IT-296, DIA no. 157A, reel T-9940.

[27] Treaty 7, September 22, 1877, LAC, RG10, vol. 1848, D-10-a, IT-310, DIA no. 163, reel T-99340.

[28] Jean Friesen, "Magnificent Gifts: The Treaties of Canada with the Indians of the Northwest 1869–1876," in *The Spirit of the Alberta Indian Treaties*, ed. Richard Price (Edmonton: University of Alberta Press, 1999), 207.

of settlers instead of the needs of Indigenous peoples in the west. Following a strict interpretation of the treaty terms as defined by the written text, the fulfilment of the treaty by the Department of Indian Affairs was nowhere near the expectation of signatory nations.[29] In the opinion of departmental officials, anything provided by the government that was beyond the narrow wording of the treaty text was due to the Crown's "bounty and benevolence." With the collapse of bison stocks and a goal of transforming the Northwest Territories into Canada's agricultural heartland, that benevolence proved to be very meagre. As James Daschuk describes in *Clearing of the Plains*, government policies and practices were increasingly harsh and controlling, reducing and withholding rations both as a cost-cutting measure and as a mechanism of social control.[30] Expecting both aid and support from government officials after the signing of treaties, signatory nations instead heard accusations of ungratefulness, orders to work on government farms to receive rations, and punishment for acts of resistance. They were forced to settle on reserves in order to receive any form of assistance, conditions worsened rapidly, and starvation was a common occurrence throughout the territories.[31] As Cree historian Joseph Dion states in *My Tribe, the Crees*, the Indigenous nations of the Plains, who believed they had signed the treaties as equals, saw themselves as being starved into subjugation.[32]

Whether they were aware of it or not, the act of signing a treaty brought Indigenous nations of the northwest under the jurisdiction of the Dominion of Canada and its laws.[33] The early Numbered Treaties – Treaties 1 through 7 – became the vehicle by which the Department of Indian Affairs implemented existing and future assimilation policies in the northwest, and the treaties concluded after 1899 allowed for the opening of the north and access to valuable natural resources.

ORAL AND WRITTEN ACCOUNTS OF TREATY 6, 1876

Within the first five years after asserting its authority over Rupert's Land, the government in Ottawa had instructed its officials to conclude five agreements with Indigenous nations. Initially, Ottawa's plan had

---

[29] Ray et al., *Bounty and Benevolence*, 200.
[30] Daschuk, *Clearing the Plains*, 133.
[31] Joseph F. Dion, *My Tribe, the Crees* (Calgary: Glenbow-Alberta Institute, 1979), 89.
[32] Ibid., 81.
[33] John Tobias, "Canada's Subjugation of the Plains Cree, 1879–1885" *Canadian Historical Review* 64, no. 4 (1983): 527.

been to spread the cost of the treaty-making process over several years to match it to the pace of non-Indigenous settlement. The Indigenous nations of what was now the Northwest Territories (NWT), however, had other ideas. As Alexander Morris, lieutenant-governor of Manitoba and the NWT, reported, they wanted to conclude agreements well in advance of the arrival of settlers and were unhappy with the government's delay in addressing their claims.[34] An area of specific concern was the land between the north and south branches of the Saskatchewan River, which had a very large Cree population. In a letter to the minister of the Interior in 1873, Morris estimated that there were some 5,000 "Plains Cree" and that a treaty should be concluded with them as soon as possible.[35] While there was a soft agreement from Ottawa that a treaty should be made, no firm direction was sent until 1875, when Morris reported that a crew from the Geological Survey had been stopped on the North Saskatchewan and told that they could proceed no further as the lands had not been dealt with through treaty.[36] Finally getting Ottawa's consent, Morris called for treaty meetings to be held in August and September of 1876 at Fort Carlton and Fort Pitt near the HBC trading posts. Negotiated over some seven days, a final agreement was reached and signed on August 23, 1876, at Fort Carlton, and just over two weeks later, on September 9, at Fort Pitt. The agreement covered some 121,000 square miles (313,388 square kilometres), which, according to the terms of the written text, "yielded, ceded and surrendered" the signatories' rights to the Crown.[37]

The negotiations that took place in the summer of 1876 quickly became part of the oral traditions and history of the Indigenous communities who signed the agreement. Despite the efforts to destroy Indigenous culture, knowledge, and identity through assimilationist policies such as residential schools, the oral history of the making of the treaty has been preserved by Treaty 6 Elders across Manitoba, Saskatchewan, and Alberta. In the mid-1970s, the Treaties and Right Research (TARR) program in Alberta conducted a series of interviews with Elders in Alberta and Saskatchewan "in an attempt to pin down what might be termed as

---

[34] Taylor, "Two Views," 16.
[35] Alexander Morris to Alexander Campbell, August 2, 1873, Morris Papers, PAM, MG12, B2, reel 7.
[36] Taylor, "Two Views," 16.
[37] Jill St. Germain, *Broken Treaties: United States and Canadian Relations with the Lakota and the Plains Cree, 1868–1885* (Lincoln: University of Nebraska Press, 2009), 102.

an Indian understanding of treaty."[38] They argued that the near totality of sources relating to treaties were created by the settler state and in a written form, and that these sources were "one-sided views of the treaties" that did not reflect Indigenous understanding. After several years of work, some 250 interviews were conducted, transcribed, and translated.[39] Since its creation, large portions of the interviews have been compiled by the Canadian Plains Research Centre for its "Indian History Film Project" at the University of Regina.[40]

One of the Elders interviewed was Fred Horse from Frog Lake First Nation, who was interviewed on three separate occasions by Hickey, Lightning, and Lee: the first in February 1974 and the others in March 1975. During his interviews, which were conducted in Cree, Elder Horse recounted his community's teachings and understanding of Treaty 6. Elder Horse indicated that his father had passed down this knowledge of the treaty and stressed to him the need to remember "the old stories" because "in the future, the stories would be needed, the people would use them. I don't know how he knew, but today people approach me for this information."[41] As Sharon Venne describes in "Understanding Treaty 6: An Indigenous Perspective," this method of oral transmission is the basis for learning and teaching in Cree society because "narrative is a powerful method for teaching many things, including the history of an oral people."[42] While one treaty account is discussed here, it cannot be taken as the definitive account of the treaty. As Venne states, "Elders have within their memories a collective history. No one Elder has all the information about a particular event."[43] What is presented here is but one part of the broader Indigenous understanding of Treaty 6.

---

[38] Lynn Hickey, Richard L. Lightning, and Gordon Lee, "TARR Interview with Elders Program," in *The Spirit of the Alberta Indian Treaties*, ed. Richard Price (Edmonton: University of Alberta Press, 1999), 103.
[39] Ibid., 104.
[40] The Canadian Plains Research Centre was a research institute of the University of Regina with a mandate to improve understanding and awareness of the Plains region in Canada. The Centre's collections and materials have become part of the University of Regina Press and are available on the University of Regina's website: http://ourspace.uregina.ca/handle/10294/26. Accessed June 6, 2017.
[41] Interview with Fred Horse, no. 3, March 14, 1975, interviewer: Richard L. Lightning, tape no. IH-186B, disc 25, Canadian Plains Research Centre, Indian History Film Project collection.
[42] Sharon Venne, "Understanding Treaty 6: An Indigenous Perspective," in *Aboriginal and Treaty Rights in Canada: Essays on Law, Equality, and Respect for Difference*, ed. Michael Asch (Vancouver: University of British Columbia Press, 2002), 174.
[43] Ibid., 177.

From the start of his account, Elder Horse indicated that there was skepticism toward Alexander Morris, the Queen's representative, as the treaty discussions "were made to sound encouraging."[44] The negotiations themselves lasted for a week because the Indigenous representatives did not agree with Morris's first treaty offer, so they spent considerable amounts of time discussing among themselves how best to respond. As Elder Horse stated,

> They told him [Morris] that first they would like to foresee the whole thing, as the Indian had some foresight, and were depending on it. That is what was said. That the agreement would never come to an end as long as the earth existed, that was the understanding. The representative agreed to that, so the Indians were also in agreement and accepted. That is when the elders agreed to the very important transaction.[45]

In both his 1974 and 1975 interviews, Elder Horse discussed the importance of the pipe ceremony that was conducted during the treaty negotiations. In his first interview, he stated that Morris "took the [pipe]stem in his right and raised it towards the sky." He then went into further detail about how the significance of the pipe was explained to the Queen's representative:

> They told the government officials that they were using their greatly respected power for a legal transaction (peace pipe). With the promises the Queen made, they didn't want them to ever come to an end. The government official mentioned at the time that the terms of the treaty should never come to an end. These promises were made with the smoking of the pipe. His lips touched the stem of the pipe. This wasn't done ordinarily for no reason. If one put a pipestem to his lips, that was a highly honored agreement and the government official did that. He smoked the pipestem (smoking of peace pipe).[46]

The inclusion of a pipe ceremony as part of the treaty negotiations shows the importance of the treaty process. As the interviewer Gordon Lee notes, "in the presence of the pipe, only the truth must be used and any

---

[44] Interview with Fred Horse, no. 1, February 18, 1974, interviewer: Richard L. Lightning, tape no. IH-86, disc 38, Canadian Plains Research Centre, Indian History Film Project collection.
[45] Ibid.
[46] Interview with Fred Horse, no. 3, March 14, 1975.

commitment made in its presence must be kept. In that sense, then, the only means used by the Indians to finalize an agreement or to ensure a final commitment was by use of the pipe."[47]

According to his father's teachings, the "representative" had wanted to negotiate only for land, grass, and timber, since "[t]he land would be to make a living agriculturally, the grass to feed the animals and the timber for building a home and also to keep the livestock," while the hunting of game and fish were excluded because they were needed to "make your living with." Of specific note, the amount of land to be "bought" was extremely limited. As Elder Horse described it, "the amount of land he [the treaty commissioner] bought he indicated like this, (open hand with extended thumb)."[48] This represented only the surface land that would allow for agriculture. As Hickey et al. note in their commentary on the Treaty 6 Elder interviews, this understanding was shared across the interviews, with Elders seeing the treaty as an "agreement to let white people use the land for farming," and it therefore concerned only the amount of land needed to till the soil, and nothing else.[49]

As his interview progressed, Elder Horse outlined the different promises made to the Indigenous signatories in exchange for their consent. He indicated that the treaty promised that schools would be "inside the reserve" – a likely comment of disapproval toward residential schools, which were rarely on reserve as promised in the treaty. They were also promised agricultural implements, as well as farm instructors to teach them about their use and about the grains for planting. Morris also promised that the Queen would help them in times of need, especially during times of starvation: "The Queen's arm is long and when you are faced with starvation, she will reach out to protect you. From that time on there will be rations and all kinds of things such as money, the Queen will dump them in front of you."[50] Closing his account of the treaty promises, Elder Horse stated that the treaty would improve "everything they had, including food, [which] was to have been better than the white man's" because the treaty would last "as long as the sun walks and as long as the Saskatchewan River flows."[51] Although these were "Queen's promises," Elder Horse acknowledged that what was promised was not necessarily what they got, because "the white man has manipulated us that we are confused."

---

[47] Hickey et al., "TARR Interview," 111.
[48] Interview with Fred Horse, no. 1, February 18, 1974.
[49] Hickey et al., "TARR Interview," 105.
[50] Interview with Fred Horse, no. 1, February 18, 1974.
[51] Ibid.

As indicated above, the oral history presented by Elder Horse is but one part of the Indigenous understanding of what happened during the negotiations of Treaty 6 in 1876. As Hickey et al. show, it is possible to review large number of oral histories to show the primary themes of that broader treaty understanding: the treaties were agreements to let settlers use the land for agriculture; nothing else was sold or surrendered; the treaty commissioners promised schools, agricultural tools, and assistance to transition toward a new way of life; reserves would be set aside for their "own free use ... safe from encroachment"; and medical services and aid in times of crisis were guaranteed.[52] As will be discussed below, this understanding of the treaty is "radically different from that of the government." As Lynn Hickey comments, "The point to be made here is that no one interpretation need be accepted as reflecting what really happened. It is enough to understand that the treaties have meant very different things to different groups of people, and that subsequent actions of these people have reflected their particular understanding."[53]

Whereas the Indigenous perspective of the treaty negotiations is collectively shared and passed down from and among Elders, the settler perspective is contained in the written reports, notes, and letters of government officials, members of the clergy, and other witnesses. The primary written source for what transpired in the late summer of 1876 is the report by the Dominion of Canada's official treaty commissioner, Alexander Morris.

The change in government from Conservative to Liberal meant that when Alexander Mackenzie's Liberal government was elected in 1873, it had no direct western experience and was required to depend upon officials in the northwest. Alexander Morris, appointed lieutenant-governor for Manitoba and the North-West Territories in 1872 by Macdonald, became the leading figure in Crown-Indigenous relations in the northwest.[54] As treaty commissioner in the 1870s, he would personally negotiate four treaties, and he continuously reported back to Ottawa about the state of Indigenous affairs. Morris consulted those who were most familiar with Indigenous relations, such as James McKay, former HBC trader and Métis member of the NWT executive council, and Father Albert Lacombe

---

[52] Hickey et al., "TARR Interview," 105.
[53] Ibid., 109.
[54] Robert J. Talbot, *Negotiating the Numbered Treaties: An Intellectual and Political Biography of Alexander Morris* (Saskatoon: Purich, 2009), 54.

at St. Albert, north of Fort Edmonton, who provided statistical information regarding the population, movements, and living conditions of different Indigenous groups.[55] As Robert Talbot shows in his biography, Morris had a deep interest in the well-being of the territories' Indigenous peoples, although he was heavily influenced by the paternalism of his Christian faith. As he negotiated and discussed the treaties with Indigenous leaders, he came to see that while his main goal was to secure title to the lands, the treaties were also the basis for "a positive, reciprocal relationship between the Crown and the First Nations of the North West."[56]

Based on his success with the negotiation of Treaties 3, 4, and 5, the Dominion government gave Morris the task of making another treaty with the Indigenous inhabitants of the Northwest Territories in 1875, but with remarkably little direction because the minister of the Interior, David Laird, believed that "your [Morris] large experience and past success in conducting Indian negotiations relieves me from the necessity of giving you any detailed instructions in reference to your present mission."[57] It is therefore likely that Laird expected a similarly formulaic treaty-making process. However, the lack of instruction, the discretionary powers granted to commissioners, and the stronger positions presented by First Nations made these treaty meetings more difficult than previous ones.

With full authority to negotiate for the Crown, Morris, along with W.J. Christie of the HBC and James McKay as members of the Treaty Commission, met with Indigenous leaders at Fort Carlton and Fort Pitt in August and September 1876.[58] Upon his return to Manitoba, Morris drafted a report of the treaty meetings for the minister of the Interior and included notes and summaries taken by his secretary, Dr. A.G. Jackes. The lieutenant-governor's account of the treaty negotiations bears many similarities to the oral history shared by the Elders who were interviewed a century after the signing of Treaty 6. Similarly to Elder Horse's account, Morris reported that the treaty negotiations were more difficult than expected and took several days before the parties could reach agreeable terms. As Talbot notes, Morris was quick to adopt the tone, language, and symbols of his Indigenous counterparts in his interactions.[59] This attitude brought him

---

[55] Memorandum from Father Lacombe on the Tribes of the Saskatchewan Valley, February 13, 1875, LAC RG10, vol. 3616, file 4518, reel C-10107.
[56] Talbot, *Negotiating the Numbered Treaties*, 57.
[57] David Laird to Alexander Morris, July 15, 1876, LAC, RG10, vol. 3636, file 6692–1.
[58] Morris, *Treaties of Canada*, 217–18.
[59] Talbot, *Negotiating the Numbered Treaties*, 56.

to participate in the pipe ceremony at the start of the meetings, although possibly without fully understanding its significance:

> They [the Cree representatives] then performed the dance of the "pipe stem," the stem was elevated to the north, south, west and east, a ceremonial dance was then performed by the Chiefs and headmen, the Indian men and women shouting the while … when the pipe was presented to us and stroked by our hands. After the stroking had been completed, the Indians sat down in front of the council tent, satisfied that in accordance with their custom we had accepted the friendship of the Cree nation.[60]

While recognizing that his participation in the ceremony was part of relationship building, he seems to have not fully grasped the more sacred elements of the ceremony for the Cree.[61]

As in the Treaty 6 oral history, Morris, who had introduced himself as the "Queen's Councillor" and said that he was there to "speak from her to you,"[62] started the discussions by trying to reassure the gathered leaders of the good intentions of the Crown:

> I had ascertained that the Indian mind was oppressed with vague fears; they dreaded the treaty; they had been made to believe that they would be compelled to live on the reserves wholly, and abandon their hunting, and that in time of war, they would be placed in the front and made to fight.
>
> I accordingly shaped my address, so as to give them confidence in the intentions of the Government, and to quiet their apprehensions. I impressed on them the necessity of changing their present mode of life, and commencing to make homes and gardens for themselves, so as to be prepared for the diminution of the buffalo.

While the notes kept by the commission's secretary, Dr. Jackes, provide more detail of the treaty terms, Morris, in his report to Ottawa, simply stated, "I then fully explained to them the proposals I had to make, that we did not wish to interfere with their present mode of living, but would assign them reserves and assist them as was being done

---

[60] Morris, *Treaties of Canada*, 183.
[61] Taylor, "Two Views," 18.
[62] Morris, *Treaties of Canada*, 199.

elsewhere, in commencing to farm."[63] Interestingly, Dr. Jackes recorded a more nuanced statement that protects hunting and fishing rights for the future: "I do not want to interfere with your hunting and fishing I want you to pursue it throughout the country ... but I would like your children to be able to find food for themselves and their children that come after them."[64] Jackes also provides more detail with respect to the description of reserve lands: "we wish to give to each band who will accept of it a place where they may live; we wish to give you as much or more land than you need"; schools: "When the Indians settle on a reserve and have a sufficient number of children to be taught, the Queen would maintain a school"; agricultural implements: "two hoes, one spade, one scythe"; clothing, medals, and flags for chiefs and headmen; and a provision of $500 for "ammunition and twine" and a "present to every man, woman and child, of twelve dollars."[65]

As is the case with the oral history, Morris clearly reports that the proceedings lasted several days, with separate meetings of the Indigenous leadership to discuss the various proposals from the government and make their counterproposals. Morris's official report does not provide a detailed account of these discussions or proposals but does highlight some of the main points:

> On the 22nd the Commissioners met the Indians, when I told them that we had not hurried them, but wished now to hear their Chief spokesman, The Pound Maker, then addressed me, and asked assistance when they settled on the land, and further help as they advanced in civilization. I replied that they had their own means of living, and that we could not feed the Indians, but only assist them to settle down. The Badger, Soh-ah-moos, and several other Indians all asked help when they settled, and also in case of troubles unforeseen in the future. I explained that we could not assume the charge of their every-day life, but in a time of a great national calamity they could trust to the generosity of the Queen.

It would take two more days of discussions among the Indigenous contingent and with the Treaty Commission before acceptable terms could be agreed upon. This success was due in large part to Morris's adding

---

[63] Ibid., 184.
[64] Ibid., 204.
[65] Ibid., 204–7.

terms including assistance in times of famine, more livestock and agricultural tools, as well as financial assistance to assist in the transition to agriculture:

> After an interval we again met them, and I replied, going over their demands and reiterating my statements as to our inability to grant food, and again explaining that only in a national famine did the Crown ever intervene, and agreeing to make some additions to the number of cattle and implements, as we felt it would be desirable to encourage their desire to settle.
>
> I closed by stating that, after they settled on the reserves, we would give them provisions to aid them while cultivating, to the extent of one thousand dollars' per annum, but for three years only, as after that time they should be able to support themselves.[66]

The concessions made by Morris for Treaty 6 go beyond those found in other treaties, but all are incentives to settle on reserves and take up agriculture. These concessions included $1,000 per year for three years to assist in resettlement, the famine clause, and increased supplies of agricultural implements. It should be noted that one of the additional clauses, the "medicine chest" clause, is not reported in Morris's account, although Jackes does note Morris saying, "A medicine chest will be kept at the house of each Indian agent in case of sickness amongst you." Peter Erasmus, the Métis interpreter present during the treaty conference, wrote in his memoir of his life on the prairie that the inclusion of this clause was a specific First Nation demand and was fundamental to securing Indigenous agreement to the treaty.[67] Erasmus's account is the only source indicating not only the origin of the clause but also Morris's agreement to its inclusion. These enhanced terms proved to be sufficient: Morris asked, "if they were willing to accept our modified proposals. Ah-tuk-uk-koop then addressed me, and concluded by calling on the people, if they were in favour of our offers, to say so. – This they all did by shouting assent and holding up their hands."[68]

It should be noted that the official report does not provide a complete picture of the treaty proceedings but rather a selective summary. While it does present the outcome of the discussions, it does not fully report on how

---

[66] Ibid., 186.
[67] Peter Erasmus, *Buffalo Days and Nights* (Calgary: Fifth House, 1999), 253.
[68] Morris, *Treaties of Canada*, 186.

the Treaty Commission presented the treaty to the Indigenous representatives, nor does it help the reader see how those representatives would have understood the commission's words. Interestingly, the secretary's notes provide a far better picture of the nature of the interactions, especially when considering the specific language of the treaty terms.

TREATY 6 AND THE COURTS

As with the other Numbered Treaties concluded after Confederation, Treaty 6 of 1876 has been the subject of a number of legal proceedings that have influenced both how governments implement the terms of the agreements and how Indigenous treaty signatories view the exercise of the rights and promises within the treaty. While these cases touch on different aspects of the terms, such as the extent of the medicine chest clause in the *Dreaver* (1935), *Johnson* (1966), and *Swimmer* (1970) cases,[69] the majority of the cases focus on the promised rights of continued exercise of hunting and fishing for signatory communities. One such example, *R. v. Sundown*, centres on the case of John Sundown, who was charged with illegally building a log cabin in Meadow Lake Provincial Park in Saskatchewan. This case and its subsequent rulings expand our understanding of how the rights to hunt and fish can be exercised by including incidental activities as part of the right. In 1992, Mr. Sundown had been charged with violating the Saskatchewan *Parks Regulation* of 1991, which "prohibited both the construction of a temporary or permanent dwelling on park land without permission," and with damaging trees inside the park.[70] Specifically, Sundown had cut down a number of trees in order to build a log cabin as a shelter for an extended hunting expedition. As part of his defence, Sundown argued that under the terms of Treaty 6, he had the right to hunt for food on provincial Crown land and that building a shelter for extended hunting was a long-standing practice of his community, the Joseph Bighead First Nation. The province of Saskatchewan argued before both the Provincial Court of Saskatchewan and the Court of Queen's Bench that Sundown's actions constituted an attempt to permanently occupy part of the park and that he interfered with the rights of other park users. The Provincial Court ruled in favour of the province. On appeal, both the Court of Queen's Bench and the Saskatchewan Court of Appeal ruled for Sundown, recognizing that the construction

---

[69] *Dreaver v. R.*, [1935] 5 C.N.L.C. 92; *R. v. Johnson*, [1966] 56 W.W.R. 565, 6 C.N.L.C. 447; *R. v. Swimmer*, [1970] 6 C.N.L.C. 621, 17 D.L.R. (3rd) 476.
[70] *R. v. Sundown*, [1999] 1 R.C.S., p. 397.

of a shelter was "reasonably related" or "reasonably incidental" to the act of hunting.[71]

The Supreme Court of Canada agreed to hear the province's appeal, and in 1999 Justice Peter Cory delivered a ruling on the case. In a detailed discussion, Justice Cory presents an analysis of the evolution of the traditional hunting practices of the members of the Joseph Bighead First Nation, and specifically the practice of expeditionary hunting, which he described as

> a hub-and-spoke style of hunting in which hunters set up a base camp for some extended period of time ranging from overnight to two weeks. Each day they move out from that spot to hunt. They then return to the base camp to smoke fish or game and to prepare hides. Originally these shelters were moss-covered lean-tos and later tents and log cabins.[72]

Citing previous rulings that helped define the principles of treaty interpretation and hunting rights, such as the 1996 *Badger* decision,[73] the Supreme Court reiterated that the "interpretation of each treaty must take into account the First Nation signatory and the circumstances that surrounded the signing of the treaty," and more significantly, that when applying the legal principles of treaty interpretation, "consideration should be given to the evidence as to where the hunting and fishing were done and how the members of the First Nation carried out these activities."[74] Relying on the legal test established in the 1985 *Simon* decision that the treaty right to hunt must include "those activities reasonably incidental to the act of hunting," Justice Cory writes that

> A hunting cabin is, in these circumstances, reasonably incidental to this First Nation's right to hunt in their traditional expeditionary style. This method of hunting is not only traditional but appropriate and shelter is an important component of it. Without a shelter, it would be impossible for this First Nation to exercise its traditional method of hunting and their members would be denied their treaty rights to hunt.[75]

---

[71] Saskatchewan Court of Queen's Bench, [1995] 3 C.N.L.R. 152; Saskatchewan Court of Appeal, [1997] 4 C.N.L.R. 241.
[72] *R. v. Sundown*, [1999] 1 R.C.S., p. 401.
[73] See Chapter 7.
[74] *R. v. Sundown*, [1999] 1 R.C.S., p. 408.
[75] Ibid., 411.

As a result, the Court ruled that "[t]he rights of Mr. Sundown under Treaty No. 6 permit him to build a cabin as a reasonably incidental activity to his right to hunt."

The Supreme Court's decision in *R. v. Sundown* has interesting repercussions for how treaty terms are to be understood. As outlined in its legal principles for treaty interpretation, the terms relating to rights to hunt and fish must be interpreted in a manner that would best reflect Indigenous understanding at the time of treaty making. At its core, treaty rights should not be interpreted as though they are simple property rights, or limited to the common-law interpretation of land title and usage. As a result of the *Sundown* ruling, treaty rights must also include the other activities that allow a right holder to exercise that right, and "the rights protected in a treaty [must] extend beyond the literal words" of the treaty term.[76]

Robert Mainville points out in his legal study *An Overview of Aboriginal and Treaty Rights and Compensation for Their Breach* that the *R. v. Sundown* decision helped define the nature of treaty rights and, consequently, how treaty terms are to be understood.[77] In accordance with the principles of treaty interpretation, the ruling helps the reader of treaties understand that the exercise of a right defined by a treaty goes beyond narrow wording and must include those activities supporting the right. As legal scholar Thomas Isaac notes, the ruling provides Indigenous treaty communities with "a useful tool respecting a liberal and generous approach to interpreting treaties, since a wide array of potential incidental rights could attach to the treaty rights."[78] Notably, this ruling also aligns with parts of both the Treaty 6 oral history and Alexander Morris's account of the treaty, where the promise was made not to interfere with the practices relating to hunting and fishing.[79]

FURTHER READINGS

Sarah Carter. *Lost Harvests: Prairie Indian Reserve Farmers and Government Policy*. Montreal & Kingston: McGill-Queen's University Press, 1990.

James Daschuk. *Clearing the Plains: Disease, Politics of Starvation, and the Loss of Aboriginal Life*. Regina: University of Regina Press, 2013.

---

[76] John Borrows and Leonard Rotman, *Aboriginal Legal Issues: Cases, Materials and Commentary* (Markham, ON: LexisNexis Canada, 2007), 391.

[77] Robert Mainville, *An Overview of Aboriginal and Treaty Rights and Compensation for Their Breach*, 3rd ed. (Saskatoon: Purich, 2001), 42.

[78] Thomas Isaac, *Aboriginal Law: Commentary, Cases and Materials* (Saskatoon: Purich, 2004), 83.

[79] Interview with Fred Horse, no. 1, February 18, 1974; Morris, *Treaties of Canada*, 184.

Peter Erasmus. *Buffalo Days and Nights.* Calgary: Fifth House, 1999.

Alexander Morris. *The Treaties of Canada with the Indians of Manitoba and the North-West Territories.* Toronto: Belfords, Clarke and Co., 1880.

The Spirit of the Alberta Indian Treaties. Ed. Richard Price. Edmonton: University of Alberta Press, 1999.

Sharon Venne. "Understanding Treaty 6: An Indigenous Perspective." In *Aboriginal and Treaty Rights in Canada: Essays on Law, Equality, and Respect for Difference,* ed. Michael Asch, 173–207. Vancouver: University of British Columbia Press, 2002.

QUESTIONS FOR DISCUSSION

1. Read the following excerpts and identify the different parties to Treaty 6:

   Treaty No. 6
   ARTICLES OF A TREATY made and concluded near Carlton on the 23rd day of August and on the 28th day of said month, respectively, and near Fort Pitt on the 9th day of September, in the year of Our Lord one thousand eight hundred and seventy-six, between Her Most Gracious Majesty the Queen of Great Britain and Ireland, by Her Commissioners, the Honourable Alexander Morris, Lieutenant-Governor of the Province of Manitoba and the North-west Territories, and the Honourable James McKay, and the Honourable William Joseph Christie, of the one part, and the Plain and Wood Cree and the other Tribes of Indians, inhabitants of the country within the limits hereinafter defined and described by their Chiefs, chosen and named as hereinafter mentioned, of the other part.

   Treaty Commissioner's Report, December 4, 1876, Alexander Morris, *The Treaties of Canada with the Indians of Manitoba and the North-West Territories*
   I then asked if they were willing to accept our modified proposals. Ah-tuk-uk-koop then addressed me, and concluded by calling on the people, if they were in favour of our offers, to say so. This they all did by shouting assent and holding up their hands ... The treaty was then signed by myself, Messrs. Christie and McKay, Mist-ow-as-ia and Ah-tuk-uk-koop, the head Chiefs, and by the other Chiefs and Councillors, those signing, though many Indians were absent, yet representing all the bands of any importance in the Carlton regions, except the Willow Indians.

Interview with Elder Fred Horse, Frog Lake First Nation, February 18, 1974, "Indian History Film Project," Canadian Plains Research Centre, University of Regina
"The Queen's arm is long and when you are faced with starvation, she will reach out to protect you." From that time on there will be rations and all kinds of things such as money, the Queen will dump them in front of you. They were told that the white man would look very impressive in the future. His land would be the best, but when the Indians have completed their negotiations, everything they had, including food, was to have been better than the white man's. Take a look at the sun as it walks, the Queen used it as a pledge to strengthen the promises. As long as the sun walks is as long as she would look after the Indian. Also the Saskatchewan River was referred to, as long as it was flowing. The agreement was to last as long as these two were in existence. That was the Queen's promises.

2. How do the Elders' oral histories describe the significance of the treaty meeting?
3. What does the official report of the treaty meetings tell us of Alexander Morris's goal in concluding a treaty in 1876?
4. In your opinion, how do the courts instruct us in understanding the right to hunt?

DOCUMENTS

Treaty Text Excerpts: Treaty No. 6, LAC, RG10, vol. 1847, IT 296, IA 157A, T-9940

ARTICLES OF A TREATY made and concluded near Carlton on the 23rd day of August and on the 28th day of said month, respectively, and near Fort Pitt on the 9th day of September, in the year of Our Lord one thousand eight hundred and seventy-six, between Her Most Gracious Majesty the Queen of Great Britain and Ireland, by Her Commissioners, the Honourable Alexander Morris, Lieutenant-Governor of the Province of Manitoba and the North-west Territories, and the Honourable James McKay, and the Honourable William Joseph Christie, of the one part, and the Plain and Wood Cree and the other Tribes of Indians, inhabitants of the country within the limits hereinafter defined and described by their Chiefs, chosen and named as hereinafter mentioned, of the other part.

...

And whereas the said Indians have been notified and informed by Her Majesty's said Commissioners that it is the desire of Her Majesty to open up for settlement, immigration and such other purposes as to Her Majesty may seem meet, a tract of country bounded and described as hereinafter mentioned, and to obtain the consent thereto of Her Indian subjects inhabiting the said tract, and to make a treaty and arrange with them, so that there may be peace and good will between them and Her Majesty, and that they may know and be assured of what allowance they are to count upon and receive from Her Majesty's bounty and benevolence.

And whereas the Indians of the said tract, duly convened in council, as aforesaid, and being requested by Her Majesty's said Commissioners to name certain Chiefs and Headmen, who should be authorized on their behalf to conduct such negotiations and sign any treaty to be founded thereon, and to become responsible to Her Majesty for their faithful performance by their respective Bands of such obligations as shall be assumed by them, the said Indians have thereupon named for that purpose, that is to say, representing the Indians who make the treaty at Carlton, the several Chiefs and Councillors who have subscribed hereto, and representing the Indians who make the treaty at Fort Pitt, the several Chiefs and Councillors who have subscribed hereto.

And thereupon, in open council, the different Bands having presented their Chiefs to the said Commissioners as the Chiefs and Headmen, for the purposes aforesaid, of the respective Bands of Indians inhabiting the said district hereinafter described.

And whereas, the said Commissioners then and there received and acknowledged the persons so presented as Chiefs and Headmen, for the purposes aforesaid, of the respective Bands of Indians inhabiting the said district hereinafter described.

And whereas, the said Commissioners have proceeded to negotiate a treaty with the said Indians, and the same has been finally agreed upon and concluded, as follows, that is to say:

The Plain and Wood Cree Tribes of Indians, and all other the Indians inhabiting the district hereinafter described and defined, do hereby cede, release, surrender and yield up to the Government of the Dominion of Canada, for Her Majesty the Queen and Her successors forever, all their rights, titles and privileges, whatsoever, to the lands included within the following limits ...

And also, all their rights, titles and privileges whatsoever to all other lands wherever situated in the North-west Territories, or in any other Province or portion of Her Majesty's Dominions, situated and being within the Dominion of Canada.

The tract comprised within the lines above described embracing an area of 121,000 square miles, be the same more or less.

To have and to hold the same to Her Majesty the Queen and Her successors forever.

And Her Majesty the Queen hereby agrees and undertakes to lay aside reserves for farming lands, due respect being had to lands at present cultivated by the said Indians, and other reserves for the benefit of the said Indians, to be administered and dealt with for them by Her Majesty's Government of the Dominion of Canada; provided, all such reserves shall not exceed in all one square mile for each family of five, or in that proportion for larger or smaller families, in manner following, that is to say: that the Chief Superintendent of Indian Affairs shall depute and send a suitable person to determine and set apart the reserves for each band, after consulting with the Indians thereof as to the locality which may be found to be most suitable for them.

Provided, however, that Her Majesty reserves the right to deal with any settlers within the bounds of any lands reserved for any Band as She shall deem fit, and also that the aforesaid reserves of land, or any interest therein, may be sold or otherwise disposed of by Her Majesty's Government for the use and benefit of the said Indians entitled thereto, with their consent first had and obtained; and with a view to show the satisfaction of Her Majesty with the behaviour and good conduct of Her Indians, She hereby, through Her Commissioners, makes them a present of twelve dollars for each man, woman and child belonging to the Bands here represented, in extinguishment of all claims heretofore preferred.

And further, Her Majesty agrees to maintain schools for instruction in such reserves hereby made as to Her Government of the Dominion of Canada may seem advisable, whenever the Indians of the reserve shall desire it.

Her Majesty further agrees with Her said Indians that within the boundary of Indian reserves, until otherwise determined by Her Government of the Dominion of Canada, no intoxicating liquor shall be allowed to be introduced or sold, and all laws now in force, or hereafter to be enacted, to preserve Her Indian subjects inhabiting the reserves or living elsewhere within Her North-west Territories from the evil influence of the use of intoxicating liquors, shall be strictly enforced.

Her Majesty further agrees with Her said Indians that they, the said Indians, shall have right to pursue their avocations of hunting and fishing throughout the tract surrendered as hereinbefore described, subject to such regulations as may from time to time be made by Her Government of Her Dominion of Canada, and saving and excepting such tracts as may from time to time be required or taken up for settlement, mining, lumbering or other purposes by Her said Government of the Dominion of Canada, or by any of the subjects thereof duly authorized therefor by the said Government.

It is further agreed between Her Majesty and Her said Indians, that such sections of the reserves above indicated as may at any time be required for public works or buildings, of what nature soever, may be appropriated for that purpose by Her Majesty's Government of the Dominion of Canada, due compensation being made for the value of any improvements thereon.

And further, that Her Majesty's Commissioners shall, as soon as possible after the execution of this treaty, cause to be taken an accurate census of all the Indians … and shall, in every year ensuing the date hereof, at some period in each year, to be duly notified to the Indians, and at a place or places to be appointed for that purpose within the territory ceded, pay to each Indian person the sum of $5 per head yearly.

It is further agreed between Her Majesty and the said Indians, that the sum of $1,500.00 per annum shall be yearly and every year expended by Her Majesty in the purchase of ammunition, and twine for nets, for the use of the said Indians …

It is further agreed between Her Majesty and the said Indians, that the following articles shall be supplied to any Band of the said Indians who are now cultivating the soil, or who shall hereafter commence to cultivate the land, that is to say … All the aforesaid articles to be given once and for all for the encouragement of the practice of agriculture among the Indians.

It is further agreed between Her Majesty and the said Indians, that each Chief, duly recognized as such, shall receive an annual salary of twenty-five dollars per annum; and each subordinate officer, not exceeding four for each Band, shall receive fifteen dollars per annum; and each such Chief and subordinate officer, as aforesaid, shall also receive once every three years, a suitable suit of clothing, and each Chief shall receive, in recognition of the closing of the treaty, a suitable flag and medal, and also as soon as convenient, one horse, harness and waggon.

That in the event hereafter of the Indians comprised within this treaty being overtaken by any pestilence, or by a general famine, the Queen, on being satisfied and certified thereof by Her Indian Agent or Agents, will grant to the Indians assistance of such character and to such extent as Her Chief Superintendent of Indian Affairs shall deem necessary and sufficient to relieve the Indians from the calamity that shall have befallen them.

That during the next three years, after two or more of the reserves hereby agreed to be set apart to the Indians shall have been agreed upon and surveyed, there shall be granted to the Indians included under the Chiefs adhering to the treaty at Carlton, each spring, the sum of one thousand dollars, to be expended for them by Her Majesty's Indian Agents, in the purchase of provisions for the use of such of the Band as are actually settled on the reserves and are engaged in cultivating the soil, to assist them in such cultivation.

That a medicine chest shall be kept at the house of each Indian Agent for the use and benefit of the Indians at the direction of such agent.

That with regard to the Indians included under the Chiefs adhering to the treaty at Fort Pitt, and to those under Chiefs within the treaty limits who may hereafter give their adhesion thereto (exclusively, however, of the Indians of the Carlton region), there shall, during three years, after two or more reserves shall have been agreed upon and surveyed be distributed each spring among the Bands cultivating the soil on such reserves, by Her Majesty's Chief Indian Agent for this treaty, in his discretion, a sum not exceeding one thousand dollars, in the purchase of provisions for the use of such members of the Band as are actually settled on the reserves and engaged in the cultivation of the soil, to assist and encourage them in such cultivation ...

And the undersigned Chiefs on their own behalf and on behalf of all other Indians inhabiting the tract within ceded, do hereby solemnly promise and engage to strictly observe this treaty, and also to conduct and behave themselves as good and loyal subjects of Her Majesty the Queen.

They promise and engage that they will in all respects obey and abide by the law, and they will maintain peace and good order between each other, and also between themselves and other tribes of Indians, and between themselves and others of Her Majesty's subjects, whether Indians or whites, now inhabiting or hereafter to inhabit any part of the said ceded tracts, and that they will not molest the person or property of any inhabitant of such ceded tracts, or the property of Her Majesty the Queen, or interfere with or trouble any person passing or travelling through the said tracts, or any part thereof, and that they will aid and assist the officers of Her Majesty in bringing to justice and punishment any Indian offending against the stipulations of this treaty, or infringing the laws in force in the country so ceded.

IN WITNESS WHEREOF, Her Majesty's said Commissioners and the said Indian Chiefs have hereunto subscribed and set their hands at or near Fort Carlton, on the days and year aforesaid, and near Fort Pitt on the day above aforesaid.

Excerpts from an interview with Elder Fred Horse, Frog Lake First Nation, February 18, 1974, "Indian History Film Project," Canadian Plains Research Centre, University of Regina. Reprinted by permission of The University of Regina Press.

First I'll start by saying something about the representative who was sent by the Queen. He spoke for a long time as he had much to discuss, to talk about these things with the elders. The discussions were made to sound encouraging. I'm not certain at this time but I think the representative spent a week talking to the Indians. This is what I was told, I'm not doubting what these other men have said. But that is how I was told, I was told more than once. The representative I think stayed for one week talking to the people. The Indians did not accept the terms at first, because they too were meeting, talking and getting an idea of what other people thought. When the elders had reached a decision, they approached the representative for further discussions. But it was late in the day that they accepted. They told him that first they would like to foresee the whole thing, as the Indian had some foresight, and were depending on it. That is what was said. That the agreement would never come to an end as long as the earth existed, that was the understanding. The representative agreed to that, so the Indians were also in agreement and accepted. That is when the elders agreed to the very important transaction. Once it was complete it was to last forever. It was at this time that the pipestem was brought into use, we still have that pipestem. The representative also took the pipe and smoked from it. That is when the representative took the stem in his right and raised it towards the sky.

And it is true that it was only three things that he was supposed to negotiate for. That includes the land, grass and timber. The land would be to make a living agriculturally, the grass to feed the animals and the timber for building a home and also to keep the livestock. As for other things such as birds flying and animals on the ground, they are not included. And anything underwater is also not included, and any animal in the bush you make your living with, these things the representative didn't buy from you. The amount of land he bought he indicated like this, (open hand with extended thumb). In the future the white man will explore underground but these are the things they didn't buy from the Indian. If any money should be made from it, the Indians should be entitled to it. This is the way I've heard these stories. I can't mention all the promises but those were many of them.

There would be schools on the reserve, so the children could get an education, to go as high as possible. The white man said that this would take place inside the reserve. They would also have a farm instructor; he will teach the Indian how to farm. These people would be answerable to the Indian. The farm instructor would respond to the requests of the Indian. The other thing was the farm implements, garden hoes and forks. That is that the white man could give the Indian. The Indians were told that the white man was limited in what he could give but all these things mentioned the Indians would receive. "If you want to farm, you will get some grain." When you have finished the negotiations, there should be no end to the agreement (forever). But in the future the white man will become secure and established and the Indian should be part of this. You wouldn't have to pay for anything, all this would be free to the Indians. From that time on everything will be more firmly established the Indian should be entitled to all this, because they have already paid for it. The representative said that at one time the Indian was starving to death. He told the Indians that this would not happen again, "The Queen's arm is long and when you are faced with starvation, she will reach out to protect you." From that time on there will be rations and all kinds of things such as money, the Queen will dump them in front of you. They were told that the white man would look very impressive in the future. His land would be the best, but when the Indians have completed their negotiations, everything they had, including food, was to have been better than the white man's. Take a look at the sun as it walks, the Queen used it as a pledge to strengthen the promises. As long as the sun walks is as long as she would look after the Indian. Also the Saskatchewan River was referred to, as long as it was flowing. The agreement was to last as long as these two were in existence. That was the Queen's promises. That is why I say, the white man has manipulated us that we are confused. It is not that we are really confused, it's that he promised us the money. It was a promise. The Queen was to give us money and food, to care for the Indians. It is like the Queen replaced Manitou in taking care of us.

... The reason I know all this is because my grandfather "Horse" was a headman at the time. He was given a flag and if it wore out he would receive another one. They also were given clothes and they would always get clothing. They were given medallions with the Queen's head on it, this would give the chiefs authority. The chiefs would retain this authority forever.

[Interview 3:] They told the government officials that they were using their greatly respected power for a legal transaction (peace pipe). With the promises the Queen made, they didn't want them to ever come to an end. The government official mentioned at the time that the terms of the treaty should never come to an end. These promises were made with the smoking of the pipe. His lips touched the stem of the pipe. This wasn't done ordinarily for no reason. If one put a pipestem to his lips, that was a highly honored agreement and the government official did that. He smoked the pipestem (smoking of peace pipe).

Excerpts from Treaty Commissioner's Report, December 4, 1876, Alexander Morris, *The Treaties of Canada with the Indians of Manitoba and the North-West Territories* (Toronto: Belfords, Clarke and Co., 1880), 180–96

Government House,
 Fort Garry, Manitoba, 4th December, 1876.
 Sir, – I beg to inform you that in compliance with the request of the Privy Council that I should proceed to the west to negotiate the treaties which I had last year, through the agency of the late Rev. George McDougall, promised the Plain Crees, would be undertaken, I left Fort Garry on the afternoon of the 27th of July last, with the view of prosecuting my mission. I was accompanied by one of my associates, the Hon. J. W. Christie, and by A. G. Jackes, Esq., M.D., who was to act as secretary. I selected as my guide Mr. Pierre Levailler. The Hon. James McKay, who had also been associated in the commission, it was arranged, would follow me and meet me at Fort Carlton ...

On my arrival I found that the ground had been most judiciously chosen ... On my arrival, the Union Jack was hoisted, and the Indians at once began to assemble, beating drums, discharging fire-arms, singing and dancing. In about half an hour they were ready to advance and meet me. This they did in a semicircle, having men on horseback galloping in circles, shouting, singing and discharging fire-arms.

They then performed the dance of the "pipe stem," the stem was elevated to the north, south, west and east, a ceremonial dance was then performed by the Chiefs and headmen, the Indian men and women shouting the while. They then slowly advanced, the horsemen again preceding them on their approach to my tent. I advanced to meet them, accompanied by Messrs. Christie and McKay, when the pipe was presented to us and stroked by our hands. After the stroking had been completed, the Indians sat down in front of the council tent, satisfied that in accordance with their custom we had accepted the friendship of the Cree nation.

I then addressed the Indians in suitable terms, explaining that I had been sent by the Queen, in compliance with their own wishes and the written promise I had given them last year, that a messenger would be sent to them.

I had ascertained that the Indian mind was oppressed with vague fears; they dreaded the treaty; they had been made to believe that they would be compelled to live on the reserves wholly, and abandon their hunting, and that in time of war, they would be placed in the front and made to fight.

I accordingly shaped my address, so as to give them confidence in the intentions of the Government, and to quiet their apprehensions. I impressed on them the necessity of changing their present mode of life, and commencing to make homes and gardens for themselves, so as to be prepared for the diminution of the buffalo ...

... I then fully explained to them the proposals I had to make, that we did not wish to interfere with their present mode of living, but would assign them reserves and assist them as was being done elsewhere, in commencing to farm, and that what was done would hold good for those that were away.

The Indians listened most attentively, and on the close of my remarks Mist-ow-as-is arose, took me by the hand, and said that "when a thing was thought of quietly, it was the best way," and asked "this much, that we go and think of his words."

I acquiesced at once, and expressed my hope that the Chiefs would act wisely, and thus closed the second day ... [The Chiefs] wished to have the day for consultation, and if ready would meet me on Tuesday morning. I cheerfully granted the delay from the reasonableness of the request; but I was also aware that the head Chiefs were in a position of great difficulty. The attitude of the Duck Lake Indians and of the few discontented Saulteaux embarrassed them, while a section of their own people were either averse to make a treaty or desirous of making extravagant demands. The head Chiefs were men of intelligence, and anxious that the people should act unitedly and reasonably ...

On the 22nd the Commissioners met the Indians, when I told them that we had not hurried them, but wished now to hear their Chief spokesman, The Pound Maker, then addressed me, and asked assistance when they settled on the land, and further help as they advanced in civilization. I replied that they had their own means of living, and that we could not feed the Indians, but only assist them to settle down. The Badger, Soh-ah-moos, and several other Indians all asked help when they settled, and also in case of troubles unforeseen in the future. I explained that we could not assume the charge of their every-day life, but in a time of a great national calamity they could trust to the generosity of the Queen.

After an interval we again met them, and I replied, going over their demands and reiterating my statements as to our inability to grant food, and again explaining that only in a national famine did the Crown ever intervene, and agreeing to make some additions to the number of cattle and implements, as we felt it would be desirable to encourage their desire to settle.

I closed by stating that, after they settled on the reserves, we would give them provisions to aid them while cultivating, to the extent of one thousand dollars per annum, but for three years only, as after that time they should be able to support themselves.

I told them that we could not give them missionaries, though I was pleased with their request, but that they must look to the churches, and that they saw Catholic and Protestant missionaries present at the conference. We told them that they must help their own poor, and that if they prospered they could do so. With regard to war, they would not be asked to fight unless they desired to do so, but if the Queen did call on them to protect their wives and children, I believed they would not be backward.

I then asked if they were willing to accept our modified proposals. Ah-tuk-uk-koop then addressed me, and concluded by calling on the people, if they were in favour of our offers, to say so. This they all did by shouting assent and holding up their hands.

… The treaty was then signed by myself, Messrs. Christie and McKay, Mist-ow-as-ia and Ah-tuk-uk-koop, the head Chiefs, and by the other Chiefs and Councillors, those signing, though many Indians were absent, yet representing all the bands of any importance in the Carlton regions, except the Willow Indians.

Excerpt from *R. v. Sundown*, [1999] 1 S.C.R. 393

6. It is clear from the history of the negotiations between Alexander Morris and the First Nations who signed Treaty No. 6 that the government intended to preserve the traditional Indian way of life. Hunting and fishing were of fundamental importance to that way of life. This was recognized in the treaty negotiations and in the treaties themselves.

24. … Treaties may appear to be no more than contracts. Yet they are far more. They are a solemn exchange of promises made by the Crown and various First Nations. They often formed the basis for peace and the expansion of European settlement. In many if not most treaty negotiations, members of the First Nations could not read or write English and relied completely on the oral promises made by the Canadian negotiators. There is a sound historical basis for interpreting treaties in the manner summarized in *Badger*. Anything else would amount to be a denial of fair dealing and justice between the parties.

25. Treaty rights, like aboriginal rights, are specific and may be exercised exclusively by the First Nation that signed the treaty. The interpretation of each treaty must take into account the First Nation signatory and the circumstances that surrounded the signing of the treaty … Thus, in addition to applying the guiding principles of treaty interpretation, it is necessary to take into account the circumstances surrounding the signing

of the treaty and the First Nations who later adhered to it. For example, consideration should be given to the evidence as to where the hunting and fishing were done and how the members of the First Nation carried out these activities.

26. The parties agree that Mr. Sundown has the right to hunt in the park. Like other adherents to Treaty No. 6 he is entitled to hunt for food. This he can do at any time so long as he does not endanger others and complies with the appropriate safety regulations and the conservation regulations, which are justifiable under *Sparrow*.

27. ... Both parties submitted that, in order to determine whether the right to shelter is reasonably incidental to the right to hunt, the test set out in *Simon*, *supra*, must be applied.

29. ... A form of shelter was always necessary to carry out the expeditionary hunting of the Joseph Bighead First Nation. At the time of the treaty, the shelter may have been a carefully built lean-to. That shelter appropriately evolved to a tent and then a small cabin. Thus, the reasonable person, informed of the manner of hunting at the time of the treaty, can consider it in the light of modern hunting methods and can determine whether the activity in question – the shelter – is reasonably incidental to the right to hunt.

30. In order to determine what is reasonably incidental to a treaty right to hunt, the reasonable person must examine the historical and contemporary practice of that specific treaty right by the aboriginal group in question to see how the treaty right has been and continues to be exercised. That which is reasonably incidental is something which allows the claimant to exercise the right in the manner that his or her ancestors did, taking into account acceptable modern developments or unforeseen alterations in the right. The question is whether the activity asserted as being reasonably incidental is in fact incidental to an actually practised treaty right to hunt. The inquiry is largely a factual and historical one. Its focus is not upon the abstract question of whether a particular activity is "essential" in order for hunting to be possible but rather upon the concrete question of whether the activity was understood in the past and is understood today as significantly connected to hunting. Incidental activities are not only those which are essential, or integral, but include, more broadly, activities which are meaningfully related or linked.

31. ... Without shelter, expeditionary hunting, the traditional method used by this First Nation, would be impossible. There is no doubt, in the context of this treaty and of this First Nation, that some form of shelter is in fact a necessary part of expeditionary hunting. Accordingly, shelter is also reasonably incidental to this method of hunting.

CAST OF CHARACTERS: TREATY 6

Ahtahkakoop: b. c. 1816; d. December 4, 1896

Ahtahkakoop (Starblanket) led his people through the difficult transition from hunter and warrior to farmer, and from traditional Indian spiritualism to Christianity during the last third of the nineteenth century. A Plains Cree, Ahtahkakoop was born in the Saskatchewan River country in 1816. He was raised during the era when millions of bison roamed the northern plains and parklands, and he developed into a noted leader, warrior, and buffalo hunter. By the 1860s, the bison were rapidly disappearing, and newcomers arrived in greater numbers each year. Ahtahkakoop realized that the children and grandchildren in his band would have to adopt a new way of living if they were to survive. Accordingly, in 1874 the chief invited Anglican missionary John Hines to settle with his people at Sandy Lake (Hines Lake), situated northwest of present-day Prince Albert. When Alexander Morris convened a treaty meeting in 1876, Ahtahkakoop, along with Mistawasis, was a supporter of concluding a treaty, believing that the government's promises would help his people survive the transition from plains hunters to agriculturalists. He was the second chief to sign Treaty 6 at Fort Carlton in 1876. After taking a reserve on Hines Lake, Ahtahkakoop supported the establishment of a school for the children and for the instruction of their parents in how to farm. Ahtahkakoop's community continued to increase the number of acres cultivated and sown, raising herds of cattle and building substantial homes. Unfortunately, the crops were often destroyed by frost, hail, and drought. Hunting was poor, and the people sometimes starved despite their hard work; additionally, restrictive government policies made life difficult. Ahtahkakoop and his people remained neutral during the uprising of 1885, determined to honour the treaty signed nine years earlier. Ahtahkakoop died on December 4, 1896, and was buried on the reserve that was named after him.

Alexander Morris: b. March 17, 1826; d. October 28, 1889

Alexander Morris was born and raised in the military settlement of Perth in Upper Canada in a prominent and wealthy merchant family. Educated at Glasgow, Queen's, and McGill universities, Morris became politically involved after working as a law clerk to John A. Macdonald. Elected to the House of Commons after Confederation, Morris served in Macdonald's Cabinet as minister of inland revenue. He was a strong supporter of the British Empire and a booster of Canada's role within it. A supporter of

Canada's acquisition of Rupert's Land and the northwest, he campaigned and promoted western expansion. After a decade representing the riding of Lanark in Ontario, Morris retired and was appointed chief justice of Manitoba in 1872; he was then appointed lieutenant-governor of the North-West Territories (1872–6) and also of Manitoba (1873–7). In the early years of the province, Morris sought to bring stability to Manitoba, introducing responsible government and establishing the University of Manitoba. It was in Indigenous affairs that he found the greatest satisfaction. Between 1873 and 1876, he served as the lead commissioner for the negotiation and conclusion of four treaties between 1873 and 1876 (Treaties 3 through 6), which encompassed a large portion of the territory between Lake Superior and the Rocky Mountains, and worked to resolve concerns stemming from Treaties 1 and 2. Morris later served in the Ontario legislature (1878–86), wrote a history of the treaties, and continued his life work in the Presbyterian Church. He was a governor of both McGill and Queen's.

Poundmaker (Pitikwahanapiwiyin): b. c. 1842; d. July 4, 1886

Poundmaker was born in the early 1840s into a prominent Plains Cree family from the House band, his maternal uncle being Mistawasis, a leading chief in the Eagle Hill, Alberta, area. During the Cree-Blackfoot conflict over the dwindling bison stocks of the 1860s–70s, Poundmaker was adopted by Blackfoot leader Crowfoot. His relationship with Crowfoot and time spent among his people gave Poundmaker considerable influence and respect throughout the prairie. During the negotiations for Treaty 6 at Fort Carlton in 1876, he was considered to be a councillor, or minor chief, under Red Pheasant. Poundmaker questioned the government's intent in the treaty, arguing that the government should be prepared to provide the Cree, including future generations, with instruction in farming and assistance, in exchange for their lands. After adhering to the treaty, Poundmaker formed his own band in 1878 but continued to argue for a renegotiation of the terms to better benefit Indigenous signatories. A strong and vocal critic of the government's implementation of treaty promises and Indian policy, Poundmaker was considered a "troublemaker" by officials. Members of Poundmaker's band became implicated in the 1885 Northwest Resistance/Rebellion, and although he attempted to limit confrontations, government officials held Poundmaker responsible for the violence. He was convicted of rebellion and served one year in Stoney Mountain Prison in Manitoba. He died in 1886 while visiting his adopted father Crowfoot.

Figure 6.1 Peter Hourie with Chief O'Soup (Chippewa), Chief Flying in a Circle (Ka-ka-wista-ha), Chief Big Child (Mistawasis), and Chief Starblanket (Ahtahkakoop), November 1886. Both Ahtahkakoop and Mistawasis viewed treaties as a way for the Cree to protect themselves from the growing number of settlers, as well as to ensure government support as their communities adapted to new ways of life.
Source: Provincial Archives of Saskatchewan, R-B2837.

Figure 6.2 Alexander Morris. A prominent supporter of Canadian western expansionism, Alexander Morris saw the conclusion of treaties as a way to ensure the peaceful development of the Northwest Territories.
Source: Library and Archives Canada, C-052090.

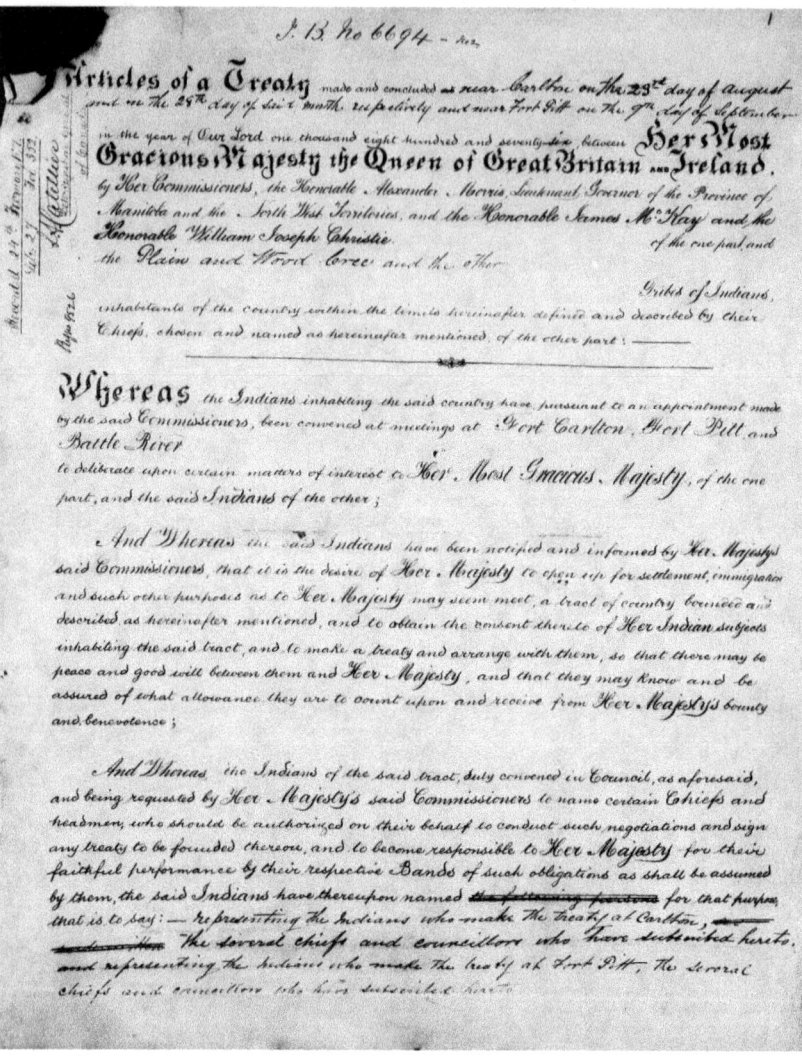

Figure 6.3 Western Treaty no. 6, August 23, 1876. Although the treaties of Western Canada have similar terms, they all have different elements, as they needed to respond to the specific needs of the nations negotiating. As a result, changes were often made during the final meetings that led to words being struck out or added in between the lines.

Source: Library and Archives Canada, e002995351.

Chapter 7
The Northern Numbered Treaties: Treaty no. 8, 1899

By 1877, there were contiguous treaties covering the southern Prairies, from the Lake Superior watershed to the Rocky Mountains, through a process that began in 1871 with Treaties 1 and 2 with the Indigenous nations of the Red and Assiniboine rivers and culminated with Treaty 7 at Blackfoot Crossing with members of the Blackfoot Confederacy and members of the Stoney communities of the foothills. As a result, the Canadian government had treaties that secured its "title" to these lands in exchange for specific rights and benefits. This process had not gone as easily as government officials would have liked, and concessions had been made in response to Indigenous demands, such as the inclusion of agricultural implements in Treaty 1,[1] or the inclusion of a clause ensuring assistance to Treaty 6 signatories in time of famine.[2] In the end, the Dominion of Canada believed it had secured the peaceful surrender of Indigenous interests throughout the agricultural districts of the Prairies and had opened the way for settlement. For their part, Indigenous signatories believed that they had concluded agreements that would allow them to survive as they transitioned out of the bison economy, through guaranteed rights and promises of support and assistance from the Crown.[3] Furthermore, they pointed out on several occasions the promises made but

---

[1] D.J. Hall, "'A Serene Atmosphere?': Treaty 1 Revisited," *Canadian Journal of Native Studies* 4, no. 2 (1984): 327.

[2] Derrick Whitehouse-Strong, "Everything Promised Had Been Included in the Writing: Indian Reserve Farming and the Spirit and Intent of Treaty Six Reconsidered," *Great Plains Quarterly* 27, no. 1 (2007): 28.

[3] Jean Friesen, "Magnificent Gifts: The Treaties of Canada with the Indians of the Northwest 1869–1876," in *The Spirit of the Alberta Indian Treaties*, ed. Richard Price (Edmonton: University of Alberta Press, 1999), 207.

not included in the final text.⁴ As J.R. Miller states in *Compact, Contract, Covenant*, the first seven treaties in the northwest "constitute an important milestone in the evolution of treaty-making in Canadian history," as they blended settler and Indigenous protocols, but also "serve as reminders of the growing strength and capacity of settler societies."⁵

A significant part of Canada's intent in concluding treaties had been to open the west to non-Indigenous settlement. Along with the establishment of the North-West Mounted Police in 1873, the promise to British Columbia that a railway would be built linking it to central Canada, and the push to survey the northwest so that it would be ready for the anticipated influx of settlers, the treaty-making process in Western Canada was a lynchpin in the government's plan for economic prosperity.⁶ Unfortunately, Canada's grand plan failed to attract the expected farmers and settlers in the 1870s and 1880s, in part due to a severe worldwide economic recession. At the same time, through a narrow interpretation of the treaty terms based on the written text, the Department of Indian Affairs sought to reduce costs by limiting rations, refused to renegotiate any aspects of the treaties, and moved to survey reserves in order to limit hunting.⁷ Meanwhile, Canada was formulating a broader Indigenous policy centred on the 1876 *Indian Act*, which transformed the Crown-Indigenous relationship into one of "trustee and ward."⁸ Based on a focus of "civilizing" the Indigenous population that also stripped community autonomy, the new policies were seen as contradictory to the relationships established by the treaty process. In the first decade after the treaty signings, Indigenous signatories quickly came to see the "strength" of the government as disagreements and conflicts about the meaning and implementation of the treaties came to the forefront of the new relationship on the prairie.⁹ Frustrated by increased hardship and a belief that the Crown was not living up to its treaty obligations, Indigenous leaders openly criticized the actions of the government, as happened with the chiefs Bobtail, Samson, Ermineskin, and Woodpecker of the Hobbema Agency, who stated in 1883 that the "government then

---

⁴ Petition to Sir John A. Macdonald, PM and Superintendent General of Indian Affairs, Letter in the *Edmonton Bulletin*, January 7, 1888, LAC, RG10, vol. 3673, file 10,986.
⁵ J.R. Miller, *Compact, Contract, Covenant: Aboriginal Treaty-Making in Canada* (Toronto; University of Toronto Press, 2009), 184.
⁶ Kenneth S. Coates, *Treaty Research Report: Treaty no. 10 (1905)* (Ottawa: Indian and Northern Affairs Canada, 1986), 3.
⁷ John Tobias, "Canada's Subjugation of the Plains Cree, 1879–1885" *Canadian Historical Review* 64, no. 4 (1983): 527.
⁸ Miller, *Compact, Contract, Covenant*, 190.
⁹ Jill St. Germain, *Broken Treaties: United States and Canadian Relations with the Lakota and the Plains Cree, 1865–1885* (Lincoln: University of Nebraska Press, 2009), 179.

can break every article of the treaty in detail or in globe and we have no redress."[10] That frustration boiled over and violence erupted in different regions of the northwest in the spring of 1885.

In the wake of the so-called "Northwest Rebellion," government officials clamped down on Indigenous activities through increasingly harsh policies.[11] At the same time, the Canadian government did not want to incur additional expenses relating to new treaties north of the agricultural areas, despite the continuous calls for treaty making by communities in the Athabasca and Peace river regions.[12] Many of these communities were facing increased hardship due to changing economic trends and the decline of the fur trade, as well as unease with the presence of surveyors, prospectors, and other settlers in their territories.[13] They saw the treaties to the south, regardless of their faults, as bringing much-needed money and assistance in a time of need. Ottawa, however, rejected the idea of more treaties in the west, stating that "the making of a treaty may be postponed for some years, or until there is a likelihood of the country being requested for settlement purposes."[14] Consequently, there was little discussion among government officials about resuming treaty making in the territories for nearly a decade. As Christine Smillie notes in her dissertation, "The People Left Out of Treaty 8," "treaties were not negotiated at the request of First Nations but when the government decided that it needed Indian land."[15] Despite a constant series of reports on the deteriorating condition of northern Indigenous communities in the last decade of the nineteenth century, it would take the identification of possible mineral wealth in the northern districts to spark the possibility of a renewed treaty process. The discovery of gold in the Klondike and the ensuing gold rush to the Yukon also played a significant role in reviving the interest in treaty making, as the North-West Mounted Police (NWMP) reported on the deteriorating conditions of First Nations and warned of increasing risks of conflict and violence along the route to the Klondike.[16]

---

[10] Petition to Sir John A. Macdonald.
[11] F. Laurie Barron, "The Indian Pass System in the Canadian West, 1882–1935," *Prairie Forum* 13, no. 1 (1988): 27.
[12] Miller, *Compact, Contract, Covenant*, 194.
[13] Lawrence Vankoughnet to John A. Macdonald, November 5, 1883, LAC, RG10, vol. 4006, file 241,209–1.
[14] Edgar Dewdney to Superintendent General of Indian Affairs, April 25, 1884, LAC, RG10, vol. 4006, file 241,209–1.
[15] Christine Smillie, "The People Left Out of Treaty 8" (MA thesis, University of Saskatchewan, 2005), 5.
[16] Report of J.D. Moodie, January 14, 1899, Annual Report of the North-West Mounted Police for 1899, Canada, Parliament, *Sessional Papers*, no. 15, pt. 2, p. 10.

As the reports from the northern regions increased calls for more treaties, the Liberal government of Wilfrid Laurier agreed that the time was right to conclude a new treaty for these territories. By the summer of 1897, Clifford Sifton, minister of the Interior and superintendent general of Indian Affairs, was "quite convinced that it will be necessary to take immediate steps to assure the Indians that the Government has no intention of ignoring their rights and has already arranged for the making of a treaty next summer."[17] On June 18, 1898, the federal cabinet resumed the long-stalled treaty-making process by appointing a treaty commission composed of David Laird, former minister, lieutenant-governor, and commissioner for Treaties 4 and 7, A.E. Forget of the Indian Department, and J.A.J. McKenna, the private secretary to the superintendent general of Indian Affairs. After a year of planning and discussions to determine the offer to be made, a first treaty meeting was held on Lesser Slave Lake, Northwest Territories, in late June 1899. The agreement made there became the basis for the adherence of other communities.

Treaty 8, being the eighth agreement since Confederation, opened a new chapter in treaty making. The circumstances of the 1899 treaty became the norm for future treaties, and despite frequent calls from Indigenous nations seeking both assistance from the government and compensation for encroachment on their unceded lands, government officials were reluctant to proceed unless there was an economic or practical need to conclude a treaty. Such was the case in 1905, when both Ontario and Ottawa formed a commission to secure land title north of the Lake Superior watershed for the construction of a railway to James Bay with Treaty 9,[18] and in 1921 in the Mackenzie Valley when Treaty 11 was negotiated only one year after the opening of the first commercial petroleum well in the north.[19]

ORAL AND WRITTEN ACCOUNTS OF TREATY 8, 1899

As with previous treaties, the treaty conferences held in 1899 and 1900 were to be negotiated between the parties; the government's treaty commissioner did not, however, arrive unprepared. As was the case with earlier treaties in the northwest, such as Treaty 6,[20] the Order-in-Council

---

[17] J.A.J. McKenna to A.E. Forget, July 6, 1898, LAC, RG10, vol. 3848, file 75,236–1.
[18] Miller, *Compact, Contract, Covenant,* 207.
[19] Ibid., 218.
[20] See Chapter 6.

establishing the Treaty Commission had few specific instructions beyond the request to secure the surrender of specific lands.[21] As a result, the task of identifying the extent of the treaty terms to be offered was left to the treaty commissioners and departmental officials. The issues of annuities, reserve lands, and rights to hunt, fish, and trap were at the heart of the discussions.[22] In a series of letters, they debated and discussed the issue of a large single payment versus a yearly annuity, and even the method of payment.[23] Aware that the Indigenous nations of the Peace and Athabasca rivers were familiar with the terms of Treaty 6 and concerned about a potential loss of their rights, the commissioners maintained many of those terms but added trapping to hunting and fishing. The importance of these rights also influenced the discussions regarding reserve lands, as the more northerly lands were less suited to agricultural pursuits. Consequently, the commissioners suggested that along with a larger reserve, additional lands to be held by individuals, known as "lands in severalty," would be made available closer to hunting and fishing sites.[24] To promote the proposed treaty meetings, public notices were printed and distributed throughout the region, while missionaries and members of the NWMP were encouraged to answer questions relating to the proposed treaty. As historian Richard Daniel comments in his article "The Spirit and Terms of Treaty Eight," reports began to surface that the region's Indigenous nations were reluctant to sign a treaty for fear of losing their hunting, fishing, and trapping rights.[25]

In the summers of 1899 and 1900, government-appointed treaty commissioners held 14 meetings with the Cree and Dene peoples of the Athabascan and Peace river watersheds. As the terms of the treaty were set during the initial meeting at Lesser Slave Lake on June 23, 1899, the other 13 meetings were considered to be adhesions to the treaty concluded, since the community leaders were only to sign the treaty without any further modifications. The treaty meetings were held during a period of rapid change throughout the Northwest Territories. Consequently, the treaty signings became a marker in

---

[21] Order-in-Council, P.C. 1703, June 27, 1898.
[22] Dennis Madill, *Treaty Research Report: Treaty Eight (1899)* (Ottawa: Indian and Northern Affairs Canada, 1986), 18.
[23] J.A.J. McKenna to David Laird, December 5, 1898, LAC, RG10, vol. 3848, file 75,236–1; J.A.J. McKenna to Clifford Sifton, April 17, 1899, LAC, RG10, vol. 3848, file 75,236–1.
[24] Arthur J. Ray, Jim Miller, and Frank Tough, *Bounty and Benevolence: A History of Saskatchewan Treaties* (Montreal & Kingston: McGill-Queen's University Press, 2000), 164.
[25] Richard Daniel, "The Spirit and Terms of Treaty Eight," in *The Spirit of the Alberta Indian Treaties*, ed. Richard Price (Edmonton: University of Alberta Press, 1999), 67.

the collective memories of the Treaty 8 communities. After decades of petitions and demands for redress and assistance, it was hoped that the treaty would be the start of renewed prosperity. Some 75 years after the treaty signings, the Treaties and Right Research (TARR) program in Alberta conducted a series of interviews with Elders in Alberta and Saskatchewan "in an attempt to pin down what might be termed as an Indian understanding of treaty."[26] Compared to the interviews for Treaties 6 and 7, concluded in the 1870s, many of the Treaty Elders were witness to the treaty meetings and shared their first-hand knowledge of the events. These oral histories also provide two different glimpses into the treaty-making process in that they capture not only the events at the first treaty meeting that set the final terms, but also how the treaty was understood at subsequent meetings.

Several Elders shared their teachings about how the meetings themselves unfolded. Elder William Okeymaw of Sucker Creek First Nation, who was 87 years old at the time, recounted how, at the age of 12, he accompanied his father and other members of his community to the first treaty meeting at Lesser Slave Lake. He recalled seeing "a huge tent at the time with many people all around it. They were from different places far and near but they travelled for that special day, the treaty. They discussed it for three days to find out how it would work best, how the Indian would make his living when he accepted treaty."[27] The terms of the treaty were not accepted without considerable amounts of persuasion from the Treaty Commission. Elder Okeymaw noted that the commission assured those at Lesser Slave Lake that because of the treaty, they would receive assistance in the future. Another oral history from Sucker Creek, shared by Elder Jean Marie Mustus, further demonstrates the need for persuasion; he recounted how Roman Catholic missionary Father Albert Lacombe urged them to sign the treaty, saying, "If you don't accept treaty, it won't be long and you will not be able to make a living. If you choose a reserve you'll have a better chance of living longer."[28]

During treaty meetings, the assembled leaders also wanted to ensure that their way of life would not be threatened by the arrival of settlers in their lands. As Elder Isador Willier explained, the commissioner stated

---

[26] Lynn Hickey, Richard L. Lightning, and Gordon Lee, "TARR Interview with Elders Program," in *The Spirit of the Alberta Indian Treaties*, ed. Richard Price (Edmonton: University of Alberta Press, 1999), 103.

[27] Interview with Elder William Okeymaw, Sucker Creek First Nation, March 27, 1975, "Indian History Film Project," Canadian Plains Research Centre, University of Regina.

[28] Interview with Jean Marie Mustus, Sucker Creek First Nation, March 26, 1975, "Indian History Film Project," Canadian Plains Research Centre, University of Regina.

that the treaty would not change their rights to hunt, fish, and trap because "no one will ever stop that form of livelihood. If you should take treaty, this is the way you will make your livelihood. Moose, cariboo [sic] and any other wild bush animals, no one will ever stop you from obtaining these animals anywhere. As long as the sun walks and the rivers flow, always and forever always, no one will ever stop you. You will always make your livelihood that way."[29] Richard Daniel comments in his analysis of Treaty 8 oral histories that the fear of losing the rights to hunt fish and trap – rights that formed the basis for the livelihood of Indigenous peoples in the region – was a driving concern during the treaty meetings. Nearly all the Elders who participated in the TARR interviews shared their understanding of the protection of these rights.[30]

While some oral histories, such as the one from Elder Willier, provide specific details of the promises to be included in the treaty, for example the number of agricultural implements and the amount of seed for the size of the reserve,[31] more frequently the accounts speak to what was not in the written terms. For instance, Elder Okeymaw indicated that doctors would be provided to communities, that they would "be cared for," and that the size of reserves would be adjusted to match a growing population:

> All those people were listening to the discussions and especially to one item. Like in my situation at my age I'm becoming concerned about that. A person who had a family and children growing should be able to get an extension of reserve. This applied to the whole band, in case they become farmers or raise livestock or any other way of livelihood or any other occupation such as the white men are doing, to be able to show something by which they make their living, such as gardening.[32]

In a review of their efforts in the Treaty 8 Elder interviews conducted by the TARR program in Alberta, Lynn Hickey, Richard Lightning, and Gordon Lee note that the oral histories contradicted the all-encompassing nature of the treaty text; anything not specifically mentioned was therefore never ceded to the Crown, such as minerals and sub-surface resources.[33]

---

[29] Interview with Elder Isador Willier, Driftpile First Nation, November 18, 1972, "Indian History Film Project," Canadian Plains Research Centre, University of Regina.
[30] Daniel, "The Spirit and Terms of Treaty Eight," 93.
[31] Interview with Elder Isador Willier, November 18, 1972.
[32] Interview with Elder William Okeymaw, March 27, 1975.
[33] Hickey et al., "TARR Interview," 107.

For example, Elder Felix Gibot of Fort Chipewyan First Nation indicated in his community's oral history of the treaty that "the commissioner never mentioned them. The only thing he mentioned was how the people would be cared for by the government as promised in the treaty. That is all which was mentioned."[34] Hickey et al.'s review of the dozens of Treaty 8 oral histories indicates that the agreement concluded in 1899 focused, on the one hand, on the establishment of a relationship between the signatory communities and the Crown, and on the other hand, the treaty would bring "opportunities for a new way of life" for the Indigenous peoples of the Athabasca and Peace rivers.[35]

In September 1899, upon their return from the treaty conference, David Laird, J.H. Ross, and J.A.J. McKenna submitted their official report for the agreement made with the Indigenous nations of "the provisional district of Athabasca and parts of the country adjacent thereto, as described in the treaty."[36] The report gives an overview of the various discussions heard during the ten treaty meetings held in the summer of 1899. It presents a condensed version of the treaty discussions that allows the reader to see how the commission responded to Indigenous proposals and their tactics in reaching an agreement. The report also lets the reader see how the commissioners viewed the Indigenous parties to the treaty as more "civilized" than those of the southern prairie regions, although in need of government assistance:

> The Indians with whom we treated differ in many respects from the Indians of the organized territories. They indulge in neither paint nor feathers, and never clothe themselves in blankets. Their dress is of the ordinary style and many of them were well clothed. In the summer they live in teepees, but many of them have log houses in which they live in winter ... Although in manners and dress the Indians of the North are much further advanced in civilization than other Indians were when treaties were made with them, they stand as much in need of the protection afforded by the law to aborigines as do any other Indians of the country, and are as fit subjects for the paternal care of the Government.[37]

---

[34] Interview with Elder Felix Gibot, Fort Chipewyan First Nation, February 5, 1974, "Indian History Film Project," Canadian Plains Research Centre, University of Regina.
[35] Hickey et al., "TARR Interview," 107.
[36] Report of Treaty Commissioners for Treaty no. 8, September 22, 1899, "Treaty no 8 made June 21 1899 and Adhesions, Reports, Etc." (Ottawa: Queen's Printer, 1966).
[37] Ibid.

Despite the advance planning to define the treaty terms in the year preceding the conference, the negotiations themselves were not as smooth as anticipated. In their opening paragraphs, the commissioners acknowledge this fact, reporting that Indigenous leaders wanted "more liberal terms than were granted to the Indians of the plains," while others sought assistance in time of need, schools for children, and medical aid. The primary concern was the fear of the "curtailment of the hunting and fishing privileges." This last issue would become a central point of discussion, the commissioners having been warned by the NWMP that there was opposition to signing a treaty due to fears of loss of hunting and fishing rights.[38] The commissioners' report stresses that the treaty "would not lead to any forced interference with their mode of life," that they "would be as free to hunt and fish after the treaty as they would be if they never entered into it," and that the only laws and regulations that would be made regarding hunting and fishing would be to protect game stocks. Despite these reassurances, agreement was reached only by increasing the provisions relating to the distribution of ammunition and twine, as this lessened "the fears of the Indians, for they admitted that it would be unreasonable to furnish the means of hunting and fishing if laws were to be enacted which would make hunting and fishing so restricted as to render it impossible to make a livelihood by such pursuits."[39]

The commissioners' report also provides a summary of their responses to requests that they believed went beyond their mandate or capacity. Always reassuring the treaty conference that they wanted to ensure the continued way of life of the communities, they state that assistance would be provided in times of need but that the government would not "maintain Indians in idleness." Contrary to the "famine clause" of Treaty 6, they refused to include specific terms relating to assistance in the text itself. Regarding requests for medical aid, they again refused to include it as a specific treaty clause, arguing that the government "would always be ready to avail itself of any opportunity of affording medical service." After a full day of negotiations on June 20, the commissioners drafted the full terms of the treaty, based partially on Treaty 6 of 1876, with clauses for reserve and severalty lands, agricultural implements, seed and livestock, salaries for school teachers, as well as the inclusion of twine and ammunition to support hunting and fishing.[40] The draft of

---

[38] Madill, *Treaty Research Report*, 21.
[39] Report of Treaty Commissioners for Treaty no. 8.
[40] Ibid.

the treaty they prepared had no references to medical aid, or to government assistance in time of crisis.[41] The commissioners did not report any of the reactions to the final terms when they were formally presented on June 21 but instead stated simply that the agreement concluded at Lesser Slave Lake would be the treaty for the entire region and that other treaty meetings would see the adherence of other communities to this treaty. The remainder of the report presents short accounts of the subsequent nine meetings held in June and July 1899.

The commissioners present a fairly straightforward account of the treaty meetings and report very little of the Indigenous response and reactions to the treaty proposals. This report is not, however, the only existing settler account of the treaty conferences. While the official report for Treaty 6 includes the notes of the commission's secretary, the same cannot be said for Treaty 8, as the notes prepared by Charles Mair, who acted as secretary to the Métis scrip commission that accompanied the Treaty Commission, were excluded. Mair, a Winnipeg-based journalist, published an account of the two commissions as they travelled through the Athabasca District in 1908. Another contemporary source was an article that appeared in the *Edmonton Bulletin* on July 10, 1899, by a reporter who accompanied the Treaty Commission. Mair's account of the Lesser Slave Lake meeting details many of the exchanges between the treaty commissioners, mostly the words of David Laird, and two chiefs, Kinosayoo and Moostoos (Mustus). One exchange notes how the terms were to be accepted without questions, with Kinosayoo stating, "Do you now allow the Indians to make their own conditions, so that they may benefit as much as possible?"[42] The *Edmonton Bulletin*, while noting the inclusion of the pipestem ceremony at the opening of the treaty conference, corroborated Mair's account of initial displeasure with the proposed terms.[43] Whereas the commissioners made no note of the discussions of the final treaty terms presented on the twenty-first, Mair reported that initially there was skepticism among the Indigenous leaders, and acceptance was achieved only after a speech by treaty commissioner J.H. Ross, who reiterated that the treaty would not change their way of life, and an intervention by missionary Father Albert Lacombe, who argued that "your forests and river

---

[41] Daniel, "The Spirit and Terms of Treaty Eight," 80.

[42] Charles Mair, *Through the Mackenzie Basin: An Account of the Signing of Treaty 8 and the Scrip Commission, 1899* (Edmonton: University of Alberta Press, 1999), 60.

[43] "Conference at Slave Lake," July 10, 1899, *Edmonton Bulletin*, LAC, RG10, vol. 3848, file 75,236–1, reel T-9941.

life will not be changed by the Treaty, and you will have your annuities, as well, year by year, as long as the sun shines and the earth remains. Therefore, I finish my speaking by saying, Accept!"[44]

As Brian Calliou notes in the preface to the 1999 reprint of Mair's account *Through the Mackenzie Basin*, settler accounts such as Mair's or the *Edmonton Bulletin* article are one-sided perspectives of the treaty negotiations and are affected by the writer's own views of Indigenous peoples in the northwest.[45] Nonetheless, when read in conjunction with the Treaty Commission's report, they can provide a clearer understanding of the treaty meetings. These other contemporary accounts also align with many of the elements of the treaty signing discussed in Treaty 8 oral histories, especially the need to persuade Indigenous signatories to accept the terms, and the role of Father Lacombe.[46] Furthermore, a comparison of the terms used in the commissioners' report and the Mair account points to the lack of a clear definition of the term "surrender" during the treaty meetings.[47] Despite these first-person accounts that bring a broader perspective of the treaty meetings, the Crown's understanding of what happened on June 20–1, 1899, was defined by the treaty text itself and the Treaty Commission's report. As with other treaties, when these settler sources are compared with oral histories, differences in the understanding of Treaty 8 become apparent. For Richard Daniel, the differences between the oral histories held by Treaty 8 Elders and the details of the Treaty 8 commissioners' report led him to conclude that beyond the broad protection of the way of life based on hunting, fishing, trapping, and the opening of the territory to settlers, there was a "failure of the meeting of minds" regarding the other aspects, such as the sharing of natural resources.[48] In his opinion, this resulted in both sides seeing the treaty favourably but misunderstanding the intent and interpretation of the other party.

TREATY 8 AND THE COURTS

Under the *British North America Act* of 1867, all lands and resources within the boundary of a province were under the jurisdiction of that specific

---

[44] Mair, *Through the Mackenzie Basin*, 62–63.
[45] Ibid., xliv–xlv.
[46] "Conference at Slave Lake," July 10, 1899.
[47] Mair, *Through the Mackenzie Basin*, 57–8.
[48] Richard Daniel, "Indian Rights and Hinterland Resources: The Case of Northern Alberta" (MA thesis, University of Alberta, 1977), 100.

provincial government.[49] Control over these resources was considered important, and they were necessary sources of revenue for the new provincial governments.[50] The federal government, therefore, had control of the resources outside of the provinces; after the transfer of Rupert's Land in 1870, this meant the entirety of the Northwest Territories. With the creation of the provinces of Manitoba (1871) and Saskatchewan and Alberta (1905), the federal government retained control over all Crown resources in the province.[51] The development of new resource sectors, especially lumber, resulted in the provinces demanding more control of the resources within their boundaries in the same manner as other provinces.[52] By 1930, the federal government and the governments of Manitoba, Saskatchewan, and Alberta had come to an agreement for the transfer of ownership to all resources rights. As historian Frank Tough notes in "The Forgotten Constitution: Natural Resources Transfer Agreements and Indian Livelihood Rights," the Natural Resources Transfer Agreements (NRTA) amended the *British North America Act* by transferring resources, but they also modified the hunting, fishing, and trapping rights described in the Numbered Treaties.[53] Specifically, the agreements extend the rights beyond the confines of the treaty boundary to the entire province and specified that hunting, fishing, and trapping can be done only for food and only on unoccupied Crown lands. Since the passage of the NRTA, the changes effected with respect to Indigenous treaty rights have been the focus of several court decisions and have influenced how the terms of the treaty are to be interpreted, such as the Supreme Court of Canada's ruling in *R. v. Badger* in 1996.

This case focused on three Indigenous men, Wayne Clarence Badger, Leroy Steven Kiyawasew, and Ernest Clarence Ominayak, all members of Treaty 8 First Nation communities who had been charged for hunting for food on private land under the Alberta *Wildlife Act*.[54] Under the defined

---

[49] *British North America Act*, 1867, 30–1 Vict., c. 3, section 109.
[50] Robert D. Cairns, "Natural Resource and Canadian Federalism: Decentralization, Recurring Conflict, and Resolution" *Publis: The Journal of Federalism* 22 (1992): 55.
[51] For example, see section 21 of *Alberta Act*, 1905, 4–5 Edw. VII, c. 3.
[52] Adam Wellstead, "The (Post) Staples Economy and the (Post) Staples State in Historical Perspective," *Canadian Political Science Review* 1, no. 1 (2007): 16.
[53] Frank J. Tough, "The Forgotten Constitution: The Natural Resources Transfer Agreements and Indian Livelihood Rights, ca. 1925–1933," *Alberta Law Review* 41, no. 4 (2004): 1000.
[54] Leonard I. Rotman, "Hunting for Answers in a Strange Kettle of Fish: Unilateralism, Paternalism and Fiduciary Rhetoric in *Badger* and *Van der Peet*," *Constitutional Forum* 8, no. 2 (1997): 41.

terms relating to hunting and fishing in Treaty 8 of 1899, the three men argued that they had a right to hunt. For its part, the province replied that the treaty rights had been extinguished and replaced by the 1930 NRTA, with a specific and more limited right to hunt for food. Continuously appealing their conviction through the provincial courts all the way to the Court of Appeal, Badger, Kiyawasew, and Ominayak called on the Supreme Court of Canada to hear their case and determine both whether the NRTA had extinguished or modified the treaty right to hunt and the extent to which legislation could be used to limit the exercise of treaty rights to hunt and fish.[55] On April 3, 1996, the Supreme Court tabled its ruling upholding the convictions of Badger and Kiyawasew; it allowed the appeal of Ominayak but ordered a new trial for him.

The decision, written by Justice Peter Cory, concluded that while Treaty 8 did guarantee Indigenous signatories a right to hunt, fish, and trap, that right was also "subject to two limitations, a geographic limitation and the right of government to make regulations for conservation purposes."[56] At the same time, the Court reiterated four essential principles of treaty interpretation: (1) treaties are exchanges of solemn promises between the Crown and Indigenous nations; (2) "the Crown must be assumed to intend to fulfil it promises"; (3) ambiguity around treaty terms must be resolved in a manner favouring Indigenous signatories without narrowly restricting treaty rights; and (4) the Crown must prove that a right has been extinguished. Contradicting the province's argument that the passage of the NRTA in 1930 had extinguished the treaty right to hunt, the Supreme Court decided that the "NRTA did not extinguish and replace the Treaty No. 8 right to hunt for food" and that the inclusion of Paragraph 12 of the NRTA relating to Indigenous hunting and fishing rights "clearly intended to extinguish the treaty protection of the right to hunt commercially but the right to hunt for food continued to be protected and, indeed, was expanded. Treaty rights, absent direct conflict with the NRTA, were not modified. The treaty right to hunt for food accordingly continues in force and effect."

Since both the treaty text and paragraph 12 of the NRTA stated that the right to hunt is limited to "unoccupied Crown lands," it was decided that the appeals for Badger and Kiyawasew would be rejected because

---

[55] Thomas Isaac, *Aboriginal Law: Commentary, Cases and Materials* (Saskatoon: Purich, 2004), 81.
[56] *R. v. Badger*, [1996] 1 R.C.S., p. 773.

they were hunting where the "land was being visibly used. Since they did not have a right of access to these particular tracts of land, their treaty right to hunt for food did not extend there."[57] As the third appellant, Ernest Ominayak, was not hunting on land that was "being put to any visible use," his appeal was granted, but a new trial would be required to determine how his rights were being infringed by the provincial legislation. Adding to the list of treaty interpretation principles to be used by the courts, the ruling also questioned how Indigenous signatories would have understood the limitations of the treaty right to hunt as a result of the negotiations in 1899. Basing its deliberation on contemporary accounts of the treaty meetings and references to conservation of game, but not on oral histories, the Court concluded that Treaty 8 First Nations "would have understood that, by the terms of the Treaty, the government would be permitted to pass regulations with respect to conservation given the existence of conservation laws existing prior to signing the Treaty." As a result of the transfer of authority to the province through the NRTA, the province could pass legislation for conservation purposes that "were not in conflict with aboriginal and treaty rights," but not without justification or undue limitations.[58]

Building on its 1990 *Horseman* decision, where it was decided that the Crown had the power to modify the Treaty 8 right to hunt commercially through the NRTA,[59] the Supreme Court stated that the NRTA "restated, merged and consolidated" treaty rights to hunt, fish, and trap, and therefore it was the "sole source for a claim involving the right to hunt for food." It then reduced the significance of the right as stated in the treaty, noting that it could be used only to assist "in the interpretation of the NRTA but it has no other legal significance." To ensure that the interpretative principles remain the same, however, the Court added that the rights stated in paragraph 12 of the NRTA had to follow the same principles as are used for all other treaties, specifically that "ambiguity in the treaty will be resolved in favour of the Indians," and "treaties should be interpreted in a manner that maintains the integrity of the Crown, particularly the Crown's fiduciary obligation toward aboriginal peoples."

As Indigenous law scholar Catherine Bell states in her commentary on the Supreme Court's ruling, the decision provides a mixed interpretation

---

[57] Ibid., 774.
[58] Ibid.
[59] Robert Reiter, *The Law of Canadian Indian Treaties* (Edmonton: Juris Analytica, 1994), part 7, p. 46.

of treaty rights. While it helps clarify the concept of "incompatible use" of lands that may allow the exercise of a treaty right to hunt on some occupied non-Crown land, it also acknowledges that the Crown can extinguish a treaty right without the consent of Indigenous signatories.[60] Her criticism rests on the fact that the ruling seems to ignore the interpretative principle that rights should reflect how those rights would have been understood by Indigenous signatories at the time of signing.[61] In this case, the ruling went against that principle and ignored both the oral histories of Treaty 8 communities and the words of the treaty commissioners, specifically that nothing would prevent their "continued livelihood" based on hunting, fishing, and trapping. Other legal commentators have also expressed concern that the ruling goes against interpretative principles for treaty rights in cases such as *Sioui* (1990).[62] As lawyer Kristy Pozniak indicates, the Supreme Court did not consider using the legal test from *Sioui* that treaty rights could be extinguished only with the consent of Indigenous signatories when it ruled that the NRTA had modified the Treaty 8 rights to hunt, fish, and trap.[63] Leonard Rotman, legal scholar at the University of Windsor, notes in his analysis that the *Badger* decision "clearly indicated that treaty rights were considered by the Supreme Court of Canada to be inferior to unilateral constitutional enactments such as the NRTA." As a result, the Supreme Court created a situation where the Crown could both breach its responsibilities under the treaty through unilateral extinguishment and uphold the "honour of the Crown" to act in a manner that fulfils its treaty responsibilities.[64]

The Supreme Court of Canada's decision in *R. v. Badger* is an example of how the courts determine the interpretation of treaties with relatively little reliance on either settler written accounts or Indigenous oral histories. Despite these gaps in information, the decision has created a specific legal interpretation of Treaty 8 that merges it with the 1930 *Natural Resources Transfer Act* – an interpretation that does not strictly correspond with the words of the Treaty Commission's report or the collective teachings of Treaty 8 Indigenous communities.

---

[60] Catherine Bell, "*R. v. Badger*: One Step Forward, Two Steps Back?," *Constitutional Forum* 8, no. 2 (1997) 21.
[61] Ibid., 23.
[62] See Chapter 2.
[63] Kristy Pozniak, "Modification, Infringement, and the 'Visible, Incompatible' Test: The Impact of *R. v. Badger* on Treaty Hunting Rights in the Prairie Provinces," *Saskatchewan Law Review* 68, no. 2 (2005): 403–34.
[64] Rotman, "Hunting for Answers," 42.

FURTHER READINGS

Harold Cardinal. *Treaty 8 – A Case Study*. Ottawa: Royal Commission on Aboriginal Peoples, 1993.

Richard Daniel. "The Spirit and Terms of Treaty 8." In *The Spirit of the Alberta Indian Treaties*, ed. Richard Price. Edmonton: University of Alberta Press, 1999.

Jean Friesen. "Magnificent Gifts: The Treaties of Canada with the Indians of the Northwest 1869–1876." In *The Spirit of the Alberta Indian Treaties*, ed. Richard Price. Edmonton: University of Alberta Press, 1999.

Dennis Madill. *Treaty Research Report: Treaty Eight (1899)*. Ottawa: Indian and Northern Affairs Canada, 1986.

Frank Tough, "The Forgotten Constitution: The Natural Resources Transfer Agreements and Indian Livelihood Rights, ca. 1925–1933." *Alberta Law Review* 41, no. 4 (2004): 999–1048.

QUESTIONS FOR DISCUSSION

1. Read the following excerpt of the treaty text and identify the reasons for concluding the treaty in 1899:

   Excerpt: Treaty No. 8
   AND WHEREAS, the said Indians have been notified and informed by Her Majesty's said Commission that it is Her desire to open for settlement, immigration, trade, travel, mining, lumbering and such other purposes as to Her Majesty may seem meet, a tract of country bounded and described as hereinafter mentioned, and to obtain the consent thereto of Her Indian subjects inhabiting the said tract, and to make a treaty, and arrange with them, so that there may be peace and good will between them and Her Majesty's other subjects, and that Her Indian people may know and be assured of what allowances they are to count upon and receive from Her Majesty's bounty and benevolence.

2. Read the following excerpts, one by Treaty 8 Elder Felix Gibot and the other by the treaty commissioner, and list the similarities and differences relating to some of the treaty promises:

   Interview with Elder Felix Gibot, Fort Chipewyan First Nation, February 5, 1974, "Indian History Film Project," Canadian Plains Research Centre, University of Regina
   Everybody arrived here at Fort Chipewyan. Everybody arrived here for a meeting and to listen. "Now," said the commissioner, "I was sent here by the government to read this document to you. Stories

have reached the government that Indians have been dying of starvation in the bush. The government would like to take control of the Indian people and care for them. The government does not want to see you living in poverty in the bush. This is the reason why I am here."

Report of Commissioners for Treaty No. 8, Winnipeg, Manitoba, September 22, 1899
We pointed out that the Government could not undertake to maintain Indians in idleness; that the same means of earning a livelihood would continue after the treaty as existed before it, and that the Indians would be expected to make use of them. We told them that the Government was always ready to give relief in cases of actual destitution, and that in seasons of distress they would without any special stipulation in the treaty receive such assistance as it was usual to give in order to prevent starvation among Indians in any part of Canada; and we stated that the attention of the Government would be called to the need of some special provision being made for assisting the old and indigent who were unable to work and dependent on charity for the means of sustaining life.

3. In your opinion, why do the Elders' oral histories focus on the issue of livelihood?
4. How do the courts interpret the rights contained in the treaty?

DOCUMENTS

Treaty Text Excerpts: Treaty No. 8, LAC, RG10, vol. 1848, IT 415, IA 428, T-9941

ARTICLES OF A TREATY made and concluded at the several dates mentioned therein, in the year of Our Lord one thousand eight hundred and ninety-nine, between Her most Gracious Majesty the Queen of Great Britain and Ireland, by Her Commissioners the Honourable David Laird, of Winnipeg, Manitoba, Indian Commissioner for the said Province and the Northwest Territories; James Andrew Joseph McKenna, of Ottawa, Ontario, Esquire, and the Honourable James Hamilton Ross, of Regina, in the Northwest Territories, of the one part; and the Cree, Beaver, Chipewyan and other Indians, inhabitants of the territory within the limits hereinafter defined and described, by their Chiefs and Headmen, hereunto subscribed, of the other part:

WHEREAS, the Indians inhabiting the territory hereinafter defined have, pursuant to notice given by the Honourable Superintendent General of Indian Affairs in the year 1898, been convened to meet a Commission representing Her Majesty's Government of the Dominion of Canada at certain places in the said territory in this present year 1899, to deliberate upon certain matters of interest of Her Most Gracious Majesty, of the one part, and the said Indians of the other.

AND WHEREAS, the said Indians have been notified and informed by Her Majesty's said Commission that it is Her desire to open for settlement, immigration, trade, travel, mining, lumbering and such other purposes as to Her Majesty may seem meet, a tract of country bounded and described as hereinafter mentioned, and to obtain the consent thereto of Her Indian subjects inhabiting the said tract, and to make a treaty, and arrange with them, so that there may be peace and good will between them and Her Majesty's other subjects, and that Her Indian people may know and be assured of what allowances they are to count upon and receive from Her Majesty's bounty and benevolence.

...

AND WHEREAS, the said Commissioners have proceeded to negotiate a treaty with the Cree, Beaver, Chipewyan and other Indians, inhabiting the district hereinafter defined and described, and the same has been agreed upon and concluded by the respective bands at the dates mentioned hereunder, the said Indians DO HEREBY CEDE, RELEASE, SURRENDER AND YIELD UP to the Government of the Dominion of Canada, for Her Majesty the Queen and Her successors for ever, all their rights, titles and privileges whatsoever, to the lands included within the following limits, that is to say:

Commencing at the source of the main branch of the Red Deer River in Alberta, thence due west to the central range of the Rocky Mountains, thence northwesterly along the said range to the point where it intersects the 60th parallel of north latitude, thence east along said parallel to the point where it intersects Hay River, thence northeasterly down said river to the south shore of Great Slave Lake, thence along the said shore northeasterly (and including such rights to the islands in said lakes as the Indians mentioned in the treaty may possess), and thence easterly and northeasterly along the south shores of Christie's Bay and McLeod's Bay to old Fort Reliance near the mouth of Lockhart's River, thence southeasterly in a straight line to and including Black Lake, thence southwesterly up the stream from Cree Lake, thence including said lake southwesterly along the height of land between the Athabasca and Churchill Rivers to where it intersects the northern boundary of Treaty Six, and along the said boundary easterly, northerly and southwesterly, to the place of commencement.

AND ALSO the said Indian rights, titles and privileges whatsoever to all other lands wherever situated in the Northwest Territories, British Columbia, or in any other portion of the Dominion of Canada.

TO HAVE AND TO HOLD the same to Her Majesty the Queen and Her successors for ever.

And Her Majesty the Queen HEREBY AGREES with the said Indians that they shall have right to pursue their usual vocations of hunting, trapping and fishing throughout the tract surrendered as heretofore described, subject to such regulations as may from time to time be made by the Government of the country, acting under the authority of Her Majesty, and saving and excepting such tracts as may be required or taken up from time to time for settlement, mining, lumbering, trading or other purposes.

And Her Majesty the Queen hereby agrees and undertakes to lay aside reserves for such bands as desire reserves, the same not to exceed in all one square mile for each family of five for such number of families as may elect to reside on reserves, or in that proportion for larger or smaller families; and for such families or individual Indians as may prefer to live apart from band reserves, Her Majesty undertakes to provide land in severalty to the extent of 160 acres to each Indian, the land to be conveyed with a proviso as to non-alienation without the consent of the Governor General in Council of Canada ...

Provided, however, that Her Majesty reserves the right to deal with any settlers within the bounds of any lands reserved for any band as She may see fit; and also that the aforesaid reserves of land, or any interest therein, may be sold or otherwise disposed of by Her Majesty's Government for the use and benefit of the said Indians entitled thereto, with their consent first had and obtained.

It is further agreed between Her Majesty and Her said Indian subjects that such portions of the reserves and lands above indicated as may at any time be required for public works, buildings, railways, or roads of whatsoever nature may be appropriated for that purpose by Her Majesty's Government of the Dominion of Canada, due compensation being made to the Indians for the value of any improvements thereon, and an equivalent in land, money or other consideration for the area of the reserve so appropriated.

And with a view to show the satisfaction of Her Majesty with the behaviour and good conduct of Her Indians, and in extinguishment of all their past claims, She hereby, through Her Commissioners, agrees to make each Chief a present of thirty-two dollars in cash, to each Headman twenty-two dollars, and to every other Indian of whatever age, of the families represented at the time and place of payment, twelve dollars.

Her Majesty also agrees that next year, and annually afterwards for ever, She will cause to be paid to the said Indians in cash, at suitable places and dates, of which the said Indians shall be duly notified, to each Chief twenty-five dollars, each Headman, not to exceed four to a large Band and two to a small Band, fifteen dollars, and to every other Indian, of whatever age, five dollars, the same, unless there be some exceptional reason, to be paid only to heads of families for those belonging thereto.

FURTHER, Her Majesty agrees that each Chief, after signing the treaty, shall receive a silver medal and a suitable flag, and next year, and every third year thereafter, each Chief and Headman shall receive a suitable suit of clothing.

FURTHER, Her Majesty agrees to pay the salaries of such teachers to instruct the children of said Indians as to Her Majesty's Government of Canada may seem advisable.

FURTHER, Her Majesty agrees to supply each Chief of a Band that selects a reserve, for the use of that Band, ten axes, five hand-saws, five augers, one grindstone, and the necessary files and whetstones.

FURTHER, Her Majesty agrees that each Band that elects to take a reserve and cultivate the soil, shall, as soon as convenient after such reserve is set aside and settled upon, and the Band has signified its choice and is prepared to break up the soil, receive two hoes, one spade, one scythe and two hay forks for every family so settled, and for every three families one plough and one harrow, and to the Chief, for the use of his Band, two horses or a yoke of oxen, and for each Band potatoes, barley, oats and wheat (if such seed be suited to the locality of the reserve), to plant the land actually broken up, and provisions for one month in the spring for several years while planting such seeds; and to every family one cow, and every Chief one bull, and one mowing-machine and one reaper for the use of his Band when it is ready for them; for such families as prefer to raise stock instead of cultivating the soil, every family of five persons, two cows, and every Chief two bulls and two mowing-machines when ready for their use, and a like proportion for smaller or larger families. The aforesaid articles, machines and cattle to be given once for all for the encouragement of agriculture and stock raising; and for such Bands as prefer to continue hunting and fishing, as much ammunition and twine for making nets annually as will amount in value to one dollar per head of the families so engaged in hunting and fishing.

And the undersigned Cree, Beaver, Chipewyan and other Indian Chiefs and Headmen, on their own behalf and on behalf of all the Indians whom they represent, DO HEREBY SOLEMNLY PROMISE and engage to strictly observe this Treaty, and also to conduct and behave themselves as good and loyal subjects of Her Majesty the Queen.

THEY PROMISE AND ENGAGE that they will, in all respects, obey and abide by the law; that they will maintain peace between each other, and between themselves and other tribes of Indians, and between themselves and others of Her Majesty's subjects, whether Indians, half-breeds or whites, this year inhabiting and hereafter to inhabit any part of the said ceded territory; and that they will not molest the person or property of any inhabitant of such ceded tract, or of any other district or country, or interfere with or trouble any person passing or travelling through the said tract or any part thereof, and that they will assist the officers of Her Majesty in bringing to justice and punishment any Indian offending against the stipulations of this Treaty or infringing the law in force in the country so ceded.

IN WITNESS WHEREOF Her Majesty's said Commissioners and the Cree Chief and Headmen of Lesser Slave Lake and the adjacent territory, HAVE HEREUNTO SET THEIR HANDS at Lesser Slave Lake on the twenty-first day of June, in the year herein first above written.

Signed by the parties hereto, in the presence of the undersigned witnesses, the same having been first explained to the Indians by Albert Tate and Samuel Cunningham, Interpreters.	DAVID LAIRD, Treaty Commissioner,
	J.A.J. McKENNA, Treaty Commissioner,
	J. H. ROSS, Treaty Commissioner,
Father A. LACOMBE,	his
GEO. HOLMES,	KEE NOO SHAY OO x Chief,
E. GROUARD, O.M.I.,	mark
W. G. WHITE,	his
JAMES WALKER,	MOOSTOOS x Headman,
J. ARTHUR COTÉ,	mark
A. E. SNYDER, Insp. N.W.M.P.,	his
H. B. ROUND,	FELIX GIROUX x Headman,
HARRISON S. YOUNG,	mark
J. F. PRUD'HOMME,	his
J. W. MARTIN,	WEE CHEE WAY SIS x Headman,
C. MAIR,	mark
H. A. CONROY,	his
PIERRE DESCHAMBEAULT,	CHARLES NEE SUE TA SIS x Headman,
J. H. PICARD,	mark
RICHARD SECORD,	his
M. MCCAULEY.	CAPTAIN x Headman, from Sturgeon Lake mark.

Report of Commissioners for Treaty No. 8

WINNIPEG, MANITOBA, 22nd September, 1899.

The Honourable
CLIFFORD SIFTON,
Superintendent General of Indian Affairs,
Ottawa.

SIR, – We have the honour to transmit herewith the treaty which, under the Commission issued to us on the 5th day of April last, we have made with the Indians of the provisional district of Athabasca and parts of the country adjacent thereto, as described in the treaty and shown on the map attached.

The date fixed for meeting the Indians at Lesser Slave Lake was the 8th of June, 1899. Owing, however, to unfavourable weather and lack of boatmen, we did not reach the point until the 19th. ... We met the Indians on the 20th, and on the 21st the treaty was signed.

As the discussions at the different points followed on much the same lines, we shall confine ourselves to a general statement of their import. There was a marked absence of the old Indian style of oratory. Only among the Wood Crees were any formal speeches made, and these were brief. The Beaver Indians are taciturn. The Chipewyans confined themselves to asking questions and making brief arguments. They appeared to be more adept at cross-examination than at speech-making, and the Chief at Fort Chipewyan displayed considerable keenness of intellect and much practical sense in pressing the claims of his band. They all wanted as liberal, if not more liberal terms, than were granted to the Indians of the plains. Some expected to be fed by the Government after the making of treaty, and all asked for assistance in season of distress and urged that the old and indigent who were no longer able to hunt and trap and were consequently often in distress should be cared for by the Government. They requested that medicines be furnished. At Vermilion, Chipewyan and Smith's Landing, an earnest appeal was made for the services of a medical man. There was expressed at every point the fear that the making of the treaty would be followed by the curtailment of the hunting and fishing privileges, and many were impressed with the notion that the treaty would lead to taxation and enforced military service. They seemed desirous of securing educational advantages for their children, but stipulated that in the matter of schools there should be no interference with their religious beliefs.

We pointed out that the Government could not undertake to maintain Indians in idleness; that the same means of earning a livelihood would continue after the treaty as existed before it, and that the Indians would be expected to make use of them. We told them that the Government was always ready to give relief in cases of actual destitution, and that in seasons of distress they would without any special stipulation in the treaty receive such assistance as it was usual to give in order to prevent starvation among Indians in any part of Canada; and we stated that the attention of the Government would be called to the need of some special provision being made for assisting the old and indigent who were unable to work and dependent on charity for the means of sustaining life. We promised that supplies of medicines would be put in the charge of persons selected by the Government at different points, and would be distributed free to those of the Indians who might require them. We explained that it would be practically impossible for the Government to arrange for regular medical attendance upon Indians so widely scattered over such an extensive territory. We assured them, however, that the Government would always be ready to avail itself of any opportunity of affording medical service just as it provided that the physician attached to the Commission should give free attendance to all Indians whom he might find in need of treatment as he passed through the country.

Our chief difficulty was the apprehension that the hunting and fishing privileges were to be curtailed. The provision in the treaty under which ammunition and twine is to be furnished went far in the direction of quieting the fears of the Indians, for they admitted that it would be unreasonable to furnish the means of hunting and fishing if laws were to be enacted which would make hunting and fishing so restricted as to render it impossible to make a livelihood by such pursuits. But over and above the provision, we had to solemnly assure them that only such laws as to hunting and fishing as were in the interest of the Indians and were found necessary in order to protect the fish and fur-bearing animals would be made, and that they would be as free to hunt and fish after the treaty as they would be if they never entered into it.

We assured them that the treaty would not lead to any forced interference with their mode of life, that it did not open the way to the imposition of any tax, and that there was no fear of enforced military service. We showed them that, whether treaty was made or not, they were subject to the law, bound to obey it, and liable to punishment for any infringements of it. We pointed out that the law was designed for the protection of all, and must be respected by all the inhabitants of the country, irrespective of colour or origin; and that, in requiring them to live at peace with white men who came into the country, and not to molest them in person or in property, it only required them to do what white men were required to do as to the Indians.

As to education the Indians were assured that there was no need of any special stipulation, as it was the policy of the Government to provide in every part of the country, as far as circumstances would permit, for the education of Indian children, and that the law, which was as strong as a treaty, provided for non-interference with the religion of the Indians in schools maintained or assisted by the Government.

...

When we conferred, after the first meeting with the Indians at Lesser Slave Lake, we came to the conclusion that it would be best to make one treaty covering the whole of the territory ceded, and to take adhesions thereto from the Indians to be met at the other points rather than to make several separate treaties. The treaty was therefore so drawn as to provide three ways in which assistance is to be given to the Indians, in order to accord with the conditions of the country and to meet the requirements of the Indians in the different parts of the territory.

In addition to the annuity, which we found it necessary to fix at the figures of Treaty Six, which covers adjacent territory, the treaty stipulates that assistance in the form of seed and implements and cattle will be given to those of the Indians who may take to farming, in the way of cattle and mowers to those who may devote themselves to cattle-raising, and that ammunition and twine will be given to those who continue to fish and hunt. The assistance in farming and ranching is only to be given when the Indians actually take to these pursuits, and it is not likely that for many years there will be a call for any considerable expenditure under these heads. The only Indians of the territory ceded who are likely to take to cattle-raising are those about Lesser Slave Lake and along the Peace River, where there is quite an extent of ranching country; and although there are stretches of cultivable land in those parts of the country, it is not probable that the Indians will, while present conditions obtain, engage in farming further than the raising of roots in a small way, as is now done to some extent. In the main the demand will be for ammunition and twine, as the great majority of the Indians will continue to hunt and fish for a livelihood. It does not appear likely that the conditions of the country on either side of the Athabasca and Slave Rivers or about Athabasca Lake will be so changed as to affect hunting or trapping, and it is safe to say that so long as the fur-bearing animals remain, the great bulk of the Indians will continue to hunt and to trap.

The Indians are given the option of taking reserves or land in severalty. As the extent of the country treated for made it impossible to define reserves or holdings, and as the Indians were not prepared to make selections, we confined ourselves to an undertaking to have reserves and holdings set apart in the future, and the Indians were satisfied with the promise that this would be done when required. There is no immediate necessity for the general laying out of reserves or the allotting of land. It will be quite time enough to do this as advancing settlement makes necessary the surveying of the land. Indeed, the Indians were generally averse to being placed on reserves. It would have been impossible to have made a treaty if we had not assured them that there was no intention of confining them to reserves. We had to very clearly explain to them that the provision for reserves and allotments of land were made for their protection, and to secure to them in perpetuity a fair portion of the land ceded, in the event of settlement advancing ...

    A detailed statement of the Indians treated with and of the money paid is appended.

We have the honour to be, sir,

> Your obedient servants,
> DAVID LAIRD,
> J. H. ROSS,
> J. A. J. McKENNA
> Indian Treaty Commissioners.

Excerpts from an interview with Elder William Okeymaw, Sucker Creek First Nation, March 27, 1975, "Indian History Film Project," Canadian Plains Research Centre, University of Regina. Reprinted by permission of The University of Regina Press.

I was about 12 years old and we travelled by foot or by boat. We crossed the river here in a boat, then we walked the rest of the way. When we arrived the commissioners were already prepared. Alongside them were about 22 North-West Mounted Police (NWMP) troops. I was frightened because I was only a child. I even held my dad's hand I was so scared. That is one thing I have in me is long memory. I can recall many things of long ago. I can recall a huge tent at the time with many people all around it. They were from different places far and near but they travelled for that special day, the treaty. They discussed it for three days to find out how it would work best, how the Indian would make his living when he accepted treaty.

    There are many things we didn't see, only a few such as the rations, very little of it. The main thing we are missing is the promises which were made to us. For example, Mustus, Key no say oo and Twin and Daniel Ferguson – he was with the Metis and he was thought of as a spokesman for the Metis. All those people were listening to the discussions and especially to one item. Like in my situation at my age I'm becoming concerned about that. A person who had a family and children growing should be able to get an extension of reserve. This applied to the whole band, in case they become farmers or raise livestock or any other way of livelihood or any other occupation such as the white men are doing, to be able to show something by which they make their living, such as gardening.

...

I don't know why they forgot the promise which they made to us. They have forgotten about that in Ottawa. These are the items we are wondering about and in need of. That is the reason a treaty was signed and our chief accepted a reserve, because there was a lot of persuasion and it sounded so realistic. I was listening there at the time. There is also another thing. If the Indian had anything of value on the reserve, it was his. It was only 6 inches of the surface of the ground that the commissioners were requesting... During the time of the negotiations nothing was asked about timber, so why is it they are taking the timber? It would have been better for the Indians to make use of it.

The Indian people still have other promises coming to them yet. The government still owes them a lot and he should get more help. We cannot say how long this earth will last. The commissioner said, "This will be in effect as long as the sun shines and the rivers flow." He used these two in sincerity. Today the river still flows and when we get up each morning we see the sun. I heard many things that time that the people could depend upon in the future for a living. We were not persuaded for nothing, like the white man was receiving assistance. He could settle any place. He would get help from the government, but whose money is it they are using? Maybe it belongs to the Indians. The Indian who gave up his land and prior to that made his own living should also get some type of help. He is entitled to it more so than anybody else. If they were not encouraged into treaty, the chief even today would not have consented because they were tricked. The Indian people were not like that. They would not say something and not do it. They didn't lie to one another or cheat.

Excerpts from an interview with Elder Felix Gibot, Fort Chipewyan First Nation, February 5, 1974, "Indian History Film Project," Canadian Plains Research Centre, University of Regina. Reprinted by permission of The University of Regina Press.

[Felix Gilbot:] I will tell you the story from the time of the treaty until what is happening today. I will tell you. I didn't hear it and I didn't read it. I saw it take place myself. I am telling the truth of what I'm saying. During a time while we were in the bush, word got around that we were all invited. We were not aware what it was for. Everybody arrived here at Fort Chipewyan. Everybody arrived here for a meeting and to listen. "Now," said the commissioner, "I was sent here by the government to read this document to you. Stories have reached the government that Indians have been dying of starvation in the bush. The government would like to take control of the Indian people and care for them. The government does not want to see you living in poverty in the bush. This it the reason why I am here."

...

The following day, there was another meeting. The same promises were reiterated. The Indian said, "You now have worked on me for 2 days, and now on the third day, I will talk to you. What you are saying is that the promises are being made in good faith. My people will now be cared for by the government. But I will tell you one thing. I don't want my people to be sent away from our land. I want them to stay here at Fort Chipewyan. It is large enough that there is room for everybody." The commissioner told him that this land which now belongs to you, that is the land you can keep. None will be restricted to you. You can make your living the way it suits you best. The chief said, "yes." That is when they put the coat on him and he was officially made chief. He indicated that since he was now chief, he didn't want the commissioners to say no to anything he said or requested. "When you make promises to me and I say yes, I have given you my word to last forever. If I agree to anything again, that is my final word and I expect the same from you. The promise you have made I want that fulfilled." The commissioner said, "On this trip when I'm representing the government, as long as the sun walks, the river flows, your request for anything will never be turned down." "I won't see any of this, but my people will see it if they're alive. There will be constant changes taking place in the future. As these children grow up, they will see the changes. Myself, I won't live very long, because I'm an old man." That old man was chief for 15 years although he was an old man. It was true about what he said, that he won't see the changes taking place. He also said, "For all of you who are here, I don't want you to forget these promises which are being long made." He also told the commissioner that they would get along with the white man as long as they lived, and that he would ho the white man would do the same. "I will think of them as my younger brothers when I see them." The chief also told the same thing to his people. "If you see a white man in need, help him. If you are kind to them, they too will be kind to you. They won't force you into anything if you have respect for them. It won't be like being forced into the water."

... What I'm saying now was not written on paper. I've seen it myself and heard people tell of it at the beginning as it was promised to us. And that is exactly how to the promises were made as I am telling it now.

Interviewer: You claim that the land you mentioned before was yours. It was allotted to you and when the commissioner came here to make treaty, were his intentions to sign on a friendly basis (peace) or was it to acquire the land?

Felix Gilbot: That is something which always puzzled me when I think of it. It appears as though he wanted to claim the land the way he spoke. They wanted to own the land from the government. That is why they took that action. This is what I thought anyway ... At times the Indian people forget about that. The white man never bought the land. If they bought it, there would be very large sums of money involved in order for them to claim the land. That is what some of the Indian people say, and as a result, they become angry.

Interviewer: Did the Indians of long ago ever imagine or think of anything valuable that would be found underground?

Felix Gilbot: You mean the elders of long ago? No, they never mentioned anything about money [gold] to be underground or even petroleum to be found below the surface. I never heard my grandfather, although he was intelligent, to mention anything.

Even after my grandfather died, I never heard anything questioned.

Interviewer: They never told stories of the commissioner to discuss these things?

Felix Gilbot: No, the commissioner never mentioned them. The only thing he mentioned was how the people would be cared for by the government as promised in the treaty. That is all which was mentioned.

Excerpt from *R. v. Badger*, [1996] 1 S.C.R. 771

Treaty No. 8 guaranteed the Indians the "right to pursue their usual vocations of hunting, trapping and fishing" subject to two limitations, a geographic limitation and the right of government to make regulations for conservation purposes.

Certain principles apply in interpreting a treaty. First, a treaty represents an exchange of solemn promises between the Crown and the various Indian nations. Second, the honour of the Crown is always at stake; the Crown must be assumed to intend to fulfil its promises. No appearance of "sharp dealing" will be sanctioned. Third, any ambiguities or doubtful expressions must be resolved in favour of the Indians and any limitations restricting the rights of Indians under treaties must be narrowly construed. Finally, the onus of establishing strict proof of extinguishment of a treaty or aboriginal right lies upon the Crown.

The NRTA did not extinguish and replace the Treaty No. 8 right to hunt for food. Paragraph 12 of the NRTA clearly intended to extinguish the treaty protection of the right to hunt commercially but the right to hunt for food continued to be protected and, indeed, was expanded. Treaty rights, absent direct conflict with the NRTA, were not modified. The Treaty right to hunt for food accordingly continues in force and effect.

Three preliminary observations were made regarding the NRTA. First, the "right of access" in the NRTA does not refer to a general right of access but, rather, is limited to a right of access for the purposes of hunting. Second, the extent of the treaty right to hunt on privately owned land may well differ from one treaty to another, given differences in wording. Finally, the applicable interpretative principles must be applied. The words must be interpreted as they would naturally have been understood by the Indians at the time of signing.

The geographical limitation on the existing hunting right should be based upon a concept of visible, incompatible land use. This approach is consistent with the oral promises made to the Indians at the time the Treaty was signed, with the oral history of the Treaty No. 8 Indians, with earlier case law and with the provisions of the Act itself. It is neither unduly vague nor unworkable. Land use must be considered on a case-by-case basis, however, because the approach focuses upon the use being made of the land.

The appeals of Messrs. Badger and Kiyawasew must be dismissed. The land was being visibly used. Since they did not have a right of access to these particular tracts of land, their treaty right to hunt for food did not extend there. The limitations on hunting set out in the Act accordingly did not infringe upon their existing right and were properly applied. The geographical limitations upon the Treaty right to hunt for food did not affect Mr. Ominayak who was hunting on land not being put to any visible use.

The Indians would have understood that, by the terms of the Treaty, the government would be permitted to pass regulations with respect to conservation given the existence of conservation laws existing prior to signing the Treaty. The provincial government's regulatory authority under the Treaty and the NRTA (which transferred regulatory authority for conservation purposes to the provincial authorities) did not extend beyond the realm of conservation. The constitutional provisions of s. 12 of NRTA authorizing provincial regulations made it unnecessary to consider s. 88 of the Indian Act which provided that provincial laws of general application applied to

Indians provided that those laws were not in conflict with aboriginal or treaty rights.

...

The treaty rights were restated, merged and consolidated in the NRTA and so their preservation was assured by being placed in a constitutional instrument. The sole source for a claim involving the right to hunt for food is, therefore, the NRTA. The Treaty may be relied on for the purpose of assisting in the interpretation of the NRTA but it has no other legal significance.

Two key interpretative principles apply to treaties. First, any ambiguity in the treaty will be resolved in favour of the Indians. Second, treaties should be interpreted in a manner that maintains the integrity of the Crown, particularly the Crown's fiduciary obligation toward aboriginal peoples. These interpretative principles apply equally to the rights protected by the NRTA.

The rights of Indians pursuant to either the Treaty or the NRTA would, at the time either was agreed to, be understood to be subject to governmental regulation for conservation purposes. The rights protected by the NRTA are not constitutional rights of an absolute nature precluding any governmental regulation.

CAST OF CHARACTERS: TREATY 8

Moostoos: b. c. 1850; d. November 19, 1918

Mostos (Moostoos, Mustus, Louis Willier) was first recorded in government records during the negotiations for Treaty 8, which covered the northern half of what is now Alberta, and parts of present-day British Columbia, Saskatchewan, and the Northwest Territories. Mostos and his younger brother Kinosew (Kinoosayo) were the key spokesmen for the Cree at talks in June 1899 at Willow Point, on Lesser Slave Lake. Kinosew was recognized that year as chief of the people who lived in the region of the lake and Mostos as the most prominent headman. Their negotiating styles were different, but both men were strong advocates of Indian interests. They sought to protect the traditional way of life and to secure additional benefits so that the survival of future generations would be assured.

David Laird: b. March 12, 1833; d. January 12, 1914

Son of a prominent PEI farmer and shipbuilder, David Laird was educated in both PEI and Nova Scotia, entered journalism in 1859, and quickly rose through the social and political ranks of Charlottetown. Like his father and brother, Laird was elected to the colonial legislature in 1871 as a member of the Liberal Party. After the entry of PEI into Confederation in 1873, he was elected to the House of Commons. When Alexander Mackenzie formed the first Liberal government in 1873, Laird was appointed minister of the Interior and superintendent general of Indian Affairs. Under his leadership, the *Indian Act* was tabled in the House of Commons and three treaties were concluded in the Northwest Territories, Laird participating in the negotiation of Treaty 4 in 1874. After his appointment as lieutenant-governor of the Northwest Territories in 1876, he participated in the negotiation of Treaty 7 in 1877. Hampered by budget shortfalls and rising expenses of Indian affairs, he remained in office until 1878, when the returning Macdonald government named Edgar Dewdney as his replacement. After leaving politics and returning to PEI, he was summoned back to the west in 1898 when he was appointed Indian commissioner for Manitoba and the northwest by the Laurier government. It is during this appointment that he was tasked with leading a commission to conclude a treaty in the Peace and Athabasca districts in 1899, with the assistance of James Ross and Father Albert Lacombe. Transferred back to Ottawa in 1909, Laird continued as Indian commissioner until his death in 1914.

Figure 7.1 David Laird explaining the terms of Treaty 8, Fort Vermilion, Alberta, 1899. When he was appointed as treaty commissioner in 1899, David Laird was considered to be highly experienced in Indigenous issues, having been superintendent general of Indian Affairs, participant in the negotiation of Treaties 4 and 7, and lieutenant-governor of the Northwest Territories.
Source: Glenbow Archives NA-949-34.

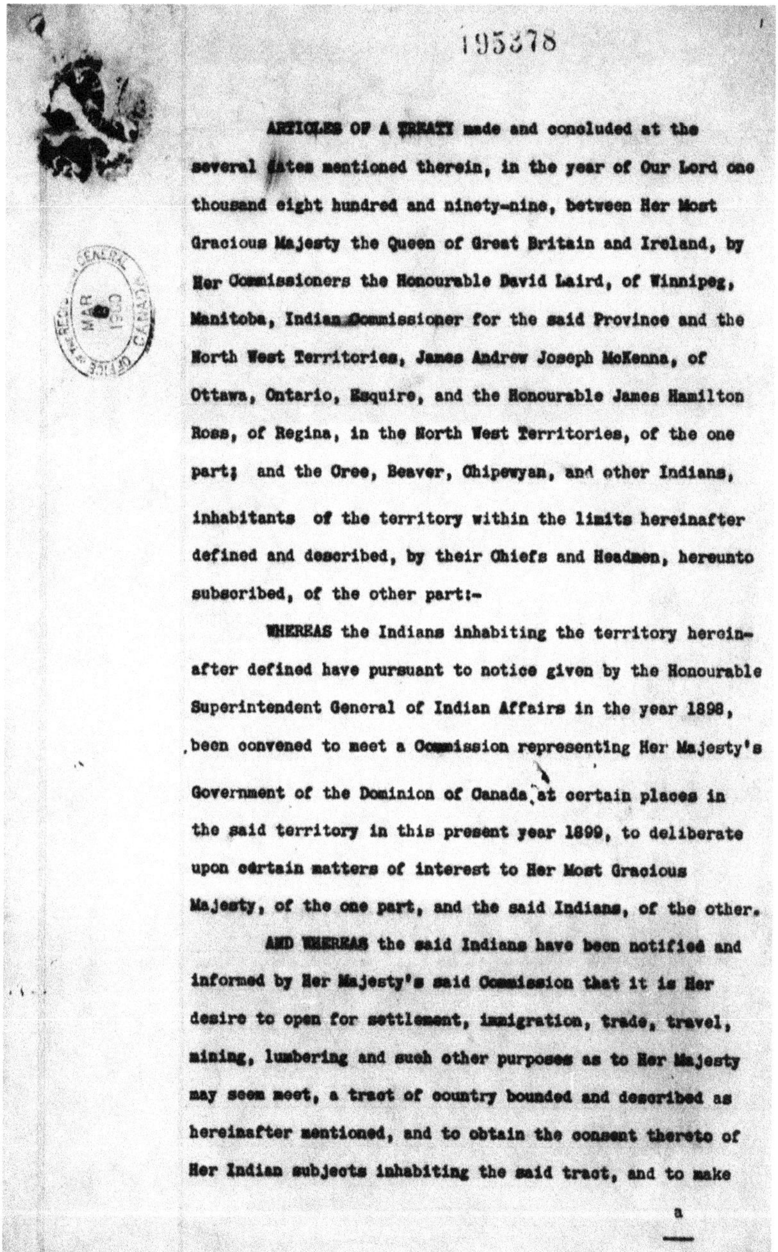

195378

ARTICLES OF A TREATY made and concluded at the several dates mentioned therein, in the year of Our Lord one thousand eight hundred and ninety-nine, between Her Most Gracious Majesty the Queen of Great Britain and Ireland, by Her Commissioners the Honourable David Laird, of Winnipeg, Manitoba, Indian Commissioner for the said Province and the North West Territories, James Andrew Joseph McKenna, of Ottawa, Ontario, Esquire, and the Honourable James Hamilton Ross, of Regina, in the North West Territories, of the one part; and the Cree, Beaver, Chipewyan, and other Indians, inhabitants of the territory within the limits hereinafter defined and described, by their Chiefs and Headmen, hereunto subscribed, of the other part:-

WHEREAS the Indians inhabiting the territory hereinafter defined have pursuant to notice given by the Honourable Superintendent General of Indian Affairs in the year 1898, been convened to meet a Commission representing Her Majesty's Government of the Dominion of Canada at certain places in the said territory in this present year 1899, to deliberate upon certain matters of interest to Her Most Gracious Majesty, of the one part, and the said Indians, of the other.

AND WHEREAS the said Indians have been notified and informed by Her Majesty's said Commission that it is Her desire to open for settlement, immigration, trade, travel, mining, lumbering and such other purposes as to Her Majesty may seem meet, a tract of country bounded and described as hereinafter mentioned, and to obtain the consent thereto of Her Indian subjects inhabiting the said tract, and to make

Figure 7.2 Treaty 8, June 21, 1899. Contrary to the treaties concluded in the 1870s, the treaty commissioners for Treaty 8 presented a fully drafted treaty text for the consideration of the signatory nations.
Source: Library and Archives Canada, e002996116.

Chapter 8
The Making of the Williams Treaties, 1923

Between 1764 and 1862, colonial officials, in an attempt to secure a continuous band of settlement along the St. Lawrence River and though the lower Great Lakes, negotiated several land-surrender treaties with the Indigenous groups of the region. The resulting agreements created a patchwork of surrenders throughout Upper Canada.[1] While the intent of British and colonial officials had been to secure the purchase of as much land as possible, in the years since Confederation it had become increasingly apparent that some lands had not been legally surrendered through treaties, most notably in central Ontario. Furthermore, discrepancies, irregularities, and possible loose dealings in some of the Upper Canada land surrenders pointed toward other potential problems throughout southern Ontario. For example, an agreement ratified in 1788, commonly known as the "Gunshot Treaty," surrendered lands along the north shore of Lake Ontario "as far as a gunshot could be heard from the water's edge."[2]

When William Benjamin Robinson concluded a treaty on behalf of the Crown with Anishinabek leaders at Sault Ste. Marie, in 1850, his mandate had been to secure a surrender of the shores of the upper Great Lakes, specifically the mineral-rich lands of the lakes Huron and Superior watershed.[3] Of the two agreements concluded in September 1850, the so-called Robinson-Huron Treaty ceded all the lands of the lakes watershed from Sault Ste. Marie to Penetanguishene on the southern shore of Georgian

---

[1] See Chapter 3.
[2] J.R. Miller, *Compact, Contract, Covenant: Aboriginal Treaty-Making in Canada* (Toronto: University of Toronto Press, 2009), 82.
[3] James Morrison, *The Robinson Treaties of 1850: A Case Study*, report prepared for the Royal Commission on Aboriginal Peoples, 1996, p. 91.

Bay.[4] The negotiations and final agreement for the treaty were with the various "Ojibway" communities from Manitoulin Island, Garden River, the French River, Lake Nipissing, and the northeastern shore of Georgian Bay.[5] On his return trip from the treaty conference, Robinson met with leaders from the Lake Simcoe and Beausoleil Island communities, chiefs Yellowhead, Snake, and Aissance, who sought compensation for some of the lands covered by the Robinson-Huron Treaty. They represented communities often referred to as the Chippewa of Lake Simcoe and Rama. Noting that he had been aware of this claim, Robinson stated in his official report that he had consulted with the Anishinabek during the meetings at Sault Ste. Marie, noting that "those chiefs had no claim on Lake Huron, that they had long since ceded their lands and were in the receipt of a large annuity."[6] While refusing their adherence to the treaty, Robinson promised to recommend further inquiry into the matter. As officials of the Indian Department likely agreed with the chiefs at Sault Ste. Marie that the Chippewa in and around Lake Simcoe had no claims due to earlier treaties, there appear to have been no inquiries into the matter.

By the 1860s, as ever-increasing settlement filled the lands around Lake Simcoe, the Anishinaabeg began to push for some kind of compensation for their lost lands. In 1866, the leaders of the Chippewa of Rama (Mnjikaning) petitioned the deputy superintendent of Indian Affairs, William Spragge, for payment of lost hunting grounds due to the government "having taken possession of their said lands" through the Robinson-Huron Treaty of 1850.[7] A few years later, the Anishinaabeg of Rice Lake, Scugog, and Curve Lake also began petitioning the government, stating that lands north of "line 45" (the 45th parallel) had never been surrendered by any treaty.[8] A decade later, Indian Affairs officials were increasingly convinced that there was an area of the province of Ontario, namely the Muskokas and the upper Ottawa Valley, that was either not covered by a treaty or that there were unsurrendered Indigenous rights.[9] As the communities continued

---

[4] See Chapter 4.

[5] Morrison, *The Robinson Treaties of 1850*, 97–8.

[6] William Benjamin Robinson, Treaty Commissioner's Report, September 24, 1850, LAC, RG10, vol. 191.

[7] Paul de la Ronde, Hester Wakaonah, and Anne Wakaonah to William Spragge, Deputy Superintendent of Indian Affairs, September 24, 1866, LAC, RG10, vol. 2329, file 67,071, pt. 1B, reel C-11202.

[8] Chiefs and Councillors of Rice Lake to William Spragge, Deputy Superintendent of Indian Affairs, December 22, 1869, LAC, RG10, vol. 2329, file 67,071, pt. 1B, reel C-11202.

[9] Joan Holmes and Associates, "Mississauga of the New Credit First Nation – Gunshot Treaty and Williams Treaties Joint Research Project," prepared for the Mississauga of the New Credit and AANDC, 2013, p. 52.

to call for compensation or payment for their unceded hunting grounds, new petitions and complaints were being heard by Indian Affairs officials relating to some of the earlier land surrenders during the colonial period. In a November 1904 letter to Frank Pedly, deputy superintendent of Indian Affairs in Ottawa, Hiawatha chief Johnson Paudash began to challenge the extent and the validity of the 1788 "Gunshot Treaty" that covered the north shore of Lake Ontario.[10] A decades-long quest for information resulted in government officials acknowledging that that there were no definitive maps of the treaties in question.[11]

By the end of the first decade of the twentieth century, both federal and provincial officials were increasingly aware of the "irregularities" in some of the early land treaties and that some areas were not covered by treaty at all. In 1916, the federal minister of justice appointed R.V. Sinclair to investigate the matter.[12] One of the primary issues that had come to light was the possible claims by the Lake Simcoe Chippewas over the southern lands ceded by the 1850 Robinson-Huron Treaty, which they had not signed. Sinclair concluded that "the Indian title to these lands has never been extinguished and I am of the opinion that some arrangement should be made for quieting the title by the payment to the claimants of compensation in the same way that the Crown has dealt with other Indians whose title has been extinguished by Treaty."[13]

Delayed by the First World War and after an internal review of the report agreed with its findings, Department of Indian Affairs officials began a process toward a new treaty. In 1921, Assistant Deputy Superintendent of Indian Affairs J.D. McLean suggested that the federal government call on the Ontario government to develop a joint approach to resolve the various claims.[14] After an exchange of letters between senior provincial and federal officials, the two levels of government hammered out a process by April 1923 that would investigate the extent of the unsurrendered land and, if deemed necessary, negotiate a treaty.[15] They then proceeded with

---

[10] Ibid., 60.
[11] J.D. McLean, Assistant Deputy and Secretary, Department of Indian Affairs, to Johnson Paudash, Lindsay, Ontario, November 24, 1920, LAC, RG10, vol. 2330, file 67,071–3, pt. 2, reel C-11202.
[12] Daniel E. Shaule, "The Disputed Boundaries of the 1923 (Williams) Treaties" (MA thesis, Trent University, 2002), 25.
[13] R.V. Sinclair to E.L. Newcombe, Deputy Minister of Justice, November 23, 1916, LAC, RG10, vol. 2330, file 67,071–3, pt. 2, reel C-11202.
[14] J.D. McLean, Assistant Deputy Minister, to Deputy Minister of Justice, July 4, 1921, LAC, RG10, vol. 2330, file 67,071–3, reel 11202.
[15] Robert Surtees, *The Williams Treaties: A Historical Perspective*, report prepared for Indian and Northern Affairs Canada, 1993, p. 32.

the appointment of a three-man commission, consisting of Department of Indian Affairs lawyer A.S. Williams as chairman, R.V. Sinclair, whose experience with the issue dated from 1916, and Uriah McFadden, a lawyer from Sault Ste. Marie.[16] Their goal was to investigate the claims and, if they deemed appropriate, to negotiate an arrangement with the Indigenous communities involved.

After a flurry of meetings and consultations in September 1923, the Treaty Commission's first report revealed that the Anishinaabeg claims were not only valid but also far more extensive than had been suggested by the 1916 Sinclair investigation.[17] The two governments, suddenly confronted with a report that not only validated the claims to the central portion of the province but also verified older claims to lands on the north shore of Lake Ontario and to a sizeable tract below Lake Simcoe, moved very quickly to extinguish the Indian title to those regions.[18] The lands in question were already being used for settlement and resources exploitation. Though part of the territory had likely been acquired by the government more than a century earlier, it was decided that new surrender agreements should be made in light of the problematic documentation for the original agreements.

Asking Williams and his colleagues to finish the process they had started, the Treaty Commission negotiated two separate treaties, known as the Williams Treaties after the head commissioner: one covering the lands between Georgian Bay and the Ottawa River and another for the lands along the shore of Lake Ontario and those up to Lake Simcoe, respectively signed on October 31 and November 21, 1923. The Williams Treaties saw the First Nation signatories surrender all their rights and title over the lands in question, including hunting and fishing rights.[19] The agreement signed on October 31 addressed the existing claims of the Lake Simcoe groups that had unresolved title claims to the lands of the Muskokas and Upper Ottawa River, as well as any underlying claims to the lands surrendered by the 1850 Robinson-Huron Treaty. Meanwhile, the November 21 treaty covered the lands implicated by some of the more problematic land cession agreements dating from the 1780s.

---

[16] Holmes and Associates, "Mississauga of the New Credit First Nation," 63.
[17] Robert Surtees, *Treaty Research Report: The Williams Treaties* (Ottawa: Indian and Northern Affairs Canada, 1986), 19.
[18] Ibid.
[19] Peggy J. Blair, *Lament for a First Nation: The Williams Treaties of Southern Ontario* (Vancouver, University of British Columbia Press, 2008), 151.

In addition to the initial payments and limited annuities, the treaties preserved the signing bands' existing reserves but did not provide for any new reserve lands. The Williams Treaties also departed from some existing practices included in earlier treaties, such as the Robinson Treaties (1850) and the Numbered Treaties. Whereas these treaties established continuing rights to hunt and fish, new reserve lands, and yearly annuities, the Williams Treaties were more like the Upper Canada Land Surrender treaties, with single cash payments, few if any reserves, and the surrender of all rights.

Not only was this a departure from what had become an established practice, but it also created some potential problems. Nearly half of land covered by the October 31 treaty overlapped with territory taken in the Robinson-Huron Treaty. This has led to a different set of rights over the same territories; the Robinson-Huron Treaty clearly recognizes a continued right to hunt and fish throughout that area. Ultimately, the conclusion of the 1923 Williams Treaties marked both the surrender of nearly all the remaining Indigenous lands to the Crown – only two small parcels of lands remain unceded – and the end of the long treaty process initiated in 1763.

ORAL AND WRITTEN ACCOUNTS OF THE WILLIAMS TREATIES, 1923

In their report of December 1, 1923, to the superintendent general of Indian Affairs, commissioners A.S. Williams, R.V. Sinclair, and Uriah McFadden concluded that "by the execution of these treaties, the Indian title which formerly covered all the lands in the old Province of Ontario has been finally released, and the taking of Treaty 9 in 1905 extinguished the Indian title up to the northern boundary of the Province of Ontario as the same existed at that date."[20] The submission of their report brought to a close not only the last treaty between the Crown and Indigenous nations for the next half-century but also one of the best-recorded treaty processes ever undertaken. For over 70 years, the Anishinaabeg of the Kawartha Lakes and Lake Simcoe, usually referred to as the Mississauga and the Chippewa, respectively, had been petitioning the Crown for protection of their unceded lands and their rights to hunt and fish. After months of discussion between Ontario and the Department of Indian Affairs – but not with the Anishinaabeg claimants themselves – about how to proceed,

---

[20] Treaty Commission to Superintendent General of Indian Affairs and Minister of Lands and Forests, Ontario, December 1, 1923, LAC, RG10, vol. 2330, file 67,071–3, pt. 1, reel C-11202.

a Memorandum of Agreement was concluded in April 1923 to establish a commission to investigate the claim to 10,719 square miles (27,762 square kilometres) of unceded land north of the 45th parallel, and to "empower the said commissioners, in the event of their determining in favour of the validity of the said claim, to negotiate a treaty with the said Indians for the surrender of the said lands upon payment of such compensation as may be fixed by such treaty."[21]

When Ontario and Canada established the commission in 1923, it was assigned a recording secretary, Kathleen Moodie, who prepared transcripts of hearings, statements, and discussions.[22] The hearings took place in each of the seven Anishinaabeg communities between September 14 and 27, 1923, starting at Georgina Island on Lake Simcoe and concluding at Alnwick (Alderville).[23] Along with the commission's two reports, the first after the hearings and the second after the treaty signing, the 288 pages of transcripts provide a unique look at how the issues of rights were discussed, how the focus of the commission shifted, and how the written text of the treaty was finalized. Furthermore, the evidence provided by community members demonstrated that despite years of interaction with them, federal and provincial officials did not understand the nature of the claims being made by Anishinaabeg leaders since the 1860s.

The settler understanding of Anishinaabeg claims and positions being limited to the "northern hunting grounds" was made evident at the very start of the hearings on September 14, 1923. In his opening statements at Georgina Island, commission chair A.S. Williams indicated that the scope of the inquiry was to focus on the claims to unsurrendered lands in the "Counties of Renfrew, Hastings, Muskoka, Parry Sound and Nipissing" in Ontario – lands north of the 45th parallel. He also added that "if the claims are established, to negotiate a Treaty of Surrender and arrange for such compensation as seems to be reasonable and proper."[24] As Daniel Shaule mentions, the commission wanted to make it clear that its mandate was focused only on lands that were not covered by other

---

[21] Memorandum of Agreement between the Dominion and the Province of Ontario, April 1923, LAC, RG10, vol. 2330, file 67,071–3, pt. 2, reel C-11202.

[22] Blair, *Lament for a First Nation*, 130.

[23] *Bound Volume of Testimony Given to a Commission, Chaired by A.S. Williams, Investigating Claims, by the Chippewas & Mississaugas of the Province of Ontario, to Compensation for Lands Not Surrendered by the Robinson Treaty of 1850*, 1923, LAC, RG10, vol. 2332, file 67,071–4C.

[24] Statement by A.S. Williams, September 14, 1923, *Bound Volume of Testimony Given to a Commission*, 1.

earlier treaties. To that effect, the commission brought a map of Ontario showing the area in question.²⁵ Despite its specific mandate to discuss only the 10,719 square miles of unsurrendered lands in Ontario, witnesses called before the commission continuously brought up claims to different areas of the province.

As Peggy Blair, a legal scholar specializing in Indigenous hunting and fishing rights, notes in *Lament for a First Nation*, when the commission arrived in a community to discuss the lands in question, discussions always turned to other lands: for the Chippewa communities of Lake Simcoe, it was seven townships directly south of that lake, while for those of Georgian Bay, it was the lands covered by the Robinson-Huron Treaty of 1850, and finally the Mississauga of the Kawarthas focused on the lands behind the 1788 "Gunshot Treaty" along Lake Ontario. During the Chippewa hearings, witnesses such as John E. Big Canoe, chief of Georgina Island, and his father, George Big Canoe, indicated that the northern hunting grounds had long been used by his community but also that their family had hunting grounds to the south of Lake Simcoe along the Holland River. In his testimony, Chief Big Canoe stated that there were lands in the townships of West and North Gwillimbury, Georgina, and Scott, where there had never been a surrender, which were still in use as hunting grounds.²⁶ As Blair points out, the claim of unsurrendered lands south of Lake Simcoe was repeated by several witnesses in different communities. Benjamin Esquabe, also of Georgina Island, stated that the seven townships had been set aside by Lieutenant-Governor Simcoe in the 1790s,²⁷ while at Scugog Lake, Isaac Johnson added that Simcoe had reserved lands south of the lake as "hunting grounds."²⁸ At Christian Island, Chief Jackson turned the commission's questions to Chippewa claims to the lands along the shore of Georgian Bay.²⁹ During the hearing held in the Kawartha region, Robert Paudash, former chief of Hiawatha and grandson of one of the signers of the 1818 Rice Lake Treaty, George Paudash, openly acknowledged that the earlier treaties reserved the northern lands for hunting.³⁰ His son, Johnson

---

[25] Shaule, "Disputed Boundaries," 117.
[26] Statement by John E. Big Canoe, September 15, 1923, *Bound Volume of Testimony Given to a Commission*, 33.
[27] Blair, *Lament for a First Nation*, 132.
[28] Ibid., 137.
[29] Statement by Chief Jackson, September 17, 1923, *Bound Volume of Testimony Given to a Commission*, 63.
[30] *Bound Volume of Testimony Given to a Commission*, 141.

Paudash, added that there was another area not covered by treaty, such as the townships south of Lake Simcoe and the lands behind the 1788 treaty along the lakefront.[31]

The Anishinaabeg testimony proved problematic for the Treaty Commission. While its mandate was clearly limited to investigating the rights over the 10,719-square-mile tract of land outside of other land cession treaties, the communities demonstrated not only their rights to these lands but also that there were a number of problems with treaties from the previous century: Chippewa rights to lands under the Robinson-Huron Treaty, the reserved lands south of Lake Simcoe, and the undefined boundaries of the 1788 "Gunshot Treaty." In their initial inquiry report, the Treaty Commission stated that the Mississauga and the Chippewa had "submitted ample and satisfactory proof of the occupation by them of the land referred to as the ancient hunting ground of the ancestors of the claimants," that being the 10,719 square miles indicated in the April 1923 Memorandum of Agreement.[32] In addition, the commission reported that the indications were strong that there were still unsurrendered lands along the western shore of Georgian Bay, in the townships south of Lake Simcoe, and along the northern shore of Lake Ontario. The Treaty Commission recommended that the scope of any treaty be broadened beyond the "northern hunting grounds":

> It is suggested by the Commission in the event of a surrender from the claimants of the large tract of hunting grounds above described [the 10,719 square miles] to include in the surrender the lands intended to be covered by the Gun Shot Treaty and the seven townships lying immediately south of Lake Simcoe, and the Commission is of the opinion that the surrender should be extended to cover the 1,000 square miles claimed by the Chippewa Indians to have been improperly included in the Robinson-Huron Treaty.[33]

The provincial and federal governments, concerned that the cost of settling the claims over these lands would only increase if further delayed,

---

[31] Statement by Johnson Paudash, September 25, 1923, *Bound Volume of Testimony Given to a Commission*, 235.
[32] Williams Commission Report, October 10, 1923, LAC, RG10, vol. 2330, file 67,071–3, pt. 1, reel C-11202.
[33] Ibid.

agreed to the commission's proposal and allocated $500,000 to cover the final agreements.[34] By the end of October, the Survey Branch of Indian Affairs was preparing a description of the lands in question, and the Treaty Commission, without further consulting with the communities, presented two treaties with identical terms to the Chippewa and the Mississauga, respectively. As Peggy Blair states, "although it had taken decades for the Chippewas and the Mississauga claims to be investigated fully, the treaties prepared by the Commissioners were signed with breathtaking speed, in less than twenty-two days" between October 31 and November 21.[35] By the terms of the treaties, the signatory communities would surrender not only all remaining unceded lands but also all rights to hunt and fish across the entire province of Ontario.

In their final report, A.S. Williams, R.V. Sinclair, and Uriah McFadden presented an account of the commission's activities, including summaries of the hearings, discussions among federal and provincial officials, and the signing of the treaties.[36] Whereas the initial hearings had recorded the various discussions, the accounts of the treaty signings are limited to the commission's final report. On the whole, the commissioners report that the signing occurred with relatively little discussion, although the representatives at Christian Island had to be "disabused" of expecting "ten million dollars" in compensation. The Treaty Commission's report spent more time describing the various schools in the communities than the signing of the treaties.[37] In the minds of government officials, what were now called the "Williams Treaties" secured the last remaining title to Indigenous lands in southern Ontario. For the Province of Ontario, this meant that Indigenous signatories to the Williams Treaties would have the same harvesting rights as all other residents and be obligated to purchase licences and observe closed seasons.

While the Crown felt secure that the 1923 treaty had resolved all outstanding or "residual" rights of the Chippewa and the Mississauga, including hunting and fishing rights, the same cannot be said for the Indigenous signatories. In the years following the signing of the treaties, members for various Anishinaabeg communities continued to hunt and fish as they had

---

[34] Surtees, *Treaty Research Report*, 19.
[35] Blair, *Lament for a First Nation*, 149.
[36] Treaty Commission to Superintendent General of Indian Affairs and Minister of Lands and Forests, Ontario, December 1, 1923.
[37] Ibid.

always done. In 1938, four men from Rama were arrested for spearfishing, their case reported across the country.[38] As government officials argued the case in Orillia, Ontario, one of the representatives from Rama who signed the 1923 treaty, Chief John Bigwin, recounted one of the growing number of Anishinaabeg perspectives of the treaty terms challenging the Crown's interpretation.

In a statement provided to the *Orillia Packet and Times* newspaper, Chief Bigwin stated,

> In September 1923, a treaty was made between the Ontario Government and Mississauga and Chippewa Indians by which the Indians gave up all rights to certain lands in the northern part of Ontario.
>
> When these Commissioners approached the Indians in a friendly manner, hunted up all the evidence and put it together, they finally came to a satisfactory settlement. Before signing the treaty each Commissioner got up and said these very words – that the Indians would still be able to hunt, fish and trap. Restrictions on fishing wasn't to be included in the treaty. "We don't want the fish of the game" they said, "Build wigwams on the river banks and hunt free without licence. As long as the grass grows and water runs you shall be free and pay no licence forever."[39]

This was not the first time that Chief Bigwin had turned to the press to argue that Chippewa hunting and fishing rights were unaffected by the 1923 Williams Treaties. When in 1928, only five years after the treaty signing, members of his community were charged with game-law violations, his statements about treaties and the protection of hunting and fishing rights appeared in the *Toronto Star*, the *Montreal Gazette*, and the *Globe*.[40] Other leaders and communities also repeated their understanding that the treaties were supposed to protect their hunting and fishing rights, not surrender them. For example, Rama Chief Alder York met with Indian Affairs officials in 1931 to argue that the "Indians were promised by the Three Commissioners who took the Chippewa treaty in 1923 that they would [have] the privilege of hunting and fishing within the bounds of the

---

[38] *Edmonton Journal*, May 12, 1938, and *Montreal Herald*, May 12, 1938, LAC, RG10, vol. 6960, file 475/20–2, pt. 1, reel C-12926.
[39] "Indians Claim Right to Fish and Hunt Not Given Up," *Orillia Packet and Times*, June 13, 1938, LAC, RG10, vol. 6960, file 475/20–2, pt. 1, reel C-12926.
[40] Blair, *Lament for a First Nation*, 160–1.

territory ceded without licence."⁴¹ For the Chippewa, the treaty interpretation by the Crown was incorrect, as it was more than just a land surrender but also a confirmation of long-standing rights. As Blair notes, "from the Aboriginal perspective ... the Williams Treaties signed ... [were] conditional on the First Nation receiving the concessions it requested when the treaty was signed, namely, the right to hunt and fish without a licence."⁴²

The Chippewa were not the only ones questioning the Crown's understanding and interpretation of the treaties. In 1931, when Arthur Whetung of the Mud Lake (Curve Lake) community was arrested for trapping, he requested a copy of the 1923 treaty he had signed so that he could use it to prove his right to trap under the terms.⁴³ Indian Affairs responded that there was no copy of the treaty available. It was only through Whetung's constant demands for a copy of the treaty to the Privy Council and Indian Affairs that a version was finally printed in 1932.⁴⁴ The printing and circulation of the treaty text did little to change the Mississauga understanding that the treaty preserved their hunting and fishing rights. A.S. Williams, the former chair of the Treaty Commission, himself recognized that the Anishinaabeg "cling persistently to the belief that they are entitled to hunt and fish over all the lands which were formerly used by their ancestors."⁴⁵

The province's understanding of the treaty terms and its continued prosecution of Anishinaabeg fishers and hunters had little impact on the communities' understanding. Oral history projects since the late 1970s have reinforced this perspective, most notably the "Oral History on the Williams Treaty of 1923" by the Indian Commission of Ontario in 1979–80,⁴⁶ and more recently "An Anishinaabeg Oral History Narrative of the Williams Treaty" by Darrel Manitowabi in 2015, as part of the evidence of the *Alderville* case.⁴⁷ These oral histories are part of the communal identity of the seven signatory communities and, as Elder Everrett Williams of Rama indicated, a topic of constant discussion: "people would come

---

⁴¹ Ibid., 162.
⁴² Ibid., 165.
⁴³ Arthur Whetung to Department of Indian Affairs, October 15, 1931, INAC, file 1/1–11–15, vol. 1.
⁴⁴ Blair, *Lament for a First Nation*, 168.
⁴⁵ A.S. Williams to Police Magistrate E.A. Jordan, County of Victoria, Provisional County, Haliburton, Lindsay, May 6, 1932, LAC, RG10, vol. 6746, file 420–8D, reel C-8103.
⁴⁶ *Oral History on the Williams Treaty of 1923*, Indian Commission of Ontario, 1979–80.
⁴⁷ Darrel Manitowabi, "An Anishinaabeg Oral Narrative of the Williams Treaties Based on 174 Interviews with Members of the Williams Treaties First Nations," *Alderville First Nation v. Canada*, [2016] FC 733 (CanLII).

over to my dad's place and talk all night and it's all they'd talk about is the Williams Treaty."[48]

In both cases, the oral history demonstrates a continuation of the treaty understanding presented in the decade after the treaty signing, specifically that promises were made so that hunting and fishing would be unaffected by the treaty and that other reserve lands would be set aside for the communities. For example, Elders from Georgina Island noted that the terms were never properly understood because there was "no way that the translators of the time could have translated the treaty – they didn't know English well enough."[49] Across all the communities, the oral history aligned with the initial goal of the Treaty Commission in 1923: the surrender of the "northern hunting grounds," and not lands or rights they may have elsewhere. Elders from Beausoleil stated that by signing the treaty, "they agreed to give up the northern lands mostly. Wanted to keep their hunting and fishing rights. Lands of the north can't fish or hunt,"[50] while those of Rama stated during the treaty meetings that the treaty commissioners "never said anything about other land in treaty,"[51] and the Anishinaabeg, as a Curve Lake Elder stated, "were working to keep their land plus all their fishing and hunting rights I don't think they were after money – what they were after was land and keeping of their hunting and fishing."[52] Almost since the very days after the treaties were signed, both sides have had radically different understandings not only of the treaty terms but also of how the treaty had been negotiated. These differing perspectives continue to affect the relationship between the Anishinaabeg of central Ontario, the province, and the federal government to the present day.

THE WILLIAMS TREATIES AND THE COURTS

In the decades following the signing of the Williams Treaties, the province of Ontario continued to apply its game laws to all members of the signatory communities. When cases made it to court, the provincial attorney general argued that hunting and fishing rights had been surrendered by treaty throughout the area described in the treaties. Until the 1970s, this legal argument was successful for the province. In 1977,

---

[48] Ibid., 95.
[49] Ibid., 59.
[50] Ibid., 71.
[51] Ibid., 84.
[52] Ibid., 119.

during the *Taylor and Williams* case, where the Anishinaabeg defendants from Curve Lake argued that they had rights to hunt on the water based on the 1818 Rice Lake Treaty,[53] the province replied that if any rights were protected by the 1818 treaty, they were subsequently surrendered by the 1923 Williams Treaties. At the divisional court, the ruling focused primarily on the matter of the oral minutes of the 1818 treaty and spent little time on the Williams Treaties, noting that these agreements may have surrendered the rights but that a new trial would be required to make that determination.[54]

The province chose not to pursue a new trial after the ruling by the Ontario Court of Appeal in 1981. A few years later in 1984, however, four men, including George Howard of Hiawatha First Nation, were charged with illegal fishing on the Otonabee River. A series of trials lasting a decade and culminating in the 1994 Supreme Court of Canada decision *R. v. Howard* focused on whether Howard, as a member of the Anishinaabeg community of Hiawatha, had treaty-protected fishing rights or if those rights had been surrendered by the Williams Treaties of 1923.[55] Whereas Howard argued that the 1818 Rice Lake Treaty protected his fishing rights and that the Hiawatha signatories would not have accepted the treaty if they had understood that it surrendered their hunting and fishing rights, the province countered that the leaders of Hiawatha in 1923 were fluent in English and understood that the so-called "blanket clause" of the Williams Treaty ceded all residual rights.[56] The Howard defence team built their argument around the research and testimony of Ian Johnson, historical researcher for the Union of Ontario Indians, while the province called upon Ralph Loucks, former chief of Hiawatha who stated no knowledge of any special rights to hunt or fish for his community. Judge Batten, in an oral ruling from the Bench, concluded that Howard's rights to hunt and fish had indeed been extinguished.[57] The case proceeded through the various courts, finally

---

[53] See Chapter 3.
[54] *R. v. Taylor and Williams*, [1981] 62 C.C.C. (2d) 227, p. 2.
[55] Blair, *Lament for a First Nation*, 181.
[56] Ibid., 183. The "blanket clause" says: "AND ALSO all the right, title, interest, claim, demand and privileges whatsoever of the said Indians, in, to, upon or in respect of all other lands situate in the Province of Ontario to which they ever had, now have, or now claim to have any right, title, interest, claim, demand or privileges, except such reserves as have heretofore been set apart for them by His Majesty the King."
[57] Oral judgment, *R. v. Howard*, R.B. Batten, Provincial Court, Peterborough, January 10, 1986.

reaching the Supreme Court. In a unanimous decision written by Justice Charles Gonthier in 1994, the Supreme Court upheld all lower court rulings, arguing that

> The historical context summarized above does not provide any basis for concluding that the terms of the 1923 Treaty are ambiguous or that they would not have been understood by the Hiawatha signatories. The basket clause was a conveyance in the broadest terms. Its wording mirrored the general terms of cession contained in the general operative clause quoted above. The lands it pertained to were clearly identified as "all other lands situate in the Province of Ontario." Furthermore, the broad nature of the clause and its wide sweeping effect is underlined by the presence of only one enumerated exception, "reserves ... set apart ... by His Majesty the King."[58]

When compared to other court decisions relating to treaty interpretation, the *Howard* decision stands out as one of the few losses for Indigenous defendants. As legal scholars John Borrows and Leonard I. Rotman note, this decision, along with the decision in *R. v. Horse* in 1988,[59] brought a certain level of confusion to principles of treaty interpretation. In their opinion,

> In *Howard*, the Court stated that a 1923 treaty ought not to be interpreted according to the canons of treaty interpretation because the treaty concerned lands close to urbanized Ontario and the Hiawatha signatories included businessmen and a civil servant and all were literate.[60]

As a result of this decision, it appeared that principles such as that terms should be liberally understood and that ambiguity should favour Indigenous interpretation could be set aside based on the "perceived or presumed knowledge" and literacy of Indigenous signatories.[61] In light of the ruling and with the goal of mitigating further conflicts between

---

[58] *R. v. Howard*, [1994] 2 S.C.R. 299, p. 306.
[59] See Chapter 7.
[60] John J. Borrows and Leonard I. Rotman, *Aboriginal Legal Issues: Cases, Materials and Commentary*, 3rd ed. (Markham, ON: LexisNexis Canada, 2007), 354.
[61] Ibid.

the province and the Williams Treaties communities, in 1994 Ontario participated in the federal "Aboriginal communal fishing licence" regime that would provide these specific communities with equivalent harvesting rights as other First Nations in the province, although the change in government the following year resulted in the province cancelling its participation.[62]

The 1994 Supreme Court decision in *R. v. Howard* has not brought a clearer understanding of the terms of the treaty or how best to reconcile the differing perspectives of the Crown, both federal and provincial, and the seven signatory communities. Since this ruling was handed down, new proceedings have been started, most notably in 1992 when the Williams Treaties communities, led by the Alderville First Nation, filed claim that they had not been fairly compensated for the lands surrendered, that promised reserves had never been set aside, and that their harvesting rights were not protected by the treaty terms.[63] As a result of the court process, in 2012 Ontario and Canada began to reconsider their position and agreed on an "interim basis" that harvesting rights in the 1818 Rice Lake Treaty are recognized for the Williams Treaties First Nations.[64] Other remaining issues in the claim, however, remain unresolved but in negotiation.

FURTHER READINGS

Peggy J. Blair. *Lament for a First Nation: The Williams Treaties of Southern Ontario*. Vancouver, University of British Columbia Press, 2008.

Daniel E. Shaule. "The Disputed Boundaries of the 1923 (Williams) Treaties." MA Thesis, Trent University, 2002.

Robert Surtees. *The Williams Treaties: A Historical Perspective*. Report prepared for Indian and Northern Affairs Canada, 1993.

QUESTIONS FOR DISCUSSION

1. According to the treaty text, why were the treaties concluded in 1923?

---

[62] Julie Jai, "Bargains Made in Bad Times: How Principles from Modern Treaties Can Reinvigorate Historic Treaties," in *The Right Relationship: Reimagining the Implementation of Historical Treaties*, eds. John Borrows and Michael Coyle (Toronto: University of Toronto Press, 2017), 142.

[63] *Alderville Indian Band et al. v. Her Majesty the Queen*, Federal Court No. T-195-92.

[64] "Backgrounder: Negotiations with the Williams Treaties First Nations toward a Negotiated Resolution of the *Alderville* Litigation," Indian and Northern Affairs Canada, https://www.aadnc-aandc.gc.ca/eng/1490649757949/1490649854322, accessed June 1, 2017.

2. Read the following excerpts and identify the similarities and differences in the understandings relating to the continued rights of hunting and fishing:

> **Statement by Chief John Bigwin, "Indians Claim Right to Fish and Hunt Not Given Up,"** *Orillia Packet and Times,* **June 13, 1938, LAC, RG10, vol. 6960, file 475/20–2, pt. 1**
> For upwards of 70 years the Chippewa Indians of Lakes Simcoe and Huron, and the Mississauga Indians of Rice Lake, Mud Lake, Scugog Lake and Alderville, have constantly pressed upon the attention of the government a claim to compensation in respect of their ancient hunting limits situated in the northern part of the Province of Ontario and lying between the Georgina Bay and the Ottawa River, and bounded approximately on the North by the French River, Lake Nipissing and the Ottawa River, and on the South by the 45th parallel of latitude ... By the execution of these treaties, the Indian title which formerly covered all the lands in the old Province of Ontario has been finally released, and the taking of Treaty 9 in 1905 extinguished the Indian title up to the northern boundary of the Province of Ontario as the same existed at that date.

> **Williams Commission Report, December 1, 1923, LAC, RG10, vol. 2330, file 67,071–3, pt. 1, reel C-11202**
> In September 1923, a treaty was made between the Ontario Government and Mississauga and Chippewa Indians by which the Indians gave up all rights to certain lands in the northern part of Ontario ... When these Commissioners approached the Indians in a friendly manner, hunted up all the evidence and put it together, they finally came to a satisfactory settlement. Before signing the treaty each Commissioner got up and said these very words – that the Indians would still be able to hunt, fish and trap. Restrictions on fishing wasn't to be included in the treaty. "We don't want the fish of the game" they said, "Build wigwams on the river banks and hunt free without licence. As long as the grass grows and water runs you shall be free and pay no licence forever." Fishing and hunting were not included in the sale of land. It's the resource for our living.

3. In your opinion, what does the Court say about Indigenous hunting rights?

DOCUMENTS

Treaty Text Excerpts: Treaty Made November 15, 1923, between His Majesty the King and the Mississauga of Rice Lake, Mud Lake, Scugog Lake, and Alderville, LAC, RG10, vol. 1853, IT 483, IA 1080, T-9941

ARTICLES OF A TREATY made and concluded on the fifteenth day of November in the year of Our Lord One thousand nine hundred and twenty-three, between His Most Gracious Majesty, George the Fifth, of the United Kingdom of Great Britain and Ireland, King, Defender of the Faith, Emperor of India, by His Commissioners ... Angus Seymour Williams, Chairman of the said Commission, representing the Dominion of Canada, and ... Robert Victor Sinclair and Uriah McFadden, representing the Province of Ontario, of the One Part, and the members of the Mississauga Tribe, inhabiting, as members of bands thereof, reserves at Rice Lake, Mud Lake, Scugog Lake and Alderville, all in the Province of Ontario, by their chiefs and headmen, of the Other Part.

WHEREAS, the Mississauga Tribe above described, having claimed to be entitled to certain interests in the lands in the Province of Ontario, hereinafter described, such interests being the Indian title of the said tribe to fishing, hunting and trapping rights over the said lands, of which said rights, His Majesty, through His said Commissioners, is desirous of obtaining a surrender, and for such purpose has appointed the said Commissioners, with power on behalf of His said Majesty, to enquire into the validity of the claims of the said tribe, and, in the event of the said Commissioners determining in favour of the validity thereof, to negotiate a treaty with the said tribe for the surrender of the said rights upon the payment of such compensation therefor as may seem to the said Commissioners to be just and proper:

AND WHEREAS the said Commissioners, having duly made the said enquiry, have determined in favour of the validity of the said rights.

AND WHEREAS the Indians belonging to the said tribe, having been duly convened in Council, at the respective places named hereunder, and having been requested by the said Commissioners to name certain chiefs and headmen to be authorized on their behalf to conduct negotiations with the said Commissioners for a surrender of the said rights and to sign a treaty in respect thereof and to become responsible to His Majesty for the faithful performance by the said tribe and by the respective bands thereof inhabiting the said reserves, of such obligations as shall be assumed by them under such treaty, the said Indians have therefore appointed for the purposes aforesaid the several chiefs and headmen who have subscribed to this treaty:

AND WHEREAS the said Commissioners, acting under the powers in them reposed as aforesaid, have negotiated the present treaty with the said tribe:

NOW THEREFORE THIS TREATY WITNESSETH that the said tribe and the Indians composing the same, occupying as members of bands the said reserves, by their chiefs and headmen, duly authorized thereunto as aforesaid, do hereby cede, release, surrender and yield up to the Government of the Dominion of Canada for His Majesty the King and His Successors forever, all their right, title, interest, claim, demand and privileges whatsoever, in, to, upon, or in respect of the lands and premises described as follows, that is to say:

FIRSTLY: All that parcel of land situate in the Province of Ontario and described as commencing on the northeasterly shore of Georgian Bay at that mouth of the French River which forms the boundary between the District of Parry Sound and the District of Sudbury ... Excepting thereout and therefrom those lands which have already been set aside as Indian reserves. The parcel hereby surrendered contains seventeen thousand, six hundred square miles, more or less.

SECONDLY: All that parcel of land situate in the Province of Ontario and described as parts of the Counties of Northumberland, Durham, Ontario and York ... Excepting thereout and therefrom those lands which have already been set aside as Indian Reserves. The land hereby conveyed contains two thousand, five hundred square miles more or less.

AND ALSO all the right, title, interest, claim, demand and privileges whatsoever of the said Indians, in, to, upon or in respect of all other lands situate in the Province of Ontario to which they ever had, now have, or now claim to have any right, title, interest, claim, demand or privileges, except such reserves as have heretofore been set apart for them by His Majesty the King.

TO HAVE AND TO HOLD the same to His Majesty the King and His Successors forever:

...

AND THE UNDERSIGNED chiefs and headmen, on their own behalf and on behalf of all the Indians whom they represent, do hereby solemnly covenant, promise and agree to strictly observe this treaty in all respects and that they will not, nor will any of them, nor will any of the Indians whom they represent, molest or interfere with the person or property of anyone who now inhabits or shall hereafter inhabit any portion of the lands covered by this treaty, or interfere with, trouble, or molest any person passing or travelling through the said lands or any part thereof, and that they will assist the officers of His Majesty in bringing to justice and punishment any Indian, party to this treaty, who may hereafter offend against the stipulations hereof or infringe the laws in force in the lands covered hereby:

AND IT IS FURTHER UNDERSTOOD that this treaty is subject to an agreement dated the – day of April, A.D. 1923, made between the Dominion of Canada and the Province of Ontario, a copy of which is hereto attached.

IN WITNESS WHEREOF, His Majesty's said Commissioners and the said chiefs and headmen have hereunto set their hands and seals at the places and times hereinafter set forth, in the year herein first above written.

SIGNED AND SEALED at Alderville on the nineteenth day of November, A.D. 1923, by His Majesty's Commissioners and the undersigned chiefs and headmen in the presence of the undersigned witnesses, after first having been interpreted and explained.

Witness:
Kathleen Moore.
W.R. Coyle.
A.S. Williams, Chairman.
R.V. Sinclair.
Uriah McFadden.
Robert Franklin.
Norman Marsden.
Frank Smoke.
Ernest Crowe.
John Lake.
Wm. Loukes.

SIGNED AND SEALED at Mud Lake on the fifteenth day of November, A.D. 1923, by His Majesty's Commissioners and the undersigned chiefs and headmen in the presence of the undersigned witnesses, after first having been interpreted and explained.

Witness:
Kathleen Moore.
R.J. McCamus.
A.S. Williams, Chairman.
R.V. Sinclair.
Uriah McFadden.
Chief D.E. Whetung.
Alfred McCue.
Joseph Whetung.
George Taylor.
Samson Fawn.
Bertram McCue.

George Coppaway.
Albert Whetung.
L.D. Taylor.

SIGNED AND SEALED at Rice Lake on the sixteenth day of November, A.D. 1923, by His Majesty's Commissioners and the undersigned chiefs and headmen in the presence of the undersigned witnesses, after first having been interpreted and explained.

Witness:
Kathleen Moore.
R.J. McCamus.
A.S. Williams, Chairman.
R.V. Sinclair.
Uriah McFadden.
Geo. Paudash.
Hanlon Howard.
J. Paudash.
Henry Cowie.
Wm. Anderson.
Alfred Crowe.
Madden Howard.

SIGNED AND SEALED at Scugog Lake on the twenty-first day of November, A.D. 1923, by His Majesty's Commissioners and the undersigned chiefs and headmen in the presence of the undersigned witnesses, after first having been interpreted and explained.

Witness:
Kathleen Moore.
Wilson Gerrow.
A.S. Williams, Chairman.
R.V. Sinclair.
Uriah McFadden.
Thos. Marseden
Austin Goose.
Isaac Johnson.
Davie Elliot.
Chas McCue.
sa X marque.
John W. Marsden.
John H. Marsden.
Norman Marsden.
Chas. F. Marsden.
Elijah Marsden.

Excerpt from Williams Commission Report, December 1, 1923, LAC, RG10, vol. 2330, file 67,071–3, pt. 1, reel C-11202

For upwards of 70 years the Chippewa Indians of Lakes Simcoe and Huron, and the Mississauga Indians of Rice Lake, Mud Lake, Scugog Lake and Alderville, have constantly pressed upon the attention of the government a claim to compensation in respect of their ancient hunting limits situated in the northern part of the Province of Ontario and lying between the Georgian Bay and the Ottawa River, and bounded approximately on the North by the French River, Lake Nipissing and the Ottawa River, and on the South by the 45th parallel of latitude.

In April of this year an agreement was made between the Dominion of Canada and the Province of Ontario for the appointment of Commissioners to investigate the foregoing claim, and, if satisfied as to its validity, to negotiate with the Indians in question for a surrender of their rights and subsequently, by an Order of His Excellency in Council of the 31st August, 1923, the undersigned were appointed Commissioners for the purposes above set forth …

During the course of the taking of evidence at Rice Lake, the Commissioners were informed by one of the witnesses that the Indian title to seven townships lying immediately south of Lake Simcoe had never been extinguished, and an investigation of the records in the Department of Indian Affairs satisfied the Commissioners that the assertion so made was correct.

On the 13th of September, 1787, a Treaty, commonly called "The Gunshot Treaty" was made by the Honourable Sir John Johnston, Baronet, on behalf of the King, with the Principal Chiefs and War Chiefs of the Mississauga Nation. This Treaty was intended to cover the land bordering on the north shore of Lake Ontario, and extending back therefrom as far as a gunshot could be heard, and covering the land lying between the Bay of Quinte and the Tobicoke River. The Commission, in the course of its researches, discovered that this Treaty was signed without a particular description of the lands intended to be surrendered having been included therein, the intention being, as appeared from the files, that the surveyor was to write into the Treaty a proper description of the lands intended to be covered thereby. It is quite clear that the surveyor failed to complete the Treaty in this regard, and the Gunshot Treaty as printed in the Volume of Indian Treaties and Surrenders published in 1905, contains no description of the lands, the title to which was intended to be surrendered. A few years after the signing of this treaty the omission in question was discovered, and a subsequent confirmatory Treaty was signed on August 1st, 1805, but by error only a portion of the land intended to be included in the Gunshot Treaty was included in the confirmatory surrender. This portion is now commonly known as the "Toronto Purchase," and included only the townships of Tobicoke, York and Vaughan, and parts of the townships of King, Whitechurch and Markham in the county of York.

In view of the foregoing, the Commissioners determined to include in the new treaty that portion of the lands originally intended to be covered by the Gunshot Treaty, but which had not been included in the confirmatory surrender of August 1st, 1805. The Commission having therefore obtained from the Surveys Branch a proper description of the lands south of Lake Simcoe, already referred to, and of the lands intended to have been included in the Gunshot Treaty, prepared two Treaties, one to be signed by the three Bands of Chippewas, and the other to be signed by the four Bands of Mississaugas, each of which Treaties covered all the ancient hunting grounds of both nations, the townships south of Lake Simcoe, and the Gunshot Treaty lands, it being felt that grave difficulty might arise particularly with respect to the ancient hunting grounds, if an attempt were made to define a boundary between the hunting limits of the Chippewas and those of the Mississaugas, as the evidence disclosed that neither of these Tribes had any very definite idea as to the actual sites of such boundary.

The Commission adjourned on Friday, the 9th, to meet again on the 13th, on which day it left for Peterborough for the purpose of negotiating with the Indians at Mud Lake, which it did on November 14th and 15th. On the latter day the Treaty was signed ... On the 16th of November the Commission went to the Hiawatha reserve, situated on the shore of Rice Lake, where, after a full explanation of the object of the visit, and some addresses by the Chief and other members of the Band, the Treaty was signed during the afternoon ... On the 20th of November the Commission went to Port Perry for the purpose of meeting the Indians at Lake Scugog reserve on the 21st, to place before them the proposals for a surrender. This took place on the latter date, when the Treaty was signed. This execution of the Treaty completed the work of the Commission so far as the Chippewa and Mississauga Indians were concerned.

By the execution of these treaties, the Indian title which formerly covered all the lands in the old Province of Ontario has been finally released, and the taking of Treaty 9 in 1905 extinguished the Indian title up to the northern boundary of the Province of Ontario as the same existed at that date.

Statement by Chief John Bigwin, "Indians Claim Right to Fish and Hunt Not Given Up," *Orillia Packet and Times*, June 13, 1938, LAC, RG10, vol. 6960, file 475/20–2, pt. 1

Chief John Bigwin, the patriarch of the Rama Reserve, visited Orillia on Saturday afternoon, to obtain publicity for his protest against the claim that the Indians had given up their alleged right to fish and hunt outside the reserve in the treaty made in 1923. Chief Bigwin, who will be one hundred years old on the 20th of August, was one of those who negotiated that treaty. Indeed, he was said to be chiefly instrumental in bringing it about, as the result of a chance interview he had on the train with the Hon. G. Howard Ferguson ...

Chief Bigwin, whose mind is remarkably clear and his memory good, notwithstanding his years though his eyesight has recently failed him almost entirely, declares that at the time the treaty was made the Indians were given to understand that it did not interfere with their right to hunt and fish. In a written statement which the Chief brought with him he says:

> "In September 1923, a treaty was made between the Ontario Government and Mississauga and Chippewa Indians by which the Indians gave up all rights to certain lands in the northern part of Ontario.
>
> When these Commissioners approached the Indians in a friendly manner, hunted up all the evidence and put it together, they finally came to a satisfactory settlement. Before signing the treaty each Commissioner got up and said these very words – that the Indians would still be able to hunt, fish and trap. Restrictions on fishing wasn't to be included in the treaty. 'We don't want the fish of the game' they said, 'Build wigwams on the river banks and hunt free without licence. As long as the grass grows and water runs you shall be free and pay no licence forever.'
>
> Fishing and hunting were not included in the sale of land. It's the resource for our living. These words were caught by schoolboys learning shorthand, and we have a lot more taken, which the Commissioners don't know what they said, but we have it here. We should have had an interpreter or a stenographer so as to take both sides of the questions. The Commissioners didn't let us have anything.
>
> The treaty shouldn't stand without an interpreter, and as it looks to have been misrepresented to the Indians and by the Government. Most of our people today realise between right and wrong.
>
> I have been appointed by the Council some years ago to fight for the hunting, trapping and fishing rights, as we don't get a fair deal. Even the Indian Department is not looking after us right and we need food on the Reserve for the winter months. Even in May and June it is really hard for us in the Reservation, and we have to do something to live. We ask the Indian Department for relief. What do they say? Go and fish and hunt. Then the inspectors or wardens stop us. We must have

some way to live. We should not be compared with the whites, to pay such licence. Licence fees should belong to the Indians in this country."

Excerpts from *R. v. Howard*, [1994] 2 S.C.R. 299, pp. 299–309

The appellant, a status Indian and a member of the Hiawatha Band whose reserve is located in Ontario, was convicted of unlawfully fishing during a prohibited period. The trial judge concluded that the treaty signed by the representatives of the Band in 1923 had extinguished the fishing rights held by the Band in the Otonabee River area where the offence occurred. Both the summary convictions appeal court and the Court of Appeal upheld the conviction. (p. 299)

The focus of the argument before this Court and the courts below was whether the appellant has an existing right to fish in the area in question. The parties agreed that a treaty entered into on November 5, 1818 (Treaty No. 20) did not extinguish the fishing rights of the Hiawatha Band on the Otonabee River. The point of controversy between the parties and the central issue which we must resolve is as to the effect of a treaty signed on November 15, 1923 ("1923 Treaty"). (p. 302)

The 1923 Treaty consists of four general "whereas" clauses and a number of paragraphs describing the lands covered by the Treaty and the various obligations of the parties. The whereas clauses describe the general background to the Treaty related by Batten Prov. Ct. J. and quoted above. The lands covered by the Treaty are described in three paragraphs ... The third paragraph is the one at the heart of this litigation ... This paragraph has been referred to as the "basket clause" and it is relied on by the Crown as extinguishing the appellant's right to fish. (p. 303–4)

The court also held that the signatories had sufficient knowledge and understanding of the terms of the 1923 Treaty to bind the Band and thereby refused to overturn the factual findings of the trial judge. The evidence of Ralph Loucks at trial and the testimony of Johnson Paudash before the Commission were pointed to in support of this result. The court found no evidence to rebut the inference of knowledge and understanding which it drew from a reading of the minutes of the Band in Council when the Treaty was signed. (p. 305)

I am in substantial agreement with the conclusions reached by the courts below. The historical context summarized above does not provide any basis for concluding that the terms of the 1923 Treaty are ambiguous or that they would not have been understood by the Hiawatha signatories. The basket clause was a conveyance in the broadest terms. Its wording mirrored the general terms of cession contained in the general operative clause quoted above. The lands it pertained to were clearly identified as "all other lands situate in the Province of Ontario." Furthermore, the broad nature of the clause and its wide sweeping effect is underlined by the presence of only one enumerated exception, "reserves ... set apart ... by His Majesty the King." (p. 306)

After carefully reviewing the factual record, I am of the view that there is no basis for overturning the result reached by the courts below. By the clear terms of the 1923 Treaty, the Hiawatha Band surrendered any remaining special rights to hunt and fish in the Otonabee River area. (p. 307)

CAST OF CHARACTERS: WILLIAMS TREATIES

Angus Seymour Williams: b. c. 1868; d. April 24, 1963

Angus Seymour Williams, originally from Southern Ontario, received his law degree at Osgoode Hall in Toronto and by the late 1910s was employed by the federal government as chief counsel for the Department of Indian Affairs. One of his primary roles was to review legal and judicial obligations of the Crown regarding Indigenous peoples. In 1923, Williams was chosen to head a commission of inquiry into the claims of the unsurrendered lands in the Muskoka region of Ontario. His commission recommended, and subsequently negotiated, the conclusion of two treaties aiming to resolve all remaining Indigenous claims in central Ontario.

Johnson Paudash: b. January 29, 1875; d. October 26, 1956

Johnson Paudash was born at the Hiawatha First Nation reserve in 1875, a member of one of the most prominent Anishinaabeg families of the Kawartha Lakes region. His great grandfather, George Cheneebeesh Paudash, was chief and signatory to the 1818 Rice Lake Treaty and a veteran of the War of 1812. Johnson Paudash served as a sniper during the First World War, where his marksmanship earned him several commendations and distinctions. After the war, he became a civil servant, working for the postal service, and served as chief of Hiawatha First Nation for several years, where he advocated for the needs of his community, their rights under treaty, and the preservation of Hiawatha's history and culture. During the Williams Treaty Commission hearings, Johnson Paudash provided strong evidence as to the long-standing practices and land use of the Anishinaabeg throughout the Kawartha and Muskoka region.

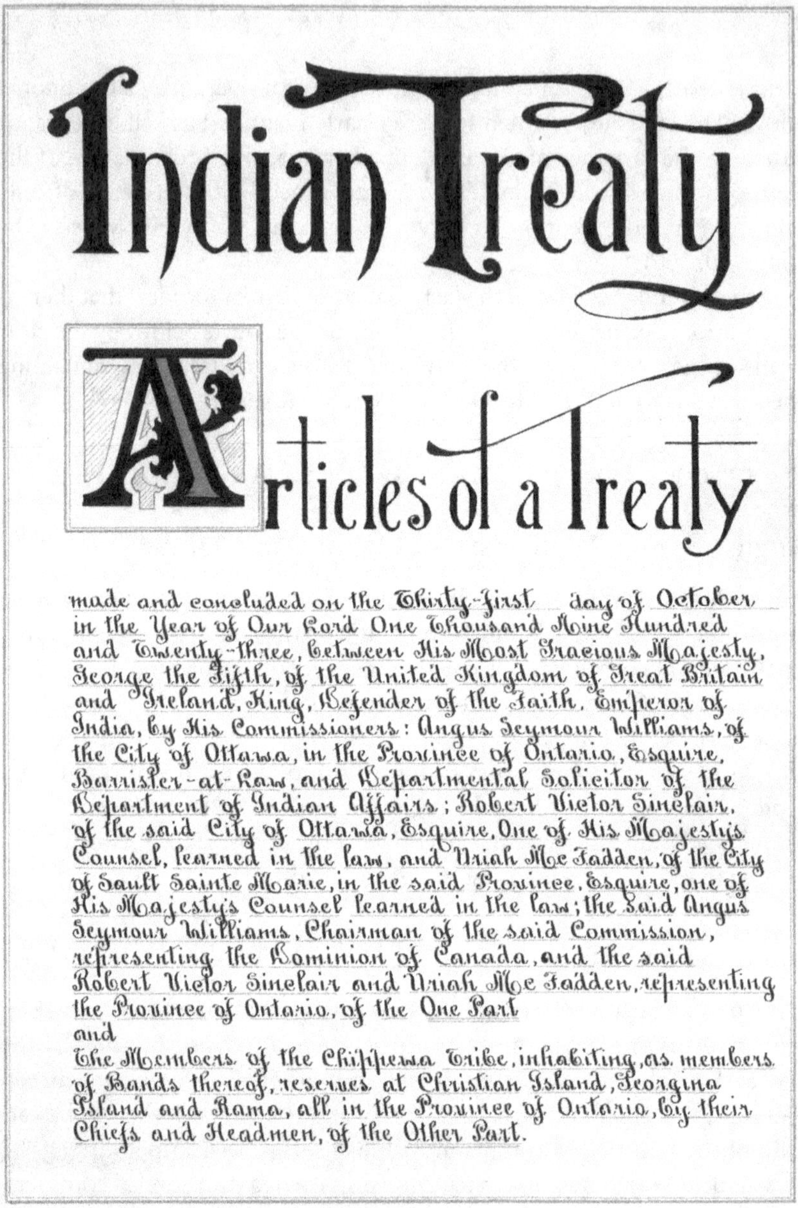

Indian Treaty

Articles of a Treaty

made and concluded on the Thirty-First day of October in the Year of Our Lord One Thousand Nine Hundred and Twenty-Three, between His Most Gracious Majesty, George the Fifth, of the United Kingdom of Great Britain and Ireland, King, Defender of the Faith, Emperor of India, by His Commissioners: Angus Seymour Williams, of the City of Ottawa, in the Province of Ontario, Esquire, Barrister-at-Law, and Departmental Solicitor of the Department of Indian Affairs; Robert Victor Sinclair, of the said City of Ottawa, Esquire, One of His Majesty's Counsel, learned in the law, and Uriah McFadden, of the City of Sault Sainte Marie, in the said Province, Esquire, one of His Majesty's Counsel learned in the law; the said Angus Seymour Williams, Chairman of the said Commission, representing the Dominion of Canada, and the said Robert Victor Sinclair and Uriah McFadden, representing the Province of Ontario, of the One Part

and

The Members of the Chippewa Tribe, inhabiting, as members of Bands thereof, reserves at Christian Island, Georgina Island and Rama, all in the Province of Ontario, by their Chiefs and Headmen, of the Other Part.

Figure 8.1 Williams Treaty, October 31, 1923. Although the treaties were concluded in 1923, no copies of the agreements were sent to the signatory nations for nearly a decade, and then only after they demanded copies be made available to them.

Source: William's Treaty - Chippewas of Christian Island, Georgina Isle and Rama - Treaty - IT 483. Library and Archives Canada/Department of Indian Affairs and Northern Development fonds, from e002996463 to e002996475. Image no. e011074097-005. © Government of Canada. Reproduced with the permission of Library and Archives Canada (2018).

Index

Aboriginal and treaty rights, and *Constitution Act, 1982* (Section 35), 34–5
Acadia, early trade and settlement, 21–2
agriculture, 77, 78, 99, 167, 172
Ahtahkakoop (Starblanket), 188, 190
Alberta, hunting and fishing rights and NRTA, 204–7
Alek, Andrew, 29
American colonies, 77
Amherst, Jeffrey, 51
Anderson, Thomas Gummersall, 84, 102–3, 109, 131–2
Anishinaabeg, land cession and surrender
  Rice Lake Treaty and fishing and hunting rights, 79, 80–1, 82–7, 239
  Williams Treaties, 228–9, 231–4, 238, 241
Anishinabek
  communities missing from negotiations, 112–15
  fur trade and land occupation, 99–100
  hunting and fishing rights, 105, 106–7
  interpretation of Robinson-Huron Treaty, 110–12
  land claims and surrender, 102–5, 227–8, 230
  land exploitation by settlers and miners, 100–3
  treaty negotiations, 103–10, 112–13
annuities. *See* payments and annuities
archival versions of treaties, as sources of examination, 8–9

Badger, Wayne Clarence, 204–6
Baker Lake test, 117
Barclay, Archibald, 136–7, 142, 150
Bartleman, Gabriel, 141

Batten, Judge, 239
Bear Island case and decisions (1991), 114–17, 129–30
Beaulieu, Alain, 55, 56, 62
Bell, Catherine, 206–7
Bernard, Andrew, 29
Big Canoe, George, 233
Big Canoe, John E., 233
Bigwin, John (chief), 236, 248–9
Blair, Peggy, 233, 235, 237
Borrows, John, 240
Bowles, Major, 80, 86, 91–2
Braddock, Edward, 50
Brant, Joseph, 79
Brant, Molly (Mary), 50, 70
Britain
  agreements with Huron-Wendat, 51–5, 56–7
  colonial competition and relationship with Indigenous peoples, 9, 21–4, 26–7, 49–52, 54, 75–6
  colonies transferred to Canada, 157, 158
  colony policy from 1763, 76
  Cope Treaty, 25–8
  Huron-British Treaty, 51–4, 60
  Indian Department or Affairs (*See* Indian Department/Affairs of Britain)
  land management and cession in Great Lakes area, 76–9, 83
  occupation and settlement of Great Lakes area, 75–6
  Peace and Friendship Treaties, 23–4
  Seven Years' War in North America, 49, 50–1, 54, 55, 56–7
  trade with Mi'kmaq, 26–7, 28
  treaty making after loss of American colonies, 77
  "truck house" (trading post) clauses, 24, 26

253

Vancouver Island colony and land ownership, 135–6
British North America Act (1867), 157, 203–4
Bruce, Colonel, 108
Buckquaquet (chief), 80, 82, 89–91, 93

Calliou, Brian, 203
Canada (Dominion)
 control of land and resources, 203–4
 creation and expansion, 157–9
 treaty making, 158–9, 163–4, 193–6
 western Prairies, 159
Canada (Province), mining and exploitation in Great Lakes area, 100–3
Canadian Plains Research Centre, 165
Cardinal, Harold, 6, 8
Chagnon, Rachel, 62
Chippewa (Anishinaabeg), land cession and surrender
 hunting and fishing rights, 228, 229, 231–2, 233–5, 236–7
 Rice Lake Treaty, 80–1
Christie, W.J., 169
Christmas, Ben, 29, 30, 41
Christmas, Joe, 29–30, 40
Chute, Janet, 31
Claus, Daniel, 54, 97
Claus, William
 biographical details, 97
 in Indian Department, 80, 97
 land cession and surrender, 80–1
 Rice Lake Treaty, 80–4, 86, 91–2
Confederacy of Seven Nations, 49–50, 51, 53
Constitution Act, 1982, and Section 35, 34–5
"Conveyance of Land to Hudson's Bay Company by Indian Tribes," 147–8
Cope, Jean Baptiste
 biographical details, 43
 conclusion of treaty, 9, 33
 in Cope Treaty, 24, 25–6, 27–8, 30, 43
Cope Treaty (1752)
 and courts, 31–5
 description, 9, 14, 24–5

historical background, 21–4
interpretation, 31–3
main characters, 43–5
minutes of council in Halifax, 25, 26, 27–8, 30, 39–40
oral accounts, 29–31, 32, 33
proclamation of treaty, 28, 47
R. v. Simon (Simon v. The Queen), 31, 32, 33–4, 41–3
signatories, 30
Sylliboy case testimony, 29–31, 40–1
text of treaty, 27–8, 36–8, 47
written accounts, 25–9, 32–3
Corntassel, Jeff, 7
Cornwallis, Edward, 24, 25, 43–4
Cory, Peter, 174–5, 205
courts
 context of treaties, 7
 evidence for treaties and use of historical materials, 61–2
 hunting and fishing and NRTA, 204–7
 interpretation of treaties, 61, 116
 legal principles for interpretation of treaties, 6–7, 12–13, 116, 117, 144, 145, 174–5, 205–7
 written text of treaties, 8
 See also law; Supreme Court of Canada
courts and specific treaties
 Cope Treaty, 31–5
 Huron-British Treaty, 58–62
 Rice Lake Treaty, 85–7
 Robinson-Huron Treaty, 112–17
 Treaty no. 6, 173–5
 Treaty no. 8, 203–7
 Vancouver Island Treaties, 144–5
 Williams Treaties, 238–41
Craft, Aimée, 7
Cree, in Treaty no. 6, 164, 166, 169
Crowe Lake, 85–6
Crown vs. Indigenous interpretation of treaties, 1–3, 4, 6, 8, 193–5

Daniel, Richard, 197, 199, 203
Daschuk, James, 159, 163
Delâge, Denys, 50, 54, 62
Dickson, Brian, 33–4
Dion, Joseph, 163

Dokis, Michel (Le Aigle/D'Aigle) (chief Migisi), 111, 113, 126–7, 131
Dominion Lands Act (1872), 158
Douglas, James
    biographical details, 136, 153–4, 156
    land cession and surrender, 139
    land ownership on Vancouver Island, 136–7
    letter to Barclay, 136, 150
    report for Vancouver Island Treaties, 139, 140, 143–4
    treaty making, 136–8, 140–2, 145
Douglas Treaties, map, 2
    See also Vancouver Island Treaties
Duff, Wilson, 137
Dummer, Governor, 23
Dummer Treaty (1725), 23

Edmonton Bulletin, 202, 203
Elgin, Lord (James Bruce), 100, 102, 104
Elliott, Dave, 138, 141–2
Erasmus, Peter, 172
Esquabe, Benjamin, 233
extinguishment
    hunting and fishing rights, 205, 207
    treaties, 60–1

fisheries legislation, impact, 84
fishing rights. *See* hunting and fishing rights
Forget, A.E., 196
Fort Carlton, 162, 164, 169
Fort Pitt, 162, 164, 169
Fort Victoria, 135, 136, 138
France
    colonial competition and relationship with Indigenous peoples, 9, 21–2, 49–52, 75
    and Mi'kmaq, 21–2, 23
    Seven Years' War in North America, 49, 50–1, 54, 56
Friesen, Gerald, 157
Friesen, Jean, 162
fur trade, Great Lakes area, 99–100

Game and Fisheries Act of Ontario, 85–6
George III, and Royal Proclamation, 76
Gertler, Franklin, 61

Gibot, Felix, 200, 218–20
Gonthier, Charles, 240
Gough, Barry, 135–6
Gould, Francis, 29, 30, 41
Gould, John, 29
governments vs. Indigenous interpretation of treaties, 1–3, 4, 6, 8, 193–5
Great Lakes area
    agricultural lands, 78, 99
    British and settler occupation, 75–6
    British relationship with Indigenous people, 54, 75–6
    fur trade, 99–100
    land cession and management, 76–9, 83, 100–5, 110–11, 227–30
    mineral resources and land claims, 100–5, 110
    terms of agreements and payments and annuities, 77–8, 79, 80, 104
    treaty making, 77, 79–80, 99
    written agreements, 77–8
"Gunshot Treaty," 81, 227, 229, 234

Haviland, William, 51
Hickey, Lynn, and colleagues, 165, 167, 168, 199–200
Hildebrandt, Walter, 6, 8
historical circumstances at time of treaties, 5–6, 31–2, 33–4, 86, 87
Historical Journal of the Campaigns in North America for the Years 1757, 1758, 1759 and 1760 by Captain John Knox, An (Doughty), 66–7
historic treaties, timeline of Indigenous peoples and Euro-Americans relationship, 13–18
    See also treaties (generally); specific treaties
history of treaties, Indigenous vs. Crown/government interpretation, 1–3, 6
Hodley, Andrew, 27
Hopson, Peregrine Thomas
    biographical details, 44
    conclusion of treaty, 9, 33
    in Cope Treaty, 24, 25, 26, 27–8, 44, 47
Horse, Fred, 165–8, 169, 181–3

Horseman decision (1990), 206
Hourie, Peter, 190
Howard, George, 239
Hudson's Bay Company (HBC)
   Rupert's Land, 158, 160
   treaties in archives, 139, 142–3
   treaty making, 136–8, 143, 144–5
   Vancouver Island colony, 135–7, 139
hunting and fishing rights
   Anishinaabeg, 81, 82–3, 84, 85–7, 239, 241
   Anishinabek, 105, 106–7
   Chippewa, 228, 231, 233–4, 235, 236–7
   extinguishment, 205, 207
   in land cession and surrender, 228–9
   legal principles for interpretation of treaties, 175, 205–7
   Mi'kmaq, 24, 26, 28, 29–30, 32, 33
   and Natural Resources Transfer Agreements (NRTA), 204–7
   Rice Lake Treaty, 81, 82–3, 84, 85–7, 239, 241
   Robinson-Huron Treaty, 105, 106–7, 231
   Sioui legal test, 35, 207
   Treaty no. 6, 171, 173–5
   Treaty no. 8, 197, 199, 201, 204–7
   Vancouver Island Treaties, 142, 144–5
   Williams Treaties, 230, 231, 234, 235–41
Huron-British Treaty (1760)
   agreements concluded, 51–2
   and courts, 58–62
   description, 9, 14, 51–2
   and external evidence, 61–2
   historical background, 49–52
   journal excerpts of British officers, 60, 61, 66–7, 68
   main characters, 69–73
   newspaper article of 1828, 55, 64–6
   oral accounts, 54–5, 57–8, 62
   paper document of treaty, 57
   R. v. Sioui, 58–62, 64, 67–9
   text of treaty, 64
   validity of treaty, 58–61, 62, 67–9
   written accounts, 52–7, 60
Huron treaty of 1850. *See* Robinson-Huron Treaty (1850)

Huron-Wendat
   agreements with British, 51–5, 56–7, 68
   awareness of treaty, 58
   oral history, 54–5, 57–8
   paper document of treaty, 57, 62
   in Seven Years' War, 51–2, 55–6
   validity of treaty, 58–60, 62, 68–9
Hutchins, Peter, 61

Indian Act, as government policy, 194
Indian Act, section 88
   hunting rights, 86
   validity of treaties, 60, 68, 69
Indian Affairs Department (after Confederation)
   interpretation of treaties, 163, 194
   land cession/surrender in Ontario, 228–30
Indian Department/Affairs of Britain (pre-Confederation)
   agricultural lands, 77
   Anishinabek and mining exploitation, 101–2
   establishment, 50
   land management, 77, 78
   Rice Lake Treaty, 80–4
   and settlement, 75–6, 78
   treaty making in Upper Canada, 79–80, 83
"Indian History Film Project," 165, 181, 217, 218
"Indian of Lorette" article, 55–6, 64–6, 69
Indian-White Relations in Nova Scotia, 1749–1761 (Patterson), 26
Indigenous vs. Crown interpretation of treaties, 1–3, 4, 6, 8, 34, 193–5
interpretation of treaties
   circumstances at time of treaties, 5–6, 31–2, 33–4, 86, 87
   and courts, 61, 116
   framework and starting points, 8
   and history of treaties, 1, 3–6
   Indigenous vs. Crown, 1–3, 4, 6, 8, 34, 193–5
   legalistic view, 6–7, 31–2
   legal principles for interpretation, 6–7, 12–13, 116, 117, 144, 145, 174–5, 205–7

and oral history, 8, 117
questions for comparison, 10–11
sources of examination, 8–9, 11–12
and text of treaties, 5–8
interpretation of specific treaties
Cope Treaty, 31–3
Numbered Treaties (1 to 7), 162–3, 193–4
Peace and Friendship Treaties, 34
Rice Lake Treaty, 83–5
Robinson-Huron Treaty, 110–12, 116–17
Treaty no. 6, 165–6, 167–8, 174
Treaty no. 8, 198–9, 203
Vancouver Island Treaties, 139–42, 143–5
Williams Treaties, 232–3, 235–8, 240–1
Ironside, George, 101, 109, 112–13
Irving, Aemilius, 111
Isaac, Thomas, 86–7, 175

Jackes, A.G., 169, 170–1, 172
Jackson (chief), 233
Jaenen, Cornelius, 62
Jeremie, François, 27
Johnson, Ian, 239
Johnson, John, 79
Johnson, William
agreements with Huron-Wendat, 52, 53, 54
biographical details, 70
in Indian Department/Affairs, 50, 70, 75–6
Seven Years' War, 51, 52
Joseph Bighead First Nation, 173–4

Kahnawake (Sault St. Louis), 56
Kawartha Lakes region, 83
Keating, John William, 110
Kinosayoo/Kinosew (chief), 202, 222
Kiyawasew, Leroy Steven, 204–6
Knighton, Janice, 141
Knox, John, journal excerpts, 52, 53, 60, 61, 67, 68

Lacombe, Albert, 168–9, 198, 202–3, 223

Laird, David
biographical details, 222–4
report of treaty commissioner, 200–2, 203, 214–17
in treaty commission, 196, 200, 202, 224
Treaty no. 6, 169
Lake Rice purchase, treaty no. 20. *See* Rice Lake Treaty, no. 20 (1818)
Lake Simcoe, 228, 230, 233–4
Lake Temagami, 113, 114
Lamer, Antonio, in *R. v. Sioui* and validity of treaties, 59–61, 67–9
land cession/surrender
Great Lakes area, 76–9, 83, 100–5, 110–11, 227–30
Numbered Treaties, 162–3
Robinson-Huron Treaty and Williams Treaties, 102–5, 227–9, 231, 232–5
terms of agreements, 77–8, 79
Treaty no. 6, 164
Vancouver Island Treaties, 139, 140–1, 143, 144
See also Anishinaabeg; Chippewa
land management and exploitation
control of land, 203–4
and Royal Proclamation of 1763, 76–7, 100–1
Latasse, Chief David, 139–41, 148–50, 154–5
law
changes in interpretation of treaties, 31, 33–4
and historical records, 60
legal tests, 35, 117, 174, 207
principles for interpretation of treaties, 6–7, 12–13, 116, 117, 144, 145, 174–5, 205–7
See also courts
Lee, Gordon, 166–7, 199–200
Le Loutre, Jean-Louis, 44–5
Lesser Slave Lake meetings (Treaty no. 8), 196, 197, 198, 202
Lightning, Richard, 199–200
Lorette village, 51, 53, 54–5, 58, 64
Lorne, Marquis, 111, 126–7
Loucks, Ralph, 239
Loyalists, and treaty making, 77
Lozier, Jean-François, 62

258 INDEX

Mackay, Joseph, 140
MacKinnon, Bert, 86, 87
Mainville, Robert, 174–5
Mair, Charles, 202–3
Maitland, Peregrine, 80
Maliseet nation, 23–4
Manitoba, resources rights, 204
Manitowabi, Darrel, 237
Martin, Andrew Hadley, 30
Martin, Gabriel, 27, 31
Mashekyash, John, 111, 128
McDonald, Archibald, 138
McDonnell, Alexander, 80, 81, 83, 84, 86
McFadden, Uriah, 230, 231, 235
McKay, James, 168, 169
McKenna, J.A.J., 196, 200
McLachlin, Beverly, legal principles for interpretation of treaties, 6–7, 34
McLean, J.D., 229
McNab, David T., 113
McNeil, Kent, 116
medicine chest clause, 172, 173
Meredith, Justice, 145
Migisi (chief). See Dokis, Michel
Mi'kma'ki lands, 21–2
Mi'kmaq of Nova Scotia
  in Cope Treaty, 27, 32
  drawing of, 46
  and early colonial presence, 21–4
  hunting and fishing in treaties, 24, 26, 28, 29–30, 32, 33
  internal divisions, 27
  oral history of treaties, 29–31
  and Peace and Friendship Treaties, 23–4
  relationship with British, 23–6
  significance of treaties, 29
  trade with British, 26–7, 28
  "truck house" (trading post) clauses, 24, 26
Mi'kmaq of Shubenacadie, in Cope Treaty (1752), 9, 24–8, 32
Miller, Bruce Granville, 117
Miller, J.R., 6, 159, 194
mining and mineral resources
  Great Lakes area, 100–5, 110
  Vancouver Island Treaties, 138
"Minutes of a Council held at Smiths Creek" (1818), 81, 86, 92–4

"Minutes of Council Held in Halifax" (1752), 25, 26, 27–8, 30, 39–40
misinterpretation of treaties. See interpretation of treaties
Mississauga nation (Anishinaabeg), land claims/surrender and hunting and fishing rights, 231, 233, 234–5, 237
Mistahimaswka (chief, aka Big Bear), 160–1
modern treaties, timeline of Indigenous peoples and Euro-Americans relationship, 18–20
Montreal, surrender in 1760, 51, 53, 54
Moodie, Kathleen, 232
Moostoos (Mostos, Mustus, Louis Willier), 202, 222
Morantz, Toby, 116–17
Morris, Alexander
  biographical details, 188–9, 191
  report of treaty commissioner, 168, 169–73, 175, 184–6
  as treaty commissioner, 168–9, 189
  treaty making and promises, 164, 166, 167, 169–73
Morrison, James, 101, 103, 105–6, 108, 110, 111
Murray, James
  agreements with Huron-Wendat, 52–3, 54, 55, 57, 58–9, 68
  biographical details, 69–70
  drawing of, 72
  journal excerpts, 52–3, 60, 61, 66–7
  in Seven Years' War, 51
  validity of treaty, 58–60, 67
"Murray Treaty." See Huron-British Treaty (1760)
Mustus, Jean Marie, 198

natural resources
  control of, 203–4
  Great Lakes area, 99–100
Natural Resources Transfer Agreements (NRTA), hunting and fishing rights in R. v. Badger, 204–7
Nebenaigoching, 108
Nebenegwune/Naibanagonai of Temaguming, 113, 115

Nenaigooching, Chief, 133
North Saanich people, 143
Northwest Territories (NWT)
 control of land and resources, 204
 establishment, 158
 treaties, 160–1
 treaty making, 164
Northwest Territories Transfer Order (1870), 158
Nova Scotia, early trade and settlement, 21–2
Nowegijick decision, 34
Numbered Treaties (generally)
 historical background, 157–63, 193–6
 hunting and fishing rights and NRTA, 204
 map, 2
 symposium, 1
Numbered Treaties (1 to 7)
 clauses and terms, 160–1, 163
 description, 160, 161–2
 differences in, 161
 historical background, 157–63, 193–4
 interpretation, 162–3, 193–4
 land cession/surrender, 162–3
 reserves, 160
 treatment of Indigenous people, 163
 treaty making, 163–4, 168–9, 194
 written source, 163
 See also specific numbered treaties
Numbered Treaties (8 to 11)
 historical background, 160, 193–6
 treaty commission, 196
 treaty making, 194–6

Office of the Treaty Commissioner of Saskatchewan, on reconciliation and treaties, 4
Okeymaw, William, 198, 199, 217–18
Old Man Told Us: Excerpts from Mi'kmaw History, 1500–1950, The (Holmes Whitehead), 40–1
Ominayak, Ernest Clarence, 204–5, 206
Ondiaraété, Étienne. *See* Petit-Étienne
"105 Years in Victoria and Saanich!" *(Victoria Daily Times)*, 139–41, 148–50

Ontario
 Bear Island case, 114–15
 See also Great Lakes area
Ontario (Attorney General) v. Bear Island Foundation (1991), 114–17, 129–30
oral history and accounts
 Cope Treaty, 29–31, 32, 33
 Huron-British Treaty, 54–5, 57–8, 62
 in interpretation of treaties, 8, 117
 Rice Lake Treaty, 83–5, 86–7
 Robinson-Huron Treaty, 113, 114, 115, 117
 Treaty no. 6, 164–8, 169–71, 175
 Treaty no. 8, 198–200, 203, 206, 207
 Vancouver Island Treaties, 139–42, 144, 145, 148–50
 Williams Treaties, 236, 237–8
Orillia Packet and Times, 236, 248
Overview of 18th Century Treaties Signed Between the Mi'kmaq and Wastukwiuk Peoples and the English Crown, An (Wicken and Reid), 27

Pagett, Frank, 148–50
Pa-pa-seance/Papasseance, 110, 111, 125–6
Papers Connected with the Indian Land Question, 1850–1875, 147–8
Papineau, Denis-Benjamin, 101
Parks Act of Quebec, 58–9
Parks Regulation of Saskatchewan, 173
Parry Island chiefs, in Robinson-Huron Treaty, 127–8
Passamaquoddy nation, 23–4
Patterson, George G., 29, 32
Patterson, Stephen, 26
Paudash, George Cheneebeesh
 account of Rice Lake Treaty, 84–5, 94–5
 biographical details, 96–7, 251
Paudash, Johnson, 84, 229, 233–4, 251
Paudash, Robert, 84, 233
Paul, Daniel, 24
payments and annuities
 Great Lakes area/Upper Canada, 77–8, 79, 80, 104
 Rice Lake Treaty, 80

260   INDEX

Robinson-Huron Treaty, 104, 105, 106-7, 109, 111-12
Treaty no. 8, 197
Peace and Friendship Treaties (1725-1779)
   description, 14, 23-4
   interpretation, 34
   map, 2
   and Mi'kmaq, 23-4, 31
   See also Cope Treaty (1752)
Peau-de-Chat, Chief, 102, 109
Pedly, Frank, 229
Pennefather, Richard, 113
Petit-Étienne (Étienne Ondiaraété)
   biographical details, 55, 69
   newspaper interview of 1828, 55-7, 62, 64-6, 69
   oral history of Huron-British Treaty, 55-7
Piggott, William, 25
Potts, Gary (chief), 114, 117
Poundmaker (Pitikwahanapiwiyin), 189
Pozniak, Kristy, 207
Prairies. *See* western Prairies
Promislow, Janna, 7
Province of Canada, mining and exploitation in Great Lakes area, 100-3
provinces, control of land and resources, 203-4

Quebec province, *Sioui* case and validity of treaty, 58-61, 62

Rama (Mnjikaning), 228, 236
"reading treaties" strategy, 11-12
reconciliation, 3-4
Reid, John G., 27
reserves and reserve lands
   Numbered Treaties (1 to 7), 160
   Rice Lake Treaty, 81, 82, 84, 85
   Robinson-Huron Treaty, 105, 110-11
   Treaty no. 6, 171
   Treaty no. 8, 197, 199
   Williams Treaties, 231
Rice Lake Treaty, no. 20 (1818)
   account by G. Paudash, 84-5, 89, 94-5
   correspondence from archives, 91-2

   and courts, 85-7
   description, 9, 16
   historical background, 75-80
   hunting and fishing, 81, 82-3, 84, 85-7, 239, 241
   interpretation, 83-5
   island reserves, 81, 82, 84, 85
   main characters, 96-7
   minutes of council at Smiths Creek, 81, 86, 92-4
   oral accounts, 83-5, 86-7
   payments and annuities, 80
   R. v. Taylor and Williams, 86, 87, 95-6
   text of treaty, 86, 89-91, 98, 112
   written accounts, 80-3, 84-5
Robinson, William Benjamin
   biographical details, 105-6, 130-1, 133
   diary entries, 108-10, 112
   report of treaty commissioner, 106-7, 108, 110-11, 112, 121-5, 228
   treaty negotiations, 103-6, 112-13
Robinson-Huron Treaty (1850)
   Bear Island case and decisions, 114-17, 129-30
   communities missing from negotiations, 112-15
   correspondence from archives, 125-8
   and courts, 112-17
   description, 9-10
   differences from earlier treaties, 105-6
   historical background, 99-105
   hunting and fishing rights, 105, 106-7, 231
   instructions from government, 104, 106, 107
   interpretation of treaties, 110-12, 116-17
   land claims and surrender, 102-5, 227-8, 229, 231
   main characters, 130-3
   map, 2
   mining exploitation and land ownership, 100-4, 110
   as model, 105, 160, 161
   oral accounts and history, 113, 114, 115, 117
   payments and annuities, 104, 105, 106-7, 109, 111-12

report by T.G. Anderson, 102–3, 109
report of treaty commissioner, 106–7, 108, 110–11, 112, 121–5, 228
reserve lands, 105, 110–11
text of treaty, 119–21, 134
treaty negotiations, 103–10, 112–13
as two treaties, 104–5, 107
written accounts, 106–12, 117
Robinson Treaties, map and description, 2, 16
Ross, J.H., 200, 202, 223
Rotman, Leonard, 207, 240
Royal Commission on Aboriginal Peoples (RCAP), 62
Royal Proclamation of 1763, 76–7, 100–1
Rupert's Land
annexation into Canada, 157–8, 160
treaty making, 160, 163–4
Rupert's Land Act (1868), 158
R. v. Badger (1996), and Treaty no. 8, 204–7, 220–2
R. v. Horse (1988), 240
R. v. Howard (1994), and Williams Treaties, 239–41, 250–1
R. v. Marshall (1999), 34
R. v. Simon (1985)
and Cope Treaty, 31, 32, 33–4, 41–3
and Treaty no. 6, 174
R. v. Sioui (1990)
and Huron-British Treaty, 58–62, 64, 67–9
Sioui legal test, 35, 207
R. v. Sundown (1999), and Treaty no. 6, 35, 173–5, 186–7
R. v. Sylliboy (1928). See *Sylliboy* case (1928)
R. v. Taylor and Williams (1981), and Rice Lake Treaty, 86, 87, 95–6

Saanich people. See WSÀNEC people
Saanichton Marina Ltd. v. Claxton (1989), and Vancouver Island Treaties, 144–5, 151–3
Saanich Treaties (1852). See Vancouver Island Treaties
Saskatchewan
resources rights, 204
Sundown case, 173–4

Sault St. Louis (Kahnawake), 56
Schmalz, Peter, 82
Scott, George, 26–7, 28
Selections of Documents from the Province of Nova Scotia (Akins), 39–40
Seneca of the Haudenosaunee Confederacy, land cession, 76–7
Seven Years' War, 49, 50–2, 54, 55–7
"Sharing the History – What Is the Future?" symposium, 1
Shaule, Daniel, 232–3
Shingwaukonse (Shingwauk, The Pine)
biographical details, 102, 130, 133
land exploitation by settlers and miners, 100, 102
Robinson-Huron Treaty, 106, 108, 109, 110
Sifton, Clifford, 196
Simon, James, 33
Simon legal test, 174
Simon v. The Queen (1985). See *R. v. Simon* (1985)
Sinclair, R.V., 229, 230, 231, 235
Sioui, George, 58
Sioui brothers, court case, 58–9
Sioui legal test, 35, 207
Six Nations Confederacy, 50
Smillie, Christine, 195
Smith, Donald, 79
Smith, Keith D., 11
South Saanich people, 142–3
"spirit and intent" of treaties, 4–5, 6
Spragge, William, 228
Star and Commercial Advertiser/L'Étoile et Journal du Commerce, 55–6, 64–6, 69
Steele, Donald, 115–16, 117
St. Lawrence river, and treaty making, 77, 99
Sundown, John, 173
Supreme Court of Canada
Bear Island case, 115–17
evidence for treaties and use of historical materials, 61–2
interpretation of treaties, 6, 61
legal principles for interpretation of treaties, 6–7, 12–13, 145, 174–5, 205–7

R. v. Badger, 205-7
R. v. Howard, 239-40, 241
R. v. Simon/Simon v. The Queen, 33-4
R. v. Sioui, 58, 59-61, 64, 67-9
R. v. Sundown, 174-5
Vancouver Island Treaties, 144, 145
White and Bob decision, 144, 145
Surtees, Robert, 108
Sylliboy, Gabriel
   biographical details, 45
   testimony in Cope Treaty, 29, 30, 40-1, 45
Sylliboy case (1928) (*R. v. Sylliboy*)
   courts and Cope Treaty, 31-2
   oral history of Cope Treaty, 29-30
   testimony in, 29-31, 40-1, 45

Taiaiake, Alfred, 7
Talbot, Robert, 169
Tawagaiwene, 114-15
Taylor, Wayne, 85-6
Taylor and Williams decision, 86, 87, 95-6, 239
Tehariolina, Marguerite Vincent, 57-8
Telford, Rhonda, 100, 101, 110
Teme-Augama Anishnabai (Temagami Band)
   Bear Island case and decisions, 114-17, 129-30
   exclusion from Robinson-Huron Treaty, 109, 113-15
Thoms, J. Michael, 84
timeline of Indigenous peoples and Euro-Americans relationship, 13-20
Tough, Frank, 204
trade, "truck house" (trading post) clauses, 24, 26
treaties (generally)
   bundling of treaties elements, 105
   differences in Robinson-Huron Treaty from earlier treaties, 105-6
   evidence for treaties and use of historical materials, 61-2
   extinguishment, 60-1
   and historical circumstances, 5-6
   as historical records, 60
   interpretation (*See* interpretation of treaties)
   map, 2
   payments and annuities, 78, 80
   questions for comparison, 10-11
   "reading treaties" strategy, 11-12
   and reconciliation, 4
   and "right" history, 1-3
   sources of examination, 8-9, 11-12
   "spirit and intent" of, 4-5, 6
   TRC views, 3-4
   validity in courts, 60-1, 62
   See also specific treaties and topics
Treaties and Right Research (TARR) program, 164-5, 198
Treaties of Canada with the Indians of Manitoba and the North-West Territories, The, 184
Treaty of Boston (1725) or Dummer Treaty, 23
Treaty of Paris (1763), 54
Treaty of Utrecht (1713), 22
Treaty no. 1 (1871), 161
Treaty no. 2 (1871), 161
Treaty no. 3 (1873), 161, 169
Treaty no. 4 (1874), 161-2, 169
Treaty no. 5 (1875), 162, 169
Treaty no. 6 (1876)
   agricultural land and agriculture, 167, 172
   clauses and terms, 160-1, 162, 164, 167, 168, 170-2
   and courts, 173-5
   description, 10, 17
   historical background, 157-63
   hunting and fishing, 171, 173-5
   interpretation, 165-6, 167-8, 174
   interview with F. Horse, 165-8, 169, 181-3
   land cession/surrender, 164
   main characters, 188-91
   map, 2
   medicine chest clause, 172, 173
   oral accounts and history, 164-8, 169-71, 175
   pipe ceremony, 166-7, 170
   report of treaty commissioner, 168, 169-73, 175, 184-6
   reserves, 171
   R. v. Sundown, 35, 173-5, 186-7

text of treaty, 177–81, 192
treaty making, 162, 164, 166–8, 169–73
written accounts, 164, 165, 168–73
Treaty no. 7 (1877), 162
Treaty no. 8 (1899)
and courts, 203–7
description, 10, 17
historical background, 193–6
hunting and fishing, 197, 199, 201, 204–7
interpretation, 198–9, 203
interviews with elders, 198–200, 217–20
main characters, 222–4
map, 2
oral accounts and history, 198–200, 203, 206, 207
payments and annuities, 197
report of treaty commissioner, 200–2, 203, 214–17
reserves, 197, 199
R. v. Badger, 204–7, 220–2
terms and clauses, 197, 198–200, 201–3, 204–5
text of treaty, 209–14, 225
treaty making, 196–9, 202–3
Treaty no. 9 (1905), 196
Treaty no. 11 (1921), 196
treaty rights, and *Constitution Act, 1982*, and Section 35, 34–5
"truck house" (trading post) clauses, 24
Trudel, Marcel, 62
Truth and Reconciliation Commission (TRC), 3–4
Tsawout First Nation, 138, 144–5

United States, expansionism, 157–8
Upper Canada
land surrenders, 227
payments and annuities for land, 77, 78–9, 80
treaty making and land settlement, 77–80, 99, 105
See also Great Lakes area
Upper Canada Land Surrenders, map, 2
See also Rice Lake Treaty (1818)

Vancouver Island
HBC licence and colony, 135–6
land ownership, 136–7
settler-Indigenous relationships, 139–40
Vancouver Island Treaties: Saanich Treaties (1852)
article in *Victoria Daily Times*, 139–41, 148–50
and courts, 144–5
as "deeds of conveyance," 138, 139, 142, 144
description, 10, 16
historical background, 135–8
hunting and fishing, 142, 144–5
interpretation, 139–42, 143–5
interview with Chief Latasse, 148–50
land cession/surrender, 139, 140–1, 143, 144
land ownership, 136–7
letter from J. Douglas, 136, 150
main characters, 153–6
map, 2
oral accounts and history, 139–42, 144, 145, 148–50
report by J. Douglas, 139, 140, 143–4
Saanich (WSÀNEC) presence, 138
Saanichton Marina Ltd. v. Claxton, 144–5, 151–3
text of treaty, 147–8
treaty making and discussions, 136–8, 140–3, 144, 145
written accounts, 137–42
Vaugeois, Denis, 62
Venne, Sharon, 165
Vidal, Alexander, 101, 103, 107, 109
Vincent, Nicolas (Tsaouenhohoui)
appearance at Legislative Assembly, 55, 57, 71
biographical details, 71, 73
oral history of Huron-Wendat, 57

Wa-ge-ma-ke/Wagemake, 110, 111, 125–6
War of 1812, 78
western Prairies, 159–60, 204
See also Numbered Treaties (1 to 7)
Whetung, Arthur, 237

White and Bob decision (1969), 34–5, 86, 144, 145
Wicken, William, 26, 27, 28, 30, 32
Wildlife Act of Alberta, 204–7
Williams, A.E., 83, 94
Williams, Angus Seymour
　biographical details, 251
　in Williams Treaties, 230, 231, 232, 235, 237, 251
Williams, Douglas, 85–6
Williams, Everett, 237–8
Williams Commission
　hearings, 232–4, 235
　mandate, 232–3, 234
　and Rice Lake Treaty, 85
　and Williams Treaties, 230, 232–4, 235, 247–8
Williams Treaties (1923)
　and courts, 238–41
　description, 10, 18, 230
　hearings of Williams Commission, 232–4, 235
　historical background, 227–31
　hunting and fishing, 230, 231, 234, 235–41
　interpretation, 232–3, 235–8, 240–1
　land claims and surrender, 230–5
　main characters, 251
　map, 2
　oral accounts, 236, 237–8
　report of Williams Commission, 230, 231, 232, 234, 235, 247–8
　reserves, 231
　R. v. Howard, 239–41, 250–1
　statement by J. Bigwin, 248–9
　terms of treaties, 231, 237, 241

　text of treaty, 237, 243–6, 252
　treaty making, 229–30, 234–5
　written accounts, 231–7
Willier, Isador, 198–9
written agreements, Great Lakes area, 77–8
written text
　and circumstances at time of treaties, 87
　interpretation, 5–8
　as source of examination, 8–9
written text and accounts of treaties
　Cope Treaty, 25–9, 32–3
　Huron-British Treaty, 52–7, 60
　Rice Lake Treaty, 80–3, 84–5
　Robinson-Huron Treaty, 106–12, 117
　Treaty no. 6, 164, 165, 168–73
　Treaty no. 8, 199, 200–3, 205–6, 207
　Vancouver Island Treaties, 137–42
　Williams Treaties, 231–7
WSÀNEC people
　interpretation of treaties, 139–42, 143–5
　land cession/surrender, 139
　oral history, 139–41, 148–50
　settlements, 138
　settler-Indigenous relationships, 139–40
　treaty making and discussion, 140–1, 142–3
　Vancouver Island Treaties, 138–43

York, Alder (chief), 236
Youngblood Henderson, James (Sakej), 7

www.ingramcontent.com/pod-product-compliance
Lightning Source LLC
Chambersburg PA
CBHW052016070526
44584CB00016B/1774